SOUTH AMERICA

SOUTH AMERICA

edited by ALICE TAYLOR

Published in cooperation with
The American Geographical Society

DAVID & CHARLES
NEWTON ABBOT

ISBN 0 7153 6197 X

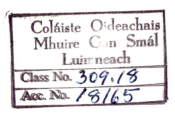
This edition published 1973

Printed in Great Britain by
Redwood Press Limited   Trowbridge   Wiltshire
for David & Charles (Holdings) Limited
South Devon House   Newton Abbot   Devon

CONTENTS

MAPS

FOREWORD

Political and social inequalities, hunger, unemployment, illiteracy, and poor health have been the lot of much of mankind throughout history. Today they are critical problems for millions of people living and working in the economically less developed nations of Asia, Africa, and South America—the so-called Third World—where new ideas, attitudes, and technology have only recently begun to challenge ancient traditions and patterns of living. Seeking solutions, these people are beginning to question political, economic, and social organizations that fail to alleviate poverty and injustice. They are becoming increasingly aware of the consequences of inequitable distribution of land, great disparities in income, rapid and chaotic urbanization, rapidly increasing population, and ecological imbalances. They see the urban rich minority retaining most of the political and economic power while the majority continues to eke out a living barely above the subsistence level. They know that in the highly industrialized affluent nations of the West the average income exceeds theirs greatly—in some cases as much as 10 to 1.

How can such problems be tackled in a nation where a privileged group pursues policies aimed at its own enrichment (the tax system, for instance) while the lowest income and employment group is unorganized and has little means to make itself heard? If there are no broadly based democratic forces that can bring pressure to change the political and economic system, how can it be changed?

Unemployment in the Third World has now reached the proportions of the Depression of the 1930's in the West. How can it be reduced when most of the people are undernourished and illiterate, when production and productivity are so low that there is little opportunity to accumulate capital investment for agricultural and industrial development? Moreover, a large portion of the foreign aid received, which might be used as capital investment, now goes to pay foreign debts and the interest on them. Unemployment spells poverty, discouragement, alienation, and unrest.

Frustration is greatest among the members of the new middle class and the young, those most imbued with ideas of equality and material progress. They seek innovations that will give them greater influence in government and society and bring a greater measure of economic well-being. Thanks to education and modern means of communication, they are more aware of injustices than their parents and grandparents, reared in societies where hierarchies in all realms were traditional and unquestioned. The political consequences of economic and social inequalities, unemployment, and increasing population pressures are likely to become more serious in the 1970's. Local governments that ignore such problems may well find it difficult to survive. Nor can any citizen of this small planet afford to ignore them.

Grateful thanks are due to the following people for their help in preparing this book: Susan R. Grande, Trina Mansfield, Chih Chwen Pinther, Attila Sioreti, and Blanca R. Uzcategui, who compiled and drew the maps; Nancy Gidwitz and Molly Laird, who assisted in the checking and editing of the articles and proofreading.

October, 1972   ALICE TAYLOR

I AN OVERVIEW

7

1 POPULATION CRISIS AND THE MARCH TO THE CITIES

Richard V. Smith and Robert N. Thomas

Factors Contributing to Population Growth • Political, Social, and Cultural Imbalances • Critical Issues • Urbanization: Some Causes and Consequences

Concern for improvement of economic and political opportunities for the millions of people living in poverty in Asia, Africa, and South America—the so-called Third World—has become widespread in the past decade, as has recognition of the complexity of their problems. Baffling questions are being raised concerning unemployment and underemployment, the rural-to-urban migration, the role of foreign capital, land and tax reforms, and regional and interregional cooperation. Central to all these factors are population growth and its impact on the evolution of the area. In the opinion of many experts, all other elements are secondary.

From a worldwide perspective, South America's population character-istics are marked by extremes. The continent has a relatively small total population; low crude population densities, per capita income, and produc-tivity levels; and a high proportion of its population involved in agricul-tural activities, although urbanization is taking place at an increasing rate. Most important, South America's annual growth rate is among the highest of the world's major regions. The current estimate is in the neighborhood of 2.3 per cent, as compared to Africa's 2.6 per cent, Asia's 2.3 per cent, Anglo-America's 1.2 per cent, and Europe's 0.8 per cent.

If current growth rates are maintained to the end of this century, one out of a little more than ten of the world's inhabitants will be in South America, as compared to one in approximately twenty-five in 1900 and one in thirteen in 1968. In absolute numbers, South America's population increased from about 63 million in 1900 to about 195 million in 1971, with a projection (based on current growth rates) to about 287 million in the year 1985.

The relationship between population growth and economic development is complex, but one aspect is quite simple: There is a race between the rate of increase in population and the rate of increase in gross national product on a per capita basis. Unless the latter rate exceeds the former, the per capita share of the gross national product will decline. Given the present low level of gross national product per capita—$425 in 1971—South American countries may find it difficult to create development policies that simultaneously improve the conditions of the present population and stimulate future development enough to meet the needs of a greatly expanded population. According to the best estimates (and figures are approximate in several nations), the yearly per capita gross national product has gone up since 1963 in all the South American nations except Bolivia and Chile, where there were drops of $4 and $3, respectively. The increases elsewhere, however, were small—over an eight-year period, slightly more than $200 in Argentina and Venezuela, slightly more than $100 in Peru, and from $18 to $54 in the poorer nations—so small as to make little difference and not enough to offset the rising prices of goods in most places.

Figures for the gross national product are somewhat unrealistic in traditional economies and societies; other elements, such as the distribution of income and employment, may be more indicative of realities. But GNP figures do nevertheless illustrate the magnitude of the problem and offer some basis for evolving population policies and incorporating them into national and regional economic planning. The urgency and scope of the population problem were given formal recognition by a meeting on "Population Policies in Relation to Development in Latin America," held in Caracas in September, 1967, under the joint sponsorship of the Organization of American States, the Pan-American Health Organization, the Population Council, and the Aspen Institute for Humanistic Studies in cooperation with the Venezuelan government. The final report contains sixty-nine declarations relating to population and development and makes forty-seven recommendations for a rational approach to the region's population-development crisis.

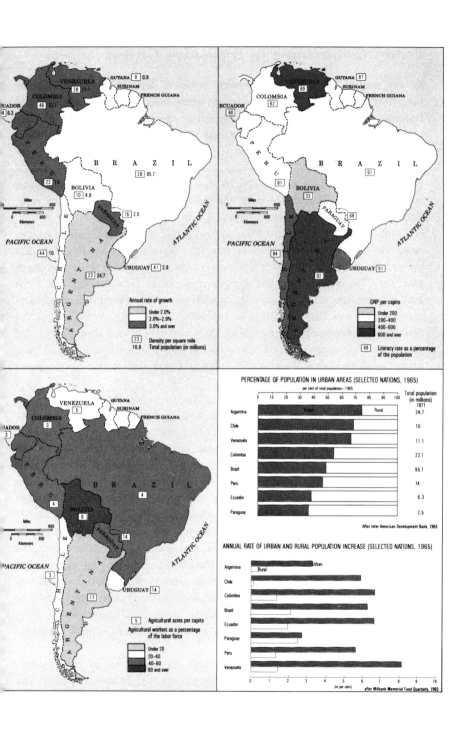

PERCENTAGE OF POPULATION IN URBAN AREAS (SELECTED NATIONS, 1965)

ANNUAL RATE OF URBAN AND RURAL POPULATION INCREASE (SELECTED NATIONS, 1965)

Factors Contributing to Population Growth

In any analysis of population growth in South America, it is essential to note that information is inadequate and often inaccurate. Few nations have had comprehensive census and vital-statistic registration systems, and data collecting and processing have been, and to a considerable degree still are, susceptible to error. Nevertheless, it appears that the population grew slowly and at a fairly regular rate until about 1900, when the rate of growth began to increase sharply. In the 1920's and 1930's the population increased by around 20 per cent; the figure for the 1940's is 25 per cent, and for the two most recent decades, about 30 per cent.

Available evidence suggests that both past and present population growth rates are largely consequences of natural increase as a result of a persistently high birth rate with a simultaneous abrupt decline in the death rate. In 1971, for example, the average crude birth rate was 32.5 per 1,000 and the average crude death rate was 9 per 1,000; the resulting natural increase rate was 23.5 per 1,000, or roughly 2.3 annually. According to the concept of compound interest, those rates will result in a doubling of the population in approximately thirty-one years. This eventuality will pose acute problems that will seriously hinder and may even defeat development efforts.

Throughout recorded South American history, a high birth rate has been characteristic, and it continues to be so. Until quite recently, South American people have been predominantly rural and village dwellers. In such a setting children are a great economic asset because they add to the family's labor pool and provide insurance for their parents' old age. The tendency toward large families has been reinforced by such other cultural and demographic phenomena as the widespread acceptance of Roman Catholicism, the concept of *machismo* (the notion that proof of masculinity requires evidence in the form of children), the relatively low socio-economic levels of the bulk of the people, the youthful age structure of the populations, with a large number of females in child-bearing age groups, and the early average age of marriage or consensual unions. In addition, the need for "fulfillment" may express itself in large families where few alternative forms are available. All these forces influence today's birth rates. All are subject to change, and, as will be noted, several programs aim at altering some of them.

The decline in the death rate, though significant in all age groups, has been most conspicuous in the younger groups. Infant mortality and childhood death rates have experienced spectacular drops. Mortality has declined because of the many programs aimed at control of communicable diseases, improved prenatal care, and improved nutrition. Death rates will no doubt experience a further decline in South America, but this will be slight in comparison with the change over the past fifty years. Formerly in the neighborhood of 25 to 30 per 1,000, the death rate now averages 9 per 1,000.

Although immigrant groups have played a notable role in the development of many parts of the continent, especially Brazil and Argentina, migration has not accounted for a major portion of the increase in population and is unlikely to do so in the future. Various experts concerned about overpopulation in other areas of the world have suggested that the vast, almost empty expanses of South America might accommodate large numbers of people from countries with limited opportunities for new settlements. But, in the opinion of the authors, local cultural and political interests and the international "climate" preclude such large-scale migrations.

From a stage of high birth and high death rates, South America is moving to a stage of high birth and moderately low death rates. Present growth trends are at the highest level in history. However, there are significant variations from nation to nation and within nations.

Political, Social, and Cultural Imbalances

Annual population growth rates range from a high of 3.4 per cent in Venezuela, Colombia, Ecuador, and Paraguay to a low of 1.2 per cent in Uruguay, with an average for the independent South American nations of about 2.3 per cent in 1971. Much evidence suggests that there is a strong correlation between population growth trends and such socio-economic indicators as per capita income, literacy, and occupation (see maps), but far more frequently the complex composition and organization of a nation's population obscure any definitive correlations when viewed from a broad perspective.

A hypothetical South American country may be thought of as having one or two focal areas which dominate the nation, not only economically, but also politically, socially, and culturally. Such areas may already have some commercial agriculture and exhibit a trend toward industrial-commercial development with related urbanization. The evolving elements of a national infrastructure tend either to be found within the focal areas or to be developed in relation to them. Transportation and communications systems tend to be most highly developed in these locations, the population is relatively concentrated, and the dissemination of information and educational efforts is more readily accomplished than in areas more remote and less well served with modern facilities. Although sizable groups of residents may have very low incomes and literacy levels, they are nevertheless exposed to a different way of life and differ in their expectations from those occupying provincial locations. They may, for example, begin to move toward smaller average family sizes.

At the other extreme are the people who live in outlying regions, mostly in rural settings or market towns. Modernization is only gradually reaching them. Fewer facilities of all kinds are available in such areas, and the probability of a rapid expansion is not great. Population growth rates may be similar to those found in the centers of dominance but are a result of higher birth and death rates. Since changes that reduce the death rate usually have an effect earlier than those influencing the birth rate, the possibility exists that the rate of population increase may *rise*. Some members of these groups will enter the migratory stream to the growth centers; in some instances, such movements have relieved population pressures locally. But the growth centers are often unable to handle the annual increment of internal migrants, even though they are, at the same time, the desired location for expanding economic activities. In a fundamental sense, the population problem of the region is a national problem. The long-run success of population programs requires some bridging of the gap between urban and rural groups. A diminution of regional differences may, in turn, foster a feeling of national identity and perhaps even of common purposes.

Regional variations are further compounded by broad socio-economic divisions. Most South American nations have a small (2–5 per cent) upper-income group, a growing but still relatively small middle group (8–20 per cent), and a very large lower-income group. Variations also prevail in literacy rates, educational attainment, health, types of housing, opportunities for jobs, social contacts, and political power, and the mobility of people, materials, and ideas. All these differences tend to reinforce barriers to the reforms considered necessary for development and to family planning. President Kennedy's original version of the Alliance for Progress required a variety of social, economic, and political reforms in order to qualify for aid. But it soon became clear that such reforms could not be achieved in the short run, and they were more or less shelved for the time being. Today, the need for such reforms is even more obvious, both for the developmental process and for the broader purpose of alleviating individual poverty and broadening individual opportunities. Unless these reforms can be achieved, there is serious doubt that present population growth patterns will be reversed. The alternative to a reduced rate of population growth seems to be both national and personal tragedy.

To date, too little research has been done on the factors that affect population growth patterns in South America. Research might explore some of the following questions: Argentina and Uruguay are among the most homogeneous countries and have relatively low growth rates. Why? Venezuela is among the most rapidly developing countries economically, yet it shows no slackening in its high growth pattern. Why? What are the real demographic differences between the Andean and coastal sections of Peru or Ecuador? There are striking contrasts between Brazil's depressed northeast region and its thriving São Paulo region in the well-being and reproductive tendencies of their respective populations. What are the dynamics of this situation?

Critical Issues

It can safely be assumed that the death rate in South America will remain at the present low levels or perhaps decline somewhat. Hence, any significant change in growth trends will have to result from a decline in birth rates. Present indications are that the birth rate will continue at a high level for the next ten to twenty years. There are, however, some reasons for a more optimistic view: surveys indicating that couples desire smaller families, the success of family-planning clinics in some urban areas, the impact of increasing urbanization and related economic changes, improved contraceptive methods, the continuing spread of education and rising literacy rates, indications that the Catholic Church is gradually liberalizing its stance on family planning, and evidence that an increasing number of national governments are including population-policy considerations in over-all national economic planning. The last of these points is perhaps the most noteworthy, for it should help in the formulation of programs aimed at attaining a growth rate commensurate with reasonable expectations of national economic expansion.

Among the important recommendations resulting from the 1967 Caracas conference, the first is especially worthy of note as a key to changing South American attitudes toward population:

That the . . . governments, the private sector, university institutions, public information media, and public and private international organizations promote the broadest possible review and study of population problems within the context of economic and social development trends and policies, taking into account the complex interrelationship between population growth and other aspects of social evolution and change.

Population policies at the national level may include efforts to encourage family planning, to study pertinent aspects of population distribution and redistribution, and to consider long-range plans. A major development problem in South America results from the low median age of the people, which in turn results in a high dependency ratio and large social overhead expenditures, not to mention the prospect of enormously high birth rates in the future if young people who will soon be entering the family-forming stage are not motivated toward family limitation.

Urbanization: Some Causes and Consequences

As we have noted, the greatest challenge for South America's future appears to hinge on the number of its people. It will also hinge on where its people live and find opportunities to make a living.

South America's population, one of the fastest growing in the world, is apparently growing faster in the cities than in the countryside despite the fact that rural families have more children than urban ones. For reasons we have mentioned earlier, the farm child can be a decided economic advantage to his family. By contrast, the urban child is generally more economically dependent on his parents and hence can be regarded as a liability.

Differences in levels of education may be associated with fertility differences between rural and urban areas. Generally speaking, the lower the level of education, the larger is the size of the family. And levels of education as a rule are lower in rural than in urban areas.

Historically, infant mortality has been high in farm families, and a large number of births was a way to assure a desired number of survivors.

With the greater diffusion of modern medical technology and improved means of sanitation, infant deaths have dropped considerably. However, rural families are still bound by the mores and folkways of their ancestors. As a result, large families tend to be the rule.

But why, in these circumstances, have the growth rates in South American cities been considerably higher than in rural areas? The answer lies mainly in two conditions: a high rate of natural increase, and rural-to-urban migration. In the September, 1965, issue of *Scientific American*, Kingsley Davis pointed out that most city growth in economically less-developed nations is due to high rates of natural increase. In South America, however, internal migration assumes such major proportions that, in several capitals, it accounts for more than 50 per cent of the increase. It appears, therefore, that South America is experiencing mobility almost opposite in direction from that occurring in North America, where most large cities are growing at lower rates than suburban areas.

One reason for the massive movement from the countryside to the city is rural poverty, stemming from rigid systems of land ownership and economic stagnation, which impede attempts by farm families to acquire land, to enlarge small holdings, and otherwise to improve their social and economic positions. Another reason is the concentration of economic activity in the large centers, particularly in the capital cities. In the last few decades, entrepreneurs have developed a number of consumer industries in these cities, which have created new jobs. Urban workers' salaries far exceed the income of farm workers. In the small, less-developed countries of South America, such as Paraguay, the capital city has the overwhelming majority of the nation's industries. Factories are located in the cities rather than outside the populated centers because the larger cities generally have the best system of highways and railroads. In many nations, electrical power is not available outside the main urban centers. City laborers are usually better educated, more technically skilled, and more motivated to work. In addition, management personnel are more easily attracted to jobs in the city than in isolated rural areas. Most of the major universities are located in the principal cities, often in the capital. A high school graduate who wishes to continue his education must live in a large urban center. Health services—hospitals, clinics, and doctors—are likewise concentrated in the cities. Most countries have some form of publicly supported medical service, and these facilities are usually located in the large cities.

Finally, once the rural visitor has had an opportunity to see the city, gaze at its bright lights, visit its parks, go window shopping, or stare at his first television program through a display window, he becomes aware of the contrast between his country environment and that of the city. He begins to think, perhaps, that the city would be a good place to live in.

Before World War II, the farmer and his family may have heard vague stories about the big city, but more likely than not they would not have visited it, for transportation routes were not highly developed, and, if they did exist, the cost of travel was likely to be prohibitive. Today, most South American nations have far more frequent bus service than most areas of the United States. Regular service extends to distant parts of the country, and, although equipment may not be luxurious, it is quite dependable. Further, most nations have undertaken extensive road-building programs in recent years; today one can drive relatively easily from Caracas through Bogotá, Quito, Lima, Santiago to Puerto Montt in southern Chile. Improved means of transportation, therefore, have made visiting the large city easier for people living in rural areas.

Another stimulus to migration is the relatively inexpensive transistor radio, which now brings urban information and propaganda to most parts of South America. It is quite common to see an illiterate rural Indian treading a dirt road in some inaccessible part of the country with his ear glued to such a radio. He is continuously bombarded with news of the big city and the many advantages it may offer. Undoubtedly, this has had a pronounced effect on the peasant, tending to uproot him from his village.

Once in the city, the typical migrant may find a life completely different from what he envisaged. Despite the number of newly created industries in the cities, jobs are still insufficient for all the people seeking them. Some return to their rural homes, but most stay on in the hope of improving their economic and social status. As a result, most cities have unemployment rates that would cause political riots in Anglo-America. It is not unusual to find jobless rates in excess of 10 per cent and in some cases near 25 per cent of the employable population. Complicating the unemployment situation is underemployment, an extremely difficult condition to measure. Many workers do not have steady work but spend their hours doing odd jobs, mostly menial tasks, such as washing cars, shining shoes, delivering packages, selling merchandise door-to-door, vending sundry articles at sidewalk displays, or selling newspapers, lottery tickets, and the like. Women and girls get a variety of low-skill, low-productivity jobs, particularly in domestic service. Real employment opportunities for women are rare on farms and in small villages; in cities, by contrast, many women are able to become economically independent and productive members of society. In fact, the relative earning power for women in cities is so much greater than that of women in rural areas that it may well explain why more women than men have migrated to cities. Teenage children frequently seek some type of work to help supplement the family income and thus deny themselves the opportunity to attend school.

Housing is another major problem in most cities. The desperately poor conditions characteristic of the typical South American slum are difficult to imagine. One wonders how people can survive crowded into one-story buildings that generally lack facilities such as electricity, water, and sewers, which are taken for granted in the United States. Children use the narrow, open-sewered paths as their playgrounds. Such an unhealthy environment presents a major problem to the health authorities, who fear massive outbreaks of disease.

One might expect that the high unemployment and underemployment rates and poor housing in the urban centers would be accompanied by serious social and political repercussions. In fact, migrants seem to adapt reasonably well to city life. It may be that their initial expectations are so low that by and large they are fulfilled. Also, any tendency of the migrant toward alienation and rootlessness may be negated by the presence of family and personal ties. Rather than develop into a politically radical group, the recent migrants show signs of adjusting well to city life and utilizing its economic and social opportunities.

According to some social scientists, the rapid rate of city growth may even have positive effects: The slum city may serve as a stepping stone for the newly arrived migrant who is fortunate enough to find an unskilled job. While living in it, he pays little or no rent, electric bills, or taxes; in many instances, he receives free water from the city. Any money he earns beyond what he spends for food, clothing, and entertainment can go toward acquiring better living conditions for his family later on. Thus, the slum city may actually be fulfilling a useful economic function.

Urban growth may also have other beneficial effects. Although the health conditions are poor in the slum cities, often they are far better than in the migrant's former home. Most urban areas have clinics where inexpensive or free medical services are available. Educational facilities, too, are undoubtedly far better in the average city than in the rural areas. Most nations have laws requiring school attendance through the sixth grade, but such laws apply primarily to people living in the city, because schools do not exist in many rural areas.

The better education facilities in the cities could have a potent, though indirect, effect on the rate of population growth. As we have noted, countries with more literate populations have lower birth rates. As a greater percentage of South American people abandon the country for the city, their level of education should increase, and population growth may slow as a result.

Cities may fulfill another vital role in the less-developed nations of South America. Specialization is generally associated with urbanization, and as specialization increases, the individual becomes more dependent upon his fellow citizens. The dependent individual usually undertakes cooperative efforts to solve his problems. When these cooperative efforts involve political decisions, and they usually do, citizens may try to take a more active part in political affairs and may initiate steps to bring greater equality of opportunities. Here, as elsewhere and in most periods of history, the urban dweller and especially the urban migrant may be the principal agents of economic, social, and political changes.

2 FOUR PROFILES*

Raymond E. Crist and Edward P. Leahy

A Rancher · *A Cosmopolitan* · *A Petroleum Worker* ·
A Subsistence Farmer

The following four profiles may make it easier to visualize South Americans —how they live, how they make a living, how they think about themselves and others. Although they are all taken from Venezuela, they are characteristic of large socio-economic groups throughout South America.

A Rancher

Don Carlos T——, sixty-nine years old, was born in Mérida, a city of about 40,000 in the uplands of western Venezuela, and moved at the age of eight to Barinas, center of a cattle-raising area, where he worked as a peon for a number of years. He is a *mestizo*—that is, of mixed parentage —but with more Indian than white blood in his veins. After his father's death he was the main support of his mother and younger brother and sisters. He gradually accumulated a little capital, with which he bought cattle from the plains to sell in the markets of the mountain towns and hamlets. By 1928 he had enough money to buy a ranch, and he has been in the cattle business ever since. Currently Don Carlos has about 1,500 head of cattle.

* Adapted from R. E. Crist and E. P. Leahy, *Venezuela: Search for a Middle Ground.* New York: Van Nostrand Reinhold, 1969.

His life on the *llanos* (the great plains of the Orinoco Basin) is a constant struggle. As a case in point, he holds 19,770 acres of land *por linderos* (according to natural boundaries) but only 14,825 *por escrituras* (according to his papers)! The discrepancy reflects the insecurity of tenure common in many parts of South America because of inadequate surveys, inexact descriptions, conflicting claims, and chicanery. There is often confusion about which lands belong to the federal government and which to private holders. Security of tenure or some proper system of title insurance would be a boon to landholders everywhere, for they would then have a personal interest in land improvement.

Don Carlos also encounters many natural hazards in cattle raising. Unexpected and protracted periods of drought or rain may dry up the natural pastures or flood them under a foot or more of water. Hoof and mouth disease is a constant menace, although its depredations have been greatly reduced. Similarly, infestation by the *gusano de monte* (larva of the warble fly), which lives under the skin of cattle until it matures and drops to the ground, was formerly so severe that many cattle died or lost a great deal of weight. Now insect pests of all kinds are being controlled by the widespread use of DDT, frequent antiseptic dipping of animals, draining stagnant pools and swamps, and frequent emptying of containers standing around dwellings to collect water.

The herd on the ranch is being improved by cross-breeding with Zebu bulls. Cattle thus cross-bred are resistant to ticks, warble flies, and horse-flies, and also to the midday heat. They gain weight more rapidly than the native animals and are better able to endure the rigors of drought. Indeed, native steers may be poor and emaciated while those with Zebu blood are sleek and fat, though both are grazing the same pasture.

There has been a gradual trend toward planting artificial pasture, which will support more stock per unit of land and make it easier to tide cattle over the dry season. Don Carlos, who has experimented with artificial pastures for some time, finds that the best all-round pasture grass is Argentinian *jaragua,* which survives the dry season and the annual burning. Don Carlos has 1,235 acres of this grass, fenced, to cut for seed, and from this he expects to harvest about a hundredweight per 2.5 acres, which he can either market or use on his own ranch.

Don Carlos also grows rice, in which he has made a considerable investment through government credit. He now has 495 acres in rice and may plant more later. He hopes to be able to pay off the machinery within three years. Furthermore, he expects that within five years his cattle will all be hybrids, and the value of his herd will just about double. In his view, his ranch cannot help increasing in value, with improved pastures and herds and fields under rice. He already has nineteen miles of fence in place to protect the rice fields and artificial pastures and mark the boundary lines. Don Carlos estimates that the ranch is now worth about $250,000; it produces an annual income of about $15,000, although this is subject to variation. Time was when Don Carlos used to work with a yoke of oxen from three o'clock in the morning until nightfall for fifteen cents a day!

Don Carlos is well aware of the need for lots of good, wholesome food to maintain the health and efficiency of his workmen. Their diet has certainly improved in the past quarter century. There is now greater variety, with emphasis on foods rich in proteins, such as meat, eggs, milk, and cheese, which help them to resist diseases.

Don Carlos is a typical Andino, frugal, hard-working, close mouthed. He tends to look down on the lowland Venezuelans as shiftless, happy-go-lucky, and improvident. He has had only two years of formal schooling, but he can read and write and he follows world happenings through the newspapers, which he reads with great interest. He has never been outside Venezuela, nor indeed has he traveled widely within the limits of that country, so his views tend to be parochial. He feels that his country needs a strong central government, but he also feels that taxes are too high, that the government gives too little back for the money it takes, and does not help the ranchers and farmers enough with revenues from the oil industry. He is Catholic, conservative, and interested in the maintenance of order and stability.

A Cosmopolitan

Dolores G—— lives in Caracas. She is twenty-three years old. Her mother came originally from Belgium, and her father is a Venezuelan of Spanish-German extraction. Dolores was born in New York, where her father was at that time attached to the Venezuelan Consulate. The family returned to Venezuela when Dolores was three and lived in Caracas until she was ten. She was then sent to Geneva, Switzerland, where she spent the next ten years, first in boarding school and then in art school, studying painting, sculpture, and architectural decoration.

Meanwhile Dolores's parents had divorced. Her mother remarried and moved to Lugano, in Switzerland. Her father stayed in Caracas, looking after his extensive and varied business interests. Dolores now maintains an apartment in Caracas (in a building owned by her father). She has a car ("but that is in Europe at the moment"), and she does art work, mostly for architects. She also has done some work in stage design and costumes.

Dolores has an independent income from the estate of her maternal grandfather. "If I had to live on what I make, I'd starve," she says. She is intelligent, engaging, and pretty enough to have been offered a film contract by a British company (which she turned down).

Dolores is now engaged to José Antonio V——, an engineer and builder who lives in Caracas. Like Dolores, he was educated in Europe (Switzerland, France, and England). José Antonio is currently erecting an apartment house in Caracas and a small hotel and restaurant on the beach near Cumaná, on a small rugged peninsula of which he is the sole owner. He is also building cottages in the hills behind the hotel, cutting roads, laying out lots, and hoping to build a yacht basin. Dolores helps in this project, doing design work. She and José Antonio fly down from Caracas in his small amphibian, spend the weekend working on his subdivision, then fly back to Caracas Monday morning.

Dolores is going to Europe for the winter. She is going via Brazil and then will fly to Dakar, where she has an invitation to go lion-hunting with the French Ambassador. Then she will visit her mother in Switzerland and do some skiing. She will be back in Caracas in the spring.

Dolores is representative of the mobile sophisticates of Venezuela—the "jet set"—and, as such, is a type one might encounter among rich people in Madrid, Paris, Rome, or Mexico City. She is well-informed and articulate within the sphere of her interests, which are the usual ones of a young woman of her social group and tastes, and is a good judge of people. She tends to be rootless, pragmatic, unsentimental.

A Petroleum Worker

Perico G—— is a twenty-two-year-old *mestizo*, with more white than Indian blood. He is medium-sized, wiry, and agile. He is taciturn, expressing himself through action rather than words. He grew up near Valencia, where his father was a sharecropper. His father died when Perico was twelve, and he had to leave school to go to work. His family had some rough years. When Perico was sixteen he joined the Venezuelan Navy, where he served for three years in the engine room of a destroyer. After his discharge he was unemployed for almost a year. He was in and around Caracas part of that time; finally he and a friend hitchhiked to Maracaibo, where Perico found work as a helper on a tank farm. He is handy mechanically and his navy training serves him in good stead. He has been in Maracaibo a year and a half now. His mother and two brothers joined him about a year ago, and the family moved into a government-sponsored housing development, where they have a four-room house made of concrete block, for which they pay a very low rent. Perico's mother is delighted with the house, which has window screens and is relatively free from insects. Perico is a union member. He believes that the unions have brought great benefits to the workers; he himself is well paid by Venezuelan standards: about $55 a week. He also gets a paid vacation, free medical care, and the privilege of taking training courses at company expense.

Perico belongs to a soccer club, which takes up a good deal of his spare time. He met a girl at one of the soccer-club parties and is seriously interested in her. Marriage presents difficulties, however, for Perico is the principal breadwinner for his family, and his girl does not wish to share a four-room house with Perico, his mother, and two brothers. Perico does not know what to do about this.

Perico takes little interest in politics. There has been some trouble around Maracaibo recently, with Castroite terrorists blowing up pipelines, for example. Also, agitators have tried to stir up resentment against the foreign-owned oil companies. None of this has troubled Perico, who is content with his life and wants no major changes. He has no interest in abstractions. He is inclined to view his friend Emilio, a Castroite activist, with amused tolerance. *"Es un loco,"* he says. Emilio is a romanticist. Perico is not.

Perico has a chance to advance to the lower levels of management. He is thus upward-mobile in a sociological sense, and he and his kind will some day fill the yawning gap between the power élite and the landless masses that now exists in Venezuela. As the country industrializes, the middle group is bound to expand. This development is necessary for the future political health of the nation, because the current situation is highly unstable and subject to violent alteration. Efforts are being made to broaden the opportunities of the poor and illiterate so that they can acquire some vested interest in the status quo and will thus add their weight and influence to the forces of order rather than anarchy.

A Subsistence Farmer

Julio R——, thirty-one years old, is a *zambo*—that is, of mixed Negro and Indian blood. He is married and has six children. He lives south of the Orinoco River near Cabruto, where he is engaged in slash-and-burn agriculture. His *modus operandi* is to clear a plot of ground in the jungle except for large trees, which he leaves standing or kills by girdling. He burns the trash when it is dry and then plants crops for from one to five years. When yields decline (owing to the leaching out of soluble plant nutrients), weeds take possession, and rodent, bird, and insect populations build up, Julio abandons this plot for another.

All the materials for Julio's house are cut in the surrounding forest: There are eight upright posts connected by cross-beams and rafters, all bound together with *bejucos,* or vines, so pliable that they can be tied when green in a knot like a rope. The thatch for the roof is made of palm leaves; not a nail is used in tying the whole structure together. Cooking is done over a wood fire in one corner of the house. The family sleeps in hammocks, using a smudge fire at night to keep mosquitoes at bay.

Julio grows maize (corn), yuca, beans, squash, and plantains. He also has two hens, which yield an occasional egg. There is a lack of animal protein in the diet of Julio and his family; he would like to have a pig but has no money to buy one. In the meantime he or his children catch fish in the nearby river, which add to the variety of their diet.

Julio and his family are all afflicted with dietary deficiencies and intestinal parasites, and Julio has chronic malaria, which saps his vitality. Modern medical treatment is not easily available to him. He endures stoically because he has no alternative.

Julio's isolation also throws him on his own resources for supplies; virtually every item he and his family use is homemade, except, of course, the ubiquitous machete. The clothing worn by the family, such as it is (the children go naked until they are six or eight years old), comes from a few cotton shrubs that grow near the house; the raw fiber is gathered, seeded by hand, spun, woven, and fashioned into the simple garments worn by Julio and his wife.

It would be exceedingly difficult for Julio to change the circumstances of his life. For one thing, he has no title to the land he is working. In fact, he has no idea to whom it belongs. Thus he has little motivation to make permanent improvements. It would be difficult for him to establish a permanent farm or ranch in his surroundings because of both poor soil conditions and remoteness of markets. There are no roads; the river is not easily or economically navigable. The humble subsistence farmer has traditionally been pushed into the least desirable areas by the more powerful elements of society. A man like Julio has neither the material resources nor the know-how to fight back. He cannot read or write. His contacts with the forces of law and order almost always work to his disadvantage; accordingly, he has a profound mistrust of city folk, with their lawyers and policemen, who tend to produce documents Julio cannot understand, or throw him into jail for little or no reason. Thus, driven back upon themselves, Julio and his family live an isolated life, and the pattern is difficult to break.

It is estimated that about a million Venezuelans are engaged in this hand-to-mouth way of life. They all live more or less as Julio does. These, incidentally, are the people who are often tempted to leave their rural surroundings to seek their fortune in the cities and often end in the shantytowns of Caracas, Rio de Janeiro, or any other large South American city. These shantytowns, appalling as they are, frequently represent an improvement to the people who live there; they are often better off than they were in the back country.

Julio's problems of adaptation to the modern world are deep and perplexing, not only to Julio, but also to government officials and planning agencies, who view his displaced, mobile group, living a marginal existence outside the money economy, as a threat to the body politic and the status quo. Venezuela and many other South American nations are taking steps to solve the problem through education, public health, public housing, and development of transportation facilities—but there is much to be done.

3 UNEMPLOYMENT
Bitter Burden of Millions[*]

David A. Morse

Taking the Glamour out of Modern Technology • Social Justice and Economic Growth

If some years ago I had had to write an article on the subject of unemployment in the less-developed nations, I would have had to begin with an explanation of why unemployment need concern us at all. "Surely," it would have been argued by those of us who had lived through the depression of the 1930's, "surely, if there is widespread unemployment in the less-developed nations today, the answer is to revitalize the economy, to stimulate demand, to inject the capital necessary to create jobs. Employment will look after itself if only we can get the economy moving."

Today we are wiser. Employment has not looked after itself, even in nations where efforts to get the economy moving have been most successful. Several less-developed nations have attained, and appear to be sustaining, quite respectable rates of growth of the gross national product, in spite of the fact that in many respects—such as foreign trade—the dice are heavily loaded against them. But, in many less-developed nations the proportion of the population that has contributed to and benefited from this achievement has barely changed, and in some of them it has actually declined. In the first Development Decade (1960–70) experts set the goal for the less-developed nations at 5 per cent annual growth in gross national product—and that goal was achieved. But as we start the 1970's several

* Adapted from a paper presented at the annual meeting of the Society for International Development, Ottawa, Canada, May 17, 1971.

hundred million human beings are still unemployed or underemployed.

It is impossible to state in precise quantitative terms just how far short the performance of less-developed nations has fallen of the goal of full or nearly full employment. To begin with, there are important conceptual difficulties of measurement. As understood in industrialized countries, the term "unemployment" applies to a person who is available for and looking for work and who in the meantime would normally be drawing unemployment benefits. In less-developed nations, a person who has no work, and hence no income from work, rarely has unemployment benefits to fall back on; he has to rely on his family, on begging, or on some barely productive activity to shield him from starvation. In these conditions, to use terms current in industrial societies, he either withdraws from the labor force (becomes a dependent) or becomes self-employed (although he may have virtually no work and be receiving barely sufficient income to live).

In an attempt to overcome this conceptual difficulty, we use the term "underemployment" to describe the situation of people who work but who work less, and earn less, than they could or would like. But how do you measure this concept? How many people in less-developed nations work and earn less than they could or would like? And how much more would they work if they could—bearing in mind that many of them have no conception of a different or better fate?

There is, therefore, an unfortunate gap in our knowledge—not merely because it would be intellectually more satisfying to be able to measure the extent and gravity of the problem but, more important, because unless we have some idea of the order of magnitude of the problem, it is difficult to devise policies and programs to deal with it or to measure progress in dealing with it.

This is not to say that we are dealing with a nonproblem. Even the most casual visitor to a less-developed nation becomes aware of the fact that the labor potential is grossly underutilized, and that, as a result, there is widespread human misery and suffering. An informed guess regarding the present magnitude of the employment problem is that something like 25 to 30 per cent of the total labor potential of less-developed nations is wasted through unemployment and underemployment.

Does it really matter? Experience has shown that there can be economic growth without anything approaching full employment. Why not, then, concentrate on growth and forget—at least temporarily—about the employment problem?

This, of course, raises a fundamental question. If we want merely to

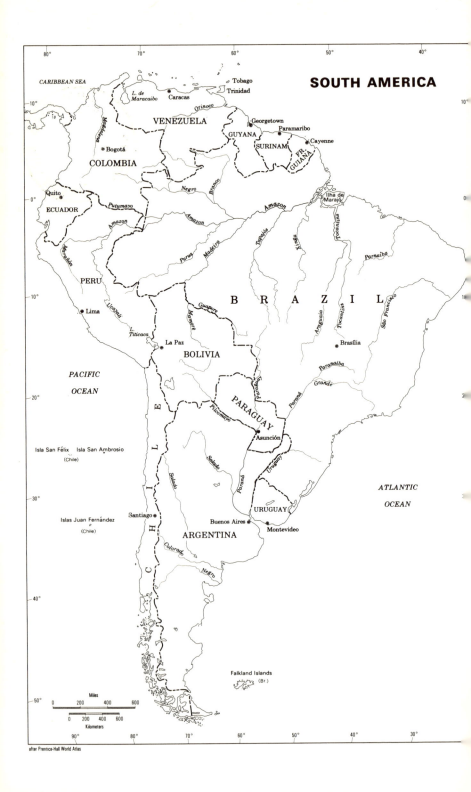

SOUTH AMERICA

CARIBBEAN SEA

Tobago
Trinidad

L. de
Maracaibo
Caracas

Orinoco

VENEZUELA

Georgetown
GUYANA
Paramaribo
SURINAM
Cayenne
FR.
GUIANA

Bogotá

COLOMBIA

Negro
Branco

Quito

ECUADOR
Putumayo

Amazon

Ilha de
Marajó

Amazon

Amazon

Purus
Madeira

Tapajós

Xingu

Tocantins

Parnaíba

PERU

Lima

Ucayali

Marañón

L.
Titicaca

Guaporé
Mamoré

B   R   A   Z   I   L

Araguaia

Tocantins

São Francisco

La Paz

BOLIVIA

Brasília

PACIFIC

OCEAN

Paranaíba

Pilcomayo

PARAGUAY

Paraná

Grande

Isla San Félix   Isla San Ambrosio
(Chile)

Asunción

Salado

Paraná

Uruguay

ATLANTIC

OCEAN

Islas Juan Fernández
(Chile)

Santiago

C
H
I
L
E

Buenos Aires

URUGUAY

Montevideo

ARGENTINA

Salado

Colorado

Negro

Miles
0   200   400   600

Falkland Islands
(Br.)

0   200   400   600
Kilometers

after Prentice-Hall World Atlas

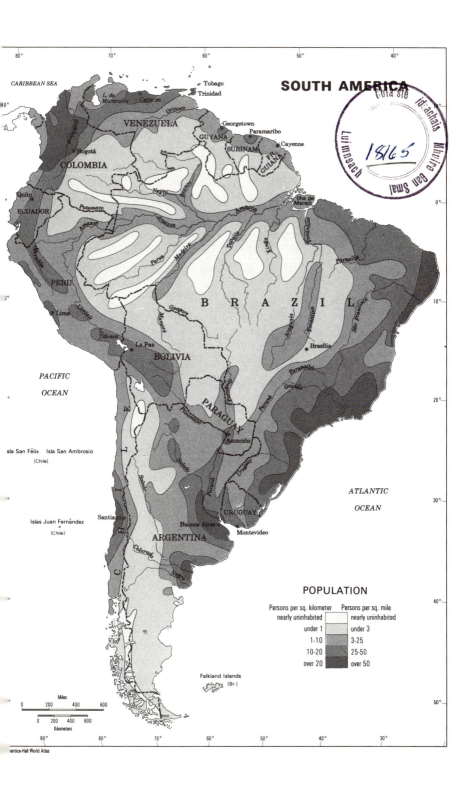

SOUTH AMERICA

CARIBBEAN SEA

Tobago
Trinidad

L. de
Maracaibo
Caracas

VENEZUELA

Orinoco

Georgetown

GUYANA

Bogotá

SURINAM

Paramaribo

COLOMBIA

Cayenne

FR.
GUIANA

Quito

Negro

Branco

Amazon

ECUADOR

Putumayo

Ilha de
Marajó

Amazon

Amazon

Japurá

Napo

Juruá

Purus

Madeira

Tapajós

Xingu

Tocantins

Araguaia

Parnaíba

Pornaíba

PERU

Lima

Ucayali

B   R   A   Z   I   L

Guaporé

Mamoré

L.
Titicaca

La Paz

São Francisco

Brasília

BOLIVIA

Paranaíba

PACIFIC

OCEAN

Grande

Paraná

sla San Félix   Isla San Ambrosio
(Chile)

Pilcomayo

PARAGUAY

Asunción

Salado

Paraná

Uruguay

ATLANTIC

OCEAN

Islas Juan Fernández
(Chile)

Santiago

C
H
I
L
E

Salado

URUGUAY

Buenos Aires

Montevideo

ARGENTINA

Colorado

POPULATION

Persons per sq. kilometer	Persons per sq. mile
nearly uninhabited	nearly uninhabited
under 1	under 3
1-10	3-25
10-20	25-50
over 20	over 50

Negro

Falkland Islands
(Br.)

Miles
0   200   400   600

0   200   400   600
Kilometers

increase the output and the material wealth of a country without regard to the means by which this is achieved or to the distribution of the increased output and wealth, this argument might have been valid; although even that is doubtful, since, even from the most narrow economic point of view, the massive unemployment and underemployment we are talking about represents a waste of human potential and human resources for economic growth. But that is, in any case, *not* the sole purpose of the developing nations. The strategy for the second Development Decade stresses as "the ultimate objective of development . . . to bring about sustained improvement in the well-being of the individual and bestow benefits on all. If undue privileges, extremes of wealth and poverty, and social injustices persist, then development fails in its essential purpose." And it is important to note that a significant reduction in unemployment and underemployment is among the major objectives of the strategy for the second Development Decade. For employment is, for most people, the only source of income; and raising employment levels is the only effective or feasible means of eliminating the most serious of all social injustices —that which deprives large numbers of people of the right to earn a decent living.

I shall not dwell any further on the rationale of an employment-oriented approach to development. My main concern will be to consider what an employment-oriented approach to development should consist of.

The question that really underlies the whole subject concerns the compatibility of employment objectives and economic-growth objectives in a development policy. A policy that places all the emphasis on employment expansion with no regard to its consequences for economic growth is certainly unthinkable: A stagnant or declining economy cannot for long provide remunerative jobs for all. It is equally certain, as the experience of recent years has shown, that a policy that places all the emphasis on growth with no regard to employment is socially unjust (and probably politically disastrous) since it widens the inequalities between the privileged few and the poverty-stricken unemployed or underemployed masses.

There may be occasions when a government is faced with a situation in a given sector in which a difficult choice has to be made between these two objectives. Such a choice would have to be a political one and would have to be made in the light of the specifics of the situation; a short-term sacrifice of a fraction of one percentage point in the growth of gross national product may in such circumstances have handsome political and social dividends (if it really does lead to the creation of higher levels of employment) as well as possibly longer-term economic dividends. However, this is, in any case, a matter of tactics rather than strategy. As far as the fundamentals of the strategy are concerned, I am convinced that a policy for economic growth is compatible with a policy for employment expansion, *provided that as much attention is devoted to the organization, the methods, and the composition of production as is currently being given to its volume.*

Taking the Glamour out of Modern Technology

This takes us to the heart of the problem. To organize production in such a way that it leads to increased employment without seriously slowing down the rate of growth will, in many cases, involve far-reaching reforms and the reversal of many long-established policies and practices. This is most obviously the case in policies relating to the choice of technology. To a very large extent, the serious unemployment and underemployment that characterize the less-developed nations of South America today are due to indiscriminate application of production techniques that have been developed in and for highly industrialized nations, where skill levels are high and labor tends to be scarce. I would, however, emphasize the word "indiscriminate." I am not suggesting that we put the clock back and invent the wheel all over again. In some cases and in some sectors, the introduction of even the most sophisticated technology may be appropriate and justifiable from the point of view of creating employment —especially when it can give rise to new employment opportunities that would not otherwise exist in other sectors.

But in an employment-oriented strategy for development, such cases are probably the exception rather than the rule. A country that seriously intends to tackle its unemployment problems needs to begin by considering how it can take the glamour out of modern technology. At present, it seems to be a matter of national pride on the part of many governments to install the most modern, automated plants and to be a matter of little concern to them that the output of such plants might have been produced more economically and with more beneficial social results if more labor and less capital had been employed.

The glamour of shiny, expensive new equipment cannot easily be dispelled, human nature being what it is. But human nature is also extremely responsive to financial and material incentives. And the fact is that in many South American nations there is every incentive, or at least few, if any, disincentives, for the private entrepreneur to adopt capital-intensive techniques—because of generous depreciation allowances, low interest rates, and so on. Labor may, however, be overpriced by comparison. Wage rates, fringe benefits, protective labor legislation, and militant trade unions may make an employer—particularly an employer not well versed or interested in personnel management and collective bargaining—think twice before increasing his labor force when this can be avoided. Thus, in many South American nations we have the paradoxical situation of a small, relatively well-paid labor force in the modern sector working long hours to get maximal returns from capital, while the remainder of the population lives in misery because it cannot find sufficiently remunerative employment.

Courtesy University of Wisconsin

A farming area on the shore of Lake Titicaca, Bolivia. This land is fallow much of the time because fertilizers are rarely used to restore its productivity. Plowing up and down the slope, instead of along the contour, is the usual practice. This is one example of the need for modern farming techniques to raise yields and rural incomes and to improve the quality of life generally in rural areas. Such measures might help to reduce migration to the cities and consequent urban unemployment.

The problem is, of course, that the unemployed have no one to promote their interests. There are plenty of persuasive salesmen to promote the purchase of machinery and equipment. The private entrepreneurs are well organized and powerful. And trade unions are concerned primarily with defending workers who are already employed—often at the expense of those who are not. But who is there to speak for the unemployed and underemployed? The Tupamaros did for a while, perhaps, but most of them are now in jail. Acts of violence and terrorism by these and other urban and rural guerrillas are but a reflection of the depths of misery and despair of millions of unemployed.

One problem we could profitably speculate on is, therefore, how to get a mix of capital and labor that will make it possible to employ more of the latter without reducing efficiency or destroying incentive. Which sectors and industries are the most likely providers of jobs in a less-developed nation?

It is clear that modern manufacturing is not a very promising sector from the employment point of view. Since this sector is the spearhead of economic growth, it would be folly to oblige it to employ more labor than it can absorb without destroying its competitive efficiency. A few thousand new jobs could and should be created in manufacturing if the biases in favor of capital were removed. A few more thousand might be created by changing production techniques in manufacturing, although in many manufacturing industries the choice of techniques is probably limited. And a further few thousand jobs could, in some cases, be found by a more widespread use of shift work in manufacturing.

These possibilities should not be overlooked. As nations develop, manufacturing will become, by definition, one of the main providers of employment. But if it is to achieve this goal in the future, its present growth must not be unduly stunted. So we must conclude that even by pursuing the most energetic policies to reduce the capital intensity of industrialization, as in my view they should do, governments can make, in the short run, only a small dent in the enormous employment problem. A small dent is, of course, better than no dent at all. But for the immediate future they will clearly have to pay a great deal more attention to other sectors, particularly agriculture and rural industries, in their search for measures to raise levels of employment.

We need new light on the immensely complex question of the optimal mix of labor and capital in nations where labor is plentiful and capital and skills are still scarce. In what circumstances, in what sectors, and in what industries are capital-intensive methods of production to be preferred, even from the point of view of employment creation?

I suggested earlier that we need to look not only at the methods but also at the *composition* of production. But the composition of production depends, of course, in large measure on demand. And the structure of domestic demand may depend to a very large extent on the distribution of income.

Social Justice and Economic Growth

Is it true that the concentration of wealth in the hands of a few, and in urban rather than rural areas, creates an excessively heavy demand for goods and services that can be produced only by large inputs of imported capital and intermediate products and of skilled labor? Is it further true that if income is more evenly distributed through taxation, social security, and social services it will create greater demand for less-sophisticated products requiring a much greater input of unskilled labor and a much lower input of capital? These ideas were put forward by a large international mission organized by the International Labour Organization (ILO) under the leadership of Dudley Seers which two years ago advised the government of Colombia on an employment strategy. If they are true, do they not represent an important breakthrough in theories of economic and social development? Do they not bring us much closer to a synthesis of economic growth and social justice?

So far, I have deliberately concentrated on steps that might be taken at the national level, by national authorities. This must, I think, be the principal focus of concern because, in the absence of a firm national commitment to employment promotion and energetic action by the nations themselves, no amount of prodding and assistance from the international community can help. But, at the same time, national employment policies, however firm, can, in this interdependent world of ours, be severely compromised if the rest of the world is pursuing the wrong sort of trade and aid policies.

Let us take a look first at international trade. The less-developed nations of South America have a tremendous potential advantage in exporting labor-intensive products. If the more-developed nations were to reduce or, even better, eliminate trade barriers for those products, employment would be stimulated in these less-developed nations. They would also be enabled to earn more foreign exchange. Is it too much to ask the more-industrialized nations to relax import restrictions on products in which they do not have the comparative advantage?

There is also, of course, the role that could be played by the giant multinational corporations which have operations in many of these developing nations. Already they are very important employers of labor; in some countries they are among the biggest employers. But do they employ all the labor they could? Is there not a tendency for them to use the production techniques—usually labor-saving techniques—that are in use in their countries of origin? How can these tendencies be checked? We must at the same time emphasize that developing nations may become markets for the industrial and agricultural products of one another—and this aspect of the problem should be constantly in the forefront of our preoccupations (see, for example, the discussion of the Andean Common Market, pages 47–60).

Then we come to the knotty problem of international aid. Could aid not be directed at sectors that have the greatest promise for employment creation—agricultural development, for example, or the development of viable small-scale industries—rather than the construction of impressive and expensive plants employing little labor? Moreover, could we not advocate a more liberal policy regarding the kind of aid that requires the importation from the donor nations of equipment that is capital-intensive? Although such aid may have impressive effects on the gross national product, it may have little effect on the employment situation in the recipient country.

And, finally, what does this employment-oriented approach to development imply for the organizations of the international community? On this question I am not, of course, a dispassionate observer, since my last years as Director General of the ILO were devoted to launching its World Employment Program. As I saw the problem at that time, and as I still see it now, employment promotion is not a matter for the ILO alone. It involves many different aspects of national development policy —food and agriculture, science and technology, industrialization, education, training, public health, housing, taxation, wages, industrial relations, and international trade. Policies in all these fields need to be looked at again in the light of the contribution they can make, not only to economic growth, but also to a better distribution of the gains of growth through higher levels of employment.

If development in the next decade merely serves to make the rich richer, bringing few or no benefits to the rapidly growing, poverty-stricken masses, we will risk seeing our efforts overtaken by a social earthquake based on the misery and despair of those who are unable to earn a decent livelihood for themselves and their families.

4 A RURAL EMPLOYMENT STRATEGY FOR SOUTH AMERICA*

Robert d'A. Shaw

Green Revolution in South America? · Pros and Cons of Mechanization · Land Reform, Power, and Status · Intensifying and Diversifying Agriculture · Creating Small Industries in Small Country Towns · Hope for the Poor?

Agriculture is so dominant in the economies of the less-developed nations that the strategies chosen to implement rural development will determine to a great extent the nature of the entire society that will emerge. This is true even of South America, where the processes of urbanization and industrialization have gone further than in any other developing region. Even in this continent, the number of people living in rural areas and the number dependent on agriculture for a living are likely to increase in absolute terms over the next generation while decreasing as a percentage of the total population.

This, then, is the setting for the need for a rural employment strategy in South America. The urgency of this need is highlighted by three addi-

* The views presented here are the author's and are not necessarily shared by any organization with which he is affiliated.

tional factors. In the first place, there is the desperate migration of millions of farm families to the squatter slums of the urban areas in search of jobs. Secondly, although agricultural output in South America has increased, *per capita* output has actually fallen by 3 per cent over the past decade. This has aggravated the problem of inflation and the foreign-exchange bottleneck to development. And, finally, the rural poor (those in most need of the benefits of development) are becoming relatively, and in some cases absolutely, worse off in terms of income distribution. In Colombia, for example, the poorest third of the rural population has probably seen *no* improvement in the standard of living in the past forty years. This not only creates severe problems of equity but also constrains the growth of the domestic markets and savings.

Yet the continent has abundant resources of land. Indeed, the United Nations has estimated that 1.2 billion acres in South America are suitable for crop production. At present fewer than 220 million acres are actually harvested in any year (though we should bear in mind that much of the rest of the land is expensive to develop, is barely accessible, or has relatively poor soils). Given this situation, some governments are becoming more aware of the need for a strategy capable of increasing agricultural output while at the same time increasing the number of decent job opportunities in the rural areas.

There are two factors in South America that could make this strategy feasible, provided that the necessary political will exists and that suitable policies and institutions can be established. The first is availability of land. According to the Indicative World Plan of the Food and Agriculture Organization (FAO), the area harvested in South America may be expected to expand by about 1 per cent per year over the period 1975–85. This in itself will allow the creation of more jobs in agriculture, not only for the farmers who settle this new land, but also for those engaged in clearing it, building roads and other forms of the infrastructure, and supplying irrigation where necessary. A possible problem is that land settlement is very expensive and therefore a major drain on overloaded development budgets. Another is that much of the land preparation and cultivation can be expected to be done by large-scale machines, which do not create many jobs.

But the principal doubt about land expansion as a solution lies in the scope of the problem. Agricultural output in South America will have to rise at 4 to 5 per cent per year to keep pace with the exploding population and rising incomes in the cities. Furthermore, land expansion

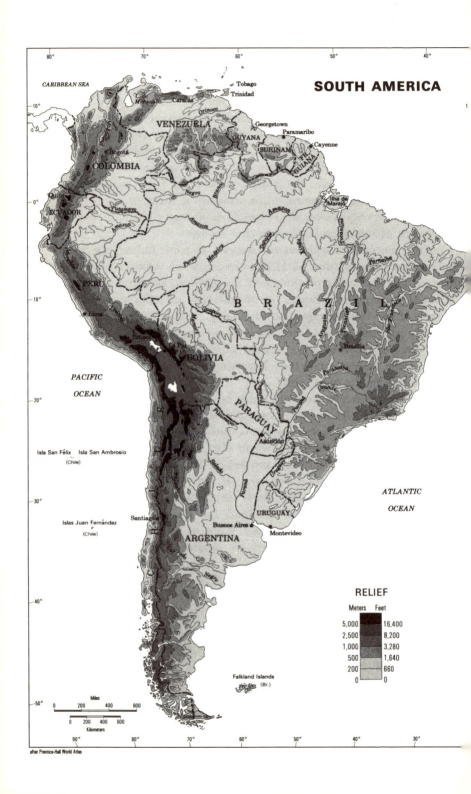

SOUTH AMERICA

CARIBBEAN SEA

Tobago
Trinidad

L. Maracaibo
Caracas
Orinoco

VENEZUELA
Georgetown
Paramaribo
GUYANA
SURINAM
Cayenne
FR. GUIANA

Bogotá

COLOMBIA

Quito
ECUADOR

Negro

Putumayo

Amazon

Amazon

Ilha de Marajó

Amazon

Parus

Madeira

Purus

Tocantins

Parnaíba

PERU

Lima

Guaporé

B   R   A   Z   I   L

Titicaca

Mamoré

BOLIVIA

Araguaia

Xingu

Tapajós

Brasília

PACIFIC

OCEAN

Paranaíba

Grande

Isla San Félix   Isla San Ambrosio
(Chile)

PARAGUAY

Pilcomayo

Asunción

Paraná

Paraguay

Islas Juan Fernández
(Chile)

Santiago

Salado

Uruguay

ATLANTIC

OCEAN

URUGUAY

Buenos Aires

Montevideo

ARGENTINA

Negro

RELIEF

Meters   Feet

5,000   16,400
2,500   8,200
1,000   3,280
500   1,640
200   660
0   0

Falkland Islands
(Br.)

Miles
0   200   400   600

0   200   400   600
Kilometers

after Prentice-Hall World Atlas

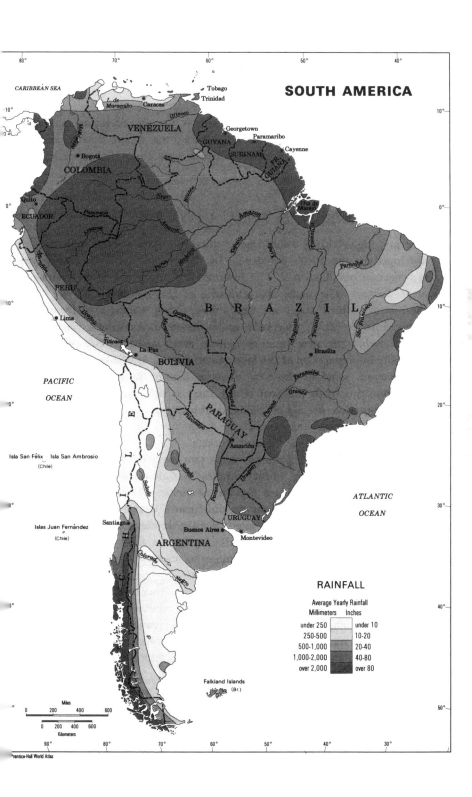

SOUTH AMERICA

CARIBBEAN SEA

Tobago
Trinidad

L. de Maracaibo
Caracas

VENEZUELA

Orinoco

Georgetown
Paramaribo
GUYANA
Cayenne
SURINAM
FR.
GUIANA

Bogotá

COLOMBIA

Quito
ECUADOR

Negro

Amazon

Ilha d.
Marajó

Putumayo

Amazon

Purús

Madeira

Parnaíba

B   R   A   Z   I   L

PERU

Tapajós

Xingu

Tocantins

Lima

Ucayali

Guaporé

Mamoré

Titicaca

La Paz

Brasília

São Francisco

BOLIVIA

PACIFIC

OCEAN

Paraná

Grande

Paraguay

Isla San Félix   Isla San Ambrosio
(Chile)

PARAGUAY

Pilcomayo

Asunción

Salado

Islas Juan Fernández
(Chile)

Santiago

Buenos Aires

Montevideo

ATLANTIC

OCEAN

URUGUAY

Uruguay

Paraná

ARGENTINA

Salado

Colorado

RAINFALL

Negro

Average Yearly Rainfall

Millimeters	Inches
under 250	under 10
250-500	10-20
500-1,000	20-40
1,000-2,000	40-80
over 2,000	over 80

Falkland Islands
(Br.)

Miles
0   200   400   600

0   200   400   600
Kilometers

Prentice-Hall World Atlas

can hardly hope to affect more than a small proportion of the many millions of small farmers in the region—and it is this vast group that forms the core of the poverty/employment problem. Thus, solution of this problem must depend largely on increasing the value of output per acre, especially on small farms. And this is the second factor making a rural employment strategy possible, namely, the recent development of cereals that yield two or even three times more than local varieties—the Green Revolution.

Green Revolution in South America?

The first high-yielding dwarf wheats suitable for subtropical regions were developed in the 1940's in Mexico by the Rockefeller Foundation (the organization now known as The International Maize and Wheat Improvement Center). The main characteristics of the new varieties are their short stems, which stand up well under strong winds, and their high response to fertilizer, especially under irrigated conditions. To obtain greater yields, the new varieties require much more careful cultivation, especially in preparation of the land, water control, fertilizing, and weeding. Furthermore, some of the new varieties mature in a shorter time, so they allow two crops per year where there is sufficient controlled water. The combination of higher yields, double-cropping, and more intensive cultivation increases the amount of labor used per acre planted, and also increases the income of farm workers.

Based on the initial research, important progress has been made in developing high-yielding wheat varieties in Colombia, Chile, Peru, and Uruguay. These varieties are capable of yields of fifteen tons per acre on irrigated land and ten tons on unirrigated lands—more than double those of the varieties normally used. Similar developments have occurred for rice, which is a staple in Brazil. Maize, the most important single cereal in South America, is also beginning to respond to research, especially that designed to increase its nutritional value.*

Cereals have a special significance in the area because they supply more than two fifths of the proteins and calories consumed and are grown by the majority of small farmers. Thus, research forms a keystone of a successful rural development strategy. Much work remains to be done to extend the area suitable for the new varieties (especially in drier places),

* Significant progress is being made in improving the protein quality of maize as a result of the discovery in the United States in 1964 of the lysine-rich mutants opaque-2 and floury-2.

to improve the nutritional content of cereals, and to develop varieties resistant to diseases and pests.

However, comparing the technologies currently available with the small number of farmers affected, we can accept the judgment of the FAO that "the constraints on the wider adoption of high-yielding varieties and other means of raising output per [acre] are mainly non-technical." * That is, the whole system of farming in South America slows the introduction of new technologies, especially to the small farmer. The question remains, what changes can be made to capitalize on the opportunities of the Green Revolution so as to increase the amounts of employment and income available to the majority of the region's farmers?

Pros and Cons of Mechanization

In all South American nations, government policies encourage the mechanization of agriculture. This is done in part through low interest rates; indeed, in a few nations on occasion the interest rate has been lower than the rate of inflation. Low interest rates and import duties and subsidized credit to large farmers have made it profitable to buy large tractors and other heavy equipment, such as combine harvesters. For these and other reasons, South America now has almost twice as many four-wheel tractors as the whole of Asia.

So important is mechanization in defining the future of the agricultural sectors in less-developed nations that their governments should give the highest priority to conceiving coherent national strategies to deal with the issues raised. The labor-displacement effects of any mechanization permitted must be carefully analyzed. Present indications are that serious labor displacements are being caused by introducing combines and tractors as in Mexico. At the same time, instead of channeling scarce foreign exchange and capital resources into large-scale mechanization it may be possible to increase agricultural production in ways more beneficial to the total society. If further research proves this to be the case, then a slowdown in farm mechanization is clearly indicated.

In order to develop a coherent mechanization strategy, the governments of the less-developed nations should establish a set of criteria to apply to demands for agricultural mechanization. The most important point to be addressed is the divergence between the net benefits accruing to farmers and those accruing to society at large. There are two main

* Provisional Indicative World Plan for Agricultural Development, I. Rome: FAO, 1970, p. 101.

elements involved in this divergence: the fact that capital investment in agricultural machinery is subsidized today in various ways, and the fact that individual employers and society evaluate labor differently.

In general, given a situation in which labor is abundant and capital is scarce, the use of capital should not be subsidized. The problem of agricultural mechanization can be treated as part of the general problem of the imbalance between the prices of capital and labor in the less-developed nations. Righting this imbalance should be the aim of these nations if they want to make the most effective use of their abundant resources. The essential elements of the solution to this problem are to raise interest rates and to value foreign exchange at a more appropriate, higher level. Where there is reluctance to do this, special policies should be devised for agricultural mechanization because of the immediate, critical danger of rural labor displacement. At the very least, taxation and pricing policies should place the full burden of all costs on those farmers who purchase the machinery. Subsidies on agricultural machinery in the form of undervalued foreign exchange, cheap subsidized credit, and similar devices should cease. Another approach would be to place heavy taxes on agricultural machinery, preferably graduated by horsepower.

An even more difficult problem is the valuation of labor. It does not cost society anything if labor is employed at a subsistence wage in the agricultural sector, but there is a definite cost for employers. On the other hand, if a laborer is displaced, there may be a net saving to the farmer who employs him, but society has to pay the cost of supporting him. And this cost rises if he moves to the city, where he requires housing, sanitation, and other social services, as well as a job. It is very difficult to devise measures to correct this difference. One could subsidize the wages of all labor employed in agriculture, but this is not economically or administratively feasible for the less-developed nations. Theoretically, it should be possible to place the costs of labor on the employer, whether or not he actually employs the labor. This possibility appears to be politically infeasible at the present time, although it should not be ruled out for the future. It might be possible to tax labor-displacing machinery heavily enough to pay for relocating and employing the redundant workers it creates. A third alternative is to increase the number of self-employed small farmers at the expense of large landowners, in which case the problem would be avoided.

Governments have a responsibility to determine where tractor mechanization is essential and to devise suitable methods for supplying it.

They could, for example, provide state-owned tractor stations with sufficient capacity to handle local needs. Services could be priced so that farmers in these areas would not obtain a competitive advantage over those in non-tractorized areas.

There is an urgent need for research in and manufacture of agricultural implements that can raise productivity and loosen labor bottlenecks, and yet be used by the great majority of small farmers without displacing vast numbers of laborers. The possibility of selective mechanization to complement labor utilization and intensify agriculture deserves special attention. Irrigation is a case in point. Pumps and tube wells to facilitate water control should be exempted from the stringent measures advocated above. In other situations where serious seasonal labor shortages occur, there may be a case for exempting other types of machinery: threshing and drying machines are good candidates for this category.

Again, with respect to small farmers, choices have to be made about the trade-off between, on the one hand, lowering their costs by developing small-scale tractors and implements and extending custom-hire services and, on the other hand, the possibly adverse labor-displacement effects of even this level of mechanization.

All these issues call for tough decisions, particularly because large- and medium-scale farmers are aware of the present advantages of mechanization and because of the power of these groups in the politics of the less-developed nations. At the same time, the rest of the rural population is becoming more sensitive to the changes in their relationships with their landlords and employers. They feel increasingly insecure, and they see a relative, if not absolute, decline in their incomes, much of which can be blamed on mechanization. This dilemma demands careful policies to maximize agricultural development while minimizing social conflicts.

Land Reform, Power, and Status

An area of major concern to political leaders and administrators is the perennially difficult problem of land reform. Inequality of land distribution is evidently worse in South America than in other less-developed regions. But the effect of this maldistribution on employment is unclear. Large farms tend to employ far fewer workers per acre than do small farms. The reasons lie in the greater tendency and ability of large landowners, most of them absentee, to buy labor-displacing machinery; differences in land quality; and the preference of many large landowners for grazing livestock extensively rather than growing more labor-intensive crops.

In a dynamic agricultural situation, sparked by new technologies, it is the large farmers who benefit most. They have capital or can borrow it against their land; they can obtain extension services more easily; and they often have better access to government infrastructure, such as roads, markets, and irrigation. All this means that they can more easily adopt new varieties.

A major study of land reforms in many countries has recently been completed.* It has strengthened the economic case for land reform by demonstrating that in most of these countries, small farms have higher productivity per acre than large farms.

A key, yet often neglected, aspect of land reform is tenancy. The evidence from many parts of the world of a deterioration in landlord-tenant relationships in areas where the new cereal varieties have been introduced on owner-operated farms and incomes have risen markedly is a strong argument for a determined program to give tenants security of tenure. This should encourage them to invest in the land they farm and to adopt the high-yielding varieties where they are suitable.

Fundamental to land reform is a willingness on the part of governments of the less-developed nations to distribute land holdings more evenly. Land redistribution by itself is not a panacea for rural problems. It alone may not bring increases in income to small farmers; its success depends on whether they can be mobilized to take advantage of the new opportunities and whether they can be provided with the necessary services to ensure their productivity.

Despite the fact that land reform is not a complete solution, it is a key link in a strategy to increase rural employment opportunities. In the first place, effective land redistribution obviates the need for mechanization of large farms. As the scale of farm units is reduced, the difficulties of managing sizable numbers of laborers on a single unit would be eliminated. Then, too, if all farms are roughly the same size, such services as marketing, credit, and irrigation can all be standardized and geared to that size. In most Asian nations today, there are essentially two agricultural service systems, one for the large commercial farmers, and the other to subsidize small farmers and tenants—with resulting inefficiencies and inequities. Land reform would also permit more even distribution of people on the land. As the new technologies are adopted in this

* U.S. Agency for International Development. *Spring Review on Land Reform,* June 2–4, 1970.

Community work projects, called *mingas,* are traditional among Indians of the Andes. Here fathers have gathered to put a new roof on their children's school. The Peruvian government contributed about $260 to the project for materials. At present the rural sector of South America is potentially the most important provider of jobs. Together with land reform and measures to increase agricultural production, public-works programs in housing, road-building, land-clearing, and construction of irrigation facilities could do much to revitalize rural areas, providing jobs for large numbers of people.

situation, each small farm could use its family labor more fully and, at the same time, employ hired hands on a regular basis. A large number of small farmers could thereby be brought into modern society, become part of the market economy, expand the demand for agricultural inputs and locally made consumer goods, and increase the supply of agricultural produce.

Land reform implies drastic revisions in patterns of income distribution, political power, and social hierarchies. All these changes will encounter strong resistance from vested interests. But what is the alternative? The value of viable farm plots is rising rapidly as a result of the Green Revolution. Power and status emanating from land ownership are increasing along with land values. Yet more people than ever before lack the benefits of land ownership. In this situation it would hardly be

A RURAL EMPLOYMENT STRATEGY   41

surprising to see more *de facto* land redistribution of the kind already taking place in parts of South America.

The introduction of the new varieties increases the urgency of the need for land reform because of its effect on land values and vested interests. At the same time, however, the Green Revolution may make it easier to convince large landowners that they can make a decent living with smaller holdings that do not expose them to the dangers of appropriation by the disadvantaged.

It is sometimes argued that progressive land taxation, preferably based on potential rather than actual output, could be a substitute for land reform. Progressive land taxes would help to equalize incomes in rural areas, and basing them on potential output would encourage production. It is, of course, extremely important for the over-all economic development of the poor countries that their agricultural sectors provide capital for the growth of the industrial sectors. Taxing agricultural output is one way of doing this. But progressive land taxes based on potential output are very hard to administer, and they fall more heavily on large farmers than small, thus raising political problems similar to those encountered in reforming land tenure. Moreover, evaluating potential and subsistence output is both complex and controversial. If changes in agricultural taxes were to follow land-reform measures, governments would still have to cope with the inefficiency of taxing a large number of small holdings. However, it can also be argued that

> While administratively it may be easier to collect taxes from a small number of landlords than from numerous peasantry, politically just the reverse may be true. Actually land reform may serve as one of the means by which it becomes politically feasible to transfer the accumulating function from the landlord to the state.*

This is particularly true if taxes are imposed and collected by local authorities who can use a portion of the revenue to undertake projects of direct benefit to local taxpayers.

Intensifying and Diversifying Agriculture

If opportunities presented by the Green Revolution to create more jobs are to be fully exploited, the area planted with the new cereals must be

---

* Alexander Eckstein, "Land Reform and Economic Development." *World Politics*, VII, no. 4 (July, 1955), p. 660.

expanded. This complex subject has been dealt with fully in other studies.* The principal measures required are as follows:

1. Expand the areas with controlled water supply
2. Maintain price incentives for producers
3. Provide adequate supplies of seeds, fertilizers, and pesticides
4. Extend credit institutions to allow farmers to purchase inputs such as seeds, fertilizers, and pesticides
5. Increase research on adapting the new cereal varieties to local ecological conditions and to local tastes
6. Provide suitable extension and education services in the rural areas
7. Create a marketing system capable of handling increased amounts of agricultural inputs and outputs.

The role of multipurpose cooperatives and farmers' associations in this expansion needs to be explored. The record of cooperatives in South America has been mixed at best, but well-run cooperatives have a significant role to play in a rural employment strategy. For example, they can allow small farmers access to the institutions of marketing and credit without which this group will have difficulty in becoming commercially viable. Secondly, the cost of providing inputs and credit to millions of small farmers can be prohibitive: The cost of administration for a $50 loan is roughly the same as for a $5,000 loan. Good cooperatives allow these small loans to be made profitably and with a high repayment rate. Finally, cooperatives can be a valuable vehicle for mobilizing savings even from very small farmers if they can pay realistic interest rates and can make a profit on their loans. A useful comparative study of farmers' cooperatives in developing countries has recently been published.† It sets out a series of principles to make these organizations viable tools for extending agricultural progress to small farmers.

However, extending the area planted to the new cereal varieties will not in itself solve the problems of rural poverty, even if every effort is made to create as many jobs as possible. Conditions are not suitable for raising the new wheats and rices in many places. Moreover, the demand for these cereals can be met relatively easily. In order to capitalize fully

---

* See, for example, Lester Brown, *Seeds of Change.* New York, N.Y.: Praeger, 1970.
† *Farmer Cooperatives in Developing Countries.* Washington, D.C.: Advisory Committee on Overseas Cooperative Development, 1971.

on employment opportunities in the rural areas, the Green Revolution must not be treated in isolation. Governments must recognize the fact that the increased productivity of the new cereals frees resources for diversifying agriculture. In particular, less-developed nations should adopt aggressive policies for diversifying their agricultural production into fruit and vegetable production, feed grains, and livestock and poultry industries. All these types of production should help to expand both directly and indirectly the available number of productive employment opportunities.

Creating Small Industries in Small Country Towns

The potential for increasing the area under the Green Revolution is closely related to the rate at which the demand for food grows. In food-deficit countries, the demand for food can grow rapidly for a few years through the displacement of imports. But once it is satisfied domestically, the growth rate of demand will be determined primarily by the population growth rate, the increase in per capita income, and food prices. It is at least possible that, with the new technologies, the increase in supply can outrun the increase in food demand resulting from these factors.

Several measures can be implemented to make full use of the more flexible situation. The most important of these are public-works programs. The principal requirement for such programs is unskilled human labor, and they therefore help to ease the unemployment problem. Moreover, since unskilled laborers spend a high proportion of their income on food, the demand for food rises with their incomes. Public-works programs also help to build the infrastructure necessary for rural regeneration—the roads, dams, houses, and schools that are essential investments for a better standard of living. And such programs tend to be far more productive and profitable in rural areas where crop yields are rapidly inceasing.

A similar argument can be used to encourage the restructuring of industry toward medium- and small-scale manufacturing. This would provide simple consumer goods such as textiles, utensils, and furniture to satisfy the increased rural purchasing power of farmers using the new cereals and of laborers employed in public works. Such industries tend to use local raw materials and employ relatively large numbers of workers for relatively small amounts of capital. Like the laborers in public-works programs, these workers spend much of their income on food.

These medium- and small-scale industries cannot, however, grow without help. Their managers often lack the knowledge and capital to expand by themselves. Governments can encourage expansion through a package of assistance, comprising research and design services, credit, joint training operations, and marketing.

Medium- and small-scale industries could form the nuclei of a network of rural growth centers, which would also help to raise the level of employment and the demand for food. This network would consist of a series of small country towns strategically placed to supply goods and needed services to rural villages. They, in turn, would be linked to service centers and supply lines in large towns. The Green Revolution presents an ideal spur to such a strategy because the new agricultural technologies encourage the growth of the market economy and increase the demand for productive investments, marketing facilities, and consumer goods. The growth centers could help meet these needs as well as provide social services quickly and cheaply to the farming community, thus raising its real income. They could have agricultural processing facilities and they could manufacture simple, improved tools for the new technologies. The centers could provide seasonal employment for laborers during the slack agricultural periods. They could also attract surplus farm workers who would otherwise move to large cities. Thus, growth centers could make a vital contribution to a rural employment strategy.

Hope for the Poor?

The Green Revolution brings opportunities for raising productivity among farmers, for intensifying and diversifying agriculture, for giving governments more flexibility in their pursuit of development, and hence for creating more jobs. It brings hope to the majority of the world's poor. But the opportunities are mixed with danger—the threats of growing inequalities between rich and poor farmers, of men being replaced by machines before other jobs are available to them, and of some regions far outpacing others in development. It should be stressed that the essence of the Green Revolution is simply the creation of a superior agricultural technology. But the effects of this technology on society will depend on the policies and institutions that implement it.

Tackling such problems will require massive international efforts. The poor nations themselves will have to face painful and difficult adjustments in their present policies. The policy decisions of the rich countries in trade, aid, private investment, and the transfer of technology will also be crucial. If the less-developed countries can at least manage to maintain their present share of world trade over the coming decades, they can generate more employment as well as boost their over-all economic growth rates. Expansion of the poor nations' exports requires a reduction of the barriers to that trade in the rich world. At the same time, the wise use of foreign aid would help to stimulate economic growth.

Private investment also brings great resources into the less-developed nations, provided that these resources are used carefully, and can make a substantial contribution to employment. Finally, the complex issue of the transfer of technology should be taken in concert with trade, aid, and investment policies. There is much room for the imaginative use of technology appropriate to unique situations in the less-developed nations. But who is to develop these technologies? Here the establishment of research funds and institutions by the rich nations could be of enormous value.

Clearly, the waste of human resources in the developing nations is a problem of international significance. To combat it will require great efforts on the part of both rich and poor countries. It is in the interest of all of us that these efforts be undertaken. As Robert McNamara asked, "Can we imagine any human order surviving with so gross a mass of misery piling up at its base?" *

* Robert S. McNamara. Address to the Board of Governors, World Bank, Copenhagen, September 21, 1970.

5 INTERNATIONAL COOPERATION FOR DEVELOPMENT
The Andean Common Market*

Kevin C. Kearns

The Andean Pact • Profile of the Andean Bloc • Plans to Reduce Competition and Increase Trade • Integrating Transport Links • Nationalism Versus Foreign Investment • Reorientation of External Trade • Political Realities

Economic cooperative movements are still in a youthful stage in South America, and it is therefore difficult to measure their impact on national economies. Yet, such measurement should be attempted, for the various forms of multinational cooperation and regional economic integration that are taking shape will certainly play an important role in the political and economic evolution of South America during the coming decade.

During the 1960's, the republics of South and Central America experienced a "collective awakening" in which superficial and exclusivist values gave way to pragmatic attitudes. Economic alliances were formed among neighbors based on the theory that a cooperative approach to common problems would benefit each of the participant countries far more than national economic self-sufficiency.

* Adapted from "The Andean Common Market: A New Thrust at Economic Integration in Latin America," *Journal of Inter-American Studies and World Affairs*, May, 1972, pp. 225–49.

The initial effort at integration was the Central American Common Market (CACM), formed in late 1960, which included all the nations of Central America except Panama. That same year the Latin American Free Trade Association (LAFTA) was created; it eventually represented 90 per cent of Latin America's population and 94 per cent of its area. A third grouping, the Caribbean Free Trade Association (CARIFTA), was established in 1968 by eleven British Commonwealth nations and territories. Cooperation to promote economic development thus became an accepted principle in Latin American thinking.

However, from its inception LAFTA had to contend with problems inherent in its organization. Regional deficiencies in transportation and telecommunications almost immediately hindered operations, highlighting the immensity of the area to be united. Equally difficult were the problems posed by governments which lacked the ability and the stability to manage domestic economies and often lacked enthusiasm for long-range and consistent international policies. To be sure, any multinational cooperative scheme encounters structural and functional difficulties, as demonstrated by the history of the European Common Market; but it quickly became obvious that LAFTA's problems were more formidable than most. The major weakness was the member nations' extremely diverse levels of development, ranging from the relatively strong economic bases and sizable markets of Brazil, Argentina, and Mexico to Ecuador's and Bolivia's attempts to establish foundations in light industry. It was the fervent hope of the poorer members that these disparities would be reduced, perhaps by the end of the first decade of cooperation.

Latin Americans who had hoped that the Free Trade Association would provide dynamic stimulus to all members were sadly disillusioned. Although appreciable increases in intra-LAFTA trade had, in fact, been realized, some basic fears of the smaller member nations were confirmed. Foremost among these was continued domination by the ABRAMEX nations—Argentina, Brazil, and Mexico—especially in the production and trade of manufactured and semifinished goods. The other nations of LAFTA became concerned that they might become mere economic vassals to the stronger powers.

Meanwhile, the enthusiasm of the ABRAMEX nations steadily waned as they turned again toward their non-LAFTA markets, which still account for nearly 90 per cent of their exports. This served only to exacerbate matters. LAFTA's image clearly reached its nadir at the end of 1967, when negotiators could not reach agreement on the second stage of a common list of products to be freed from tariffs and duties by 1973. At this point many felt that the organization had virtually collapsed.

The Andean Pact

A way out of the LAFTA impasse was suggested in 1967 when Presidents Carlos Lleras of Colombia and Eduardo Frei of Chile, seizing the opportunity presented by LAFTA's lethargy, proposed that the west coast nations of South America create a bloc as a counterforce to ABRAMEX. It was postulated that they already had some essential attributes of a successful common market—namely, a degree of physical contiguity, a limited but connecting system of transportation, similarly low income levels, a crucial need for increased market size, and even a history of common experiences and common problems, such as the integration of a sizable Indian culture group into the mainstream of national life (especially in Peru, Bolivia, and Ecuador).

On May 26, 1969, Bolivia, Chile, Colombia, Peru, and Ecuador signed the Cartagena Agreement, forming the Andean Common Market. Venezuela, one of the most ardent advocates of integration during the preliminary conferences, abruptly withdrew its application for membership at the last moment, probably a result of pressures brought to bear on the administration by private industry. But early in 1973, Venezuela decided to join ANCOM; the terms of its membership have not yet been disclosed, but apparently they are satisfactory to the other members. Venezuela's comparatively strong economy should greatly increase ANCOM's effectiveness.

The Andean Common Market is considerably more ambitious in conception than LAFTA. Its avowed goal is to raise living standards among the population of its five members within a reasonable period of time. ANCOM aspires to accomplish this by according the highest priority to

1. Harmonization of economic and social policies
2. Joint planning and execution of industrial projects predicated on multinational resources and markets, through sectorial development programs
3. Gradual and automatic elimination of all barriers to the free movement of goods among members
4. Establishment of a common external tariff to create a margin of preference for regional producers

5. Coordination of programs to speed development of the agricultural sector
6. Improvement of transportation and other facets of the region's infrastructure
7. Preferential treatment to be granted to the less-developed member nations of Bolivia and Ecuador

Profile of the Andean Bloc

In area the ANCOM region, with about 2,119,800 square miles, is more than twice as large as Argentina (1,072,067 square miles) and a good deal smaller than Brazil (3,286,470 square miles)—or about two thirds the size of the United States. With a combined population of 68.3 million, the nations of the Andean bloc range from Colombia, with 22.1 million people, to Bolivia, with a modest 4.8 million (Table 5.1). The average annual rate of population growth is about 3 per cent. At this rate of increase, the Market will be 105 million by 1985, by which time the Andean economies are expected to be well along toward integration. ANCOM's combined gross national product of $30 billion is larger than Argentina's and Mexico's and almost as large as Brazil's. With respect to GNP per person, large dis-

TABLE 5.1
NATIONAL POPULATION PROFILE OF THE ANDEAN GROUP
AND VENEZUELA (MID-1971) *

Country	Total Population (millions)	Annual Growth Rate (per cent)	Projected Population for 1985 (millions)	Per Capita Gross National Product (U.S. dollars)
Colombia	22.1	3.4	35.6	310
Ecuador	6.3	3.4	10.1	220
Peru	14.0	3.1	21.6	380
Bolivia	4.8	2.4	6.8	150
Chile	10.0	2.3	13.6	480
Total Andean Group	57.2	2.9	87.7	308
Venezuela	11.1	3.4	17.4	950
Grand total	68.3	3.0	105.1	415

SOURCE: *1971 World Population Data Sheet*, Population Reference Bureau, Washington, D.C., 1971.
* Since publication of this table, Venezuela has joined the Andean Common Market.

parities are manifest, especially between Venezuela, with $950, and Bolivia, with $150.

The cumulative resources of the bloc are a distinct asset. Andean nations lead South America in the production of many minerals, accounting for between 70 and 100 per cent of the copper, tin, molybdenum, tungsten, and bismuth. Nearly 50 per cent of the coal and 65 per cent of the iron are produced in these countries. Potential hydroelectric power is tremendous, especially in Peru and Colombia. Even in agriculture, the Andean bloc ranks high as a producer of bananas, sugar, cacao, cotton, and coffee. Simply stated, ANCOM is well endowed with resources upon which to draw for political as well as economic power in its dealings with other countries.

Plans to Reduce Competition and Increase Trade

Historically the Andean nations have traded very little with one another. Although they have attained a degree of industrial development since the end of World War II, with enterprises ranging from food-processing, textiles, clothing, cement, glass, chemicals, iron, and steel to some kinds of machinery and equipment, the national economies are still at an early stage of development; thus there are few manufactured commodities for export. Secondly, most of the mineral and agricultural products that comprise the bulk of Andean exports are items common to several or all members (oil, iron, copper, bananas, sugar, coffee). Consequently, until ANCOM generates industrial and manufactured products for exchange, there will be relatively few complementary (non-competitive) articles for intraregional trade.

Despite the fact that these countries rely heavily on agriculture, they are by no means self-sufficient in foodstuffs. Since agriculture is primarily geared toward products for export rather than domestic consumption, most nations require additional meat, feedgrains, wheat, and vegetable oils—deficiencies generally alleviated by imports from the United States. Trade with the United States has long been a salient feature of their economies. Sales by the Andean members to each other average about $65 million a year, whereas sales to the United States average fourteen times that amount—in excess of $840 million a year. In reciprocation, the United States is a major provider for Andean markets. Machinery, equipment, and manufactured goods account for over half the United States exports to ANCOM nations. The Andean governments hope that, through association, they can change this unfavorable import-export pattern and reduce dependence on the United States for their manufactured goods.

To achieve the objectives of a balanced industrial development and an equitable distribution of the benefits derived from cooperation, ANCOM proposes regional industrial programming. In accordance with this strategy, members will obligate themselves to pursue a course of industrial development for the subregion as a whole rather than just for their nation. This can mean expansion, specialization, and diversification of production, maximal utilization of regional resources, and the advantages of large-scale operations. Through such programming, the industries to be promoted in each nation are selected and the best locations for manufacturing plants are determined. Such decisions are made after taking into account factors such as accessibility to raw materials, transportation, and markets. An integral part of this coordination of industrial-production targets is a bilateral and multilateral agreement to further specialization and diversification in industry and avoid needless and costly competition or duplication of regional products. After careful study, an ANCOM commission assigns responsibility for manufacturing specific products; member nations not responsible for these commodities then pledge to prohibit, discourage, or refrain from promoting production of them within their area.

The Andean Petrochemical Agreement was the first multilateral agreement to be enacted on a complementary basis. All Andean nations produce petroleum, so a scheme was devised to avoid duplication. By unanimous approval, thirty-nine petrochemical products, many of which are primary products used in making synthetic fibers, plastics, rubber, paints, adhesives, and pesticides, were apportioned among Colombia, Peru, Chile, and Bolivia. Further production plans will cover pharmaceuticals, plastics, data-processing equipment, glass, electrical goods, domestic appliances, office equipment, and automotive parts. Savings to be effected through large-scale operations will also be emphasized. One of the traditional evils of South American economies is the prevalence of small and inefficient industrial plants. These will be discouraged in the future. Instead, one large steel rolling mill will be built to serve an area in which perhaps three smaller and less economical ones might be installed if each nation were acting on its own. The saving could be substantial. The pulp and paper industry is another example. As late as 1964, there was only one

South American plant with a capacity of 150,000 tons a year (a figure generally considered optimal), whereas some 180 pulp mills and paper factories had a capacity of less than 5,000 tons annually. ANCOM plans new mills with a minimal annual capacity of 60,000 tons. The principles for large-scale production can be applied to a wide array of processing and manufacturing plants in the region. As in all countries, small- and medium-sized industry will always have a place, often as a supplier of items for large-scale industry.

As this complementary system expands, new products and their markets will appear, thereby laying the foundation for additional intrazonal trade. The goal is to remove *all* tariffs and other restrictions from these trade items by 1980. A considerable number of goods now freely cross borders. Fifty items—manufactures, raw materials, and intermediate consumer goods—produced by Ecuador are being admitted duty-free by Chile, Colombia, and Peru. Colombia is receiving typewriters, radios, sewing machines, and printing machinery from Peru and Chile. To ensure the continued flow of this trade a common external tariff will be fixed around the region, thus converting it from a mere free-trade zone into a true Common Market. While this will not be accomplished before the mid-1980's, the initial stage, a minimum common tariff, is already in effect offering adequate protection for local products.

Integrating Transport Links

In theory, cooperation in industry and trade seems feasible in the Andean region, but in practice it is more difficult. Probably nowhere else does the landscape offer such great obstacles to commercial exchanges. The high ranges of the Andean Cordillera, the heavily forested *selva* plains, and the broad, treacherous rivers all tend to isolate people and resources. Yet these obstacles must be overcome if a regional transportation network is to be established—as indeed it must, since it is a fundamental requisite of a viable common market.

Because of the difficult terrain, maritime transport is still the principal means of shipping commodities between Andean nations, but highway and air travel are increasing. Highway transport, especially, is evolving as the major mode of travel and shipment in countries such as Colombia and Peru. The network of major South American highways does link the ANCOM nations, but away from these main arteries decent all-weather roads are scarce. And, to varying degrees, the Andean states are all plagued by a problem endemic to most developing nations: Their economy tends to be closely tied to the United States and Western Europe, fostering production for export rather than intraregional trade. Transportation systems are all too frequently directed toward foreign markets, with roads linking inland regions and cities to ports but not to one another. There is an urgent need for drastic reorientation of this pattern. A transport system must be devised to connect markets with production centers without regard to either foreign markets or national frontiers. Since the end of World War II, a number of new highway projects have been funded by international loans, but generally the Andean nations have themselves done too little to promote this part of the infrastructure.

ANCOM planners are, however, studying numerous proposals for providing direct overland transportation between regions, completely disregarding national borders. The most grandiose effort at planned transport integration is the Carretera Marginal de la Selva, the proposed highway, which, upon completion, will extend 3,000 miles along the eastern slope of the Andes from western Venezuela to southern Bolivia. When finished, this project is expected to open up vast tracts of fertile land (estimated at nearly 18.3 million acres), which so far have been untapped because of their inaccessibility. The highway should generate at least $134 million annually in additional agricultural production alone for the adjacent nations.

Ocean transportation could also benefit greatly from integration. All the ANCOM nations have shipping lines, including landlocked Bolivia, which operates through Chilean and Peruvian ports. The member nations are now considering pooling merchant fleets to form a single Andean line which would serve west coast ports and port facilities. Wider use of containerization would further facilitate the pooling of fleets. Colombia has been transporting cargo in containers since 1963 and strongly favors this type of shipping for the future.

Where land travel is slow and costly, a relatively well-developed air-cargo service is used within some nations and between these and the United States, but there is still little air-cargo traffic between one Andean country and another. A unified air transport would ensure maximum use of aircraft while a system of common schedules, equipment, and staff would promote intraregional trading. Indeed, the potentialities of an integrated regional development of land, sea, and air transport are impressive.

Nationalism Versus Foreign Investment

Among all the issues kindred to the founding of the Andean Common Market, none has raised so much controversy as the weighty matter of foreign investment—and for good reason. Recognition that many of the industrial and infrastructural development plans proposed by ANCOM planners will require funds that the member countries do not possess (even collectively) clearly points to the need for foreign capital. But formulating a foreign-investment policy acceptable to all six members may prove to be a problem not easily resolved.

The United States is the major provider of capital for the Andean countries and accounts for at least 70 per cent of all foreign investment in the three principal countries of Chile, Peru, and Colombia. Even without the $1-billion investment in mining and smelting in Peru and Chile, the U.S. investors' stake in manufacturing is nearly $400 million. This incursion of outside money from the United States and the power it wields both economically and politically has become a source of much disquietude in at least a few of these countries and has prompted the acrimonious statement of one Andean economist, "If we can't make a success of the Andean Pact, we deserve to remain subservient to Yankee imperialism." * Actually, there has been distrust on both sides: Andeans have grown increasingly resentful over U.S. capital investment and the large profits that go abroad instead of into other local economic ventures; many U.S. investors apparently regard these countries as a high-risk area. This problem has been exacerbated in recent years by the world shortage of investment money. Hostility, too, has been occasioned by the outbreak of politico-economic rifts between several of the Andean governments and the United States. Most notable have been the alleged violations by U.S. vessels of the territorial sea of Peru and Ecuador, a claim vigorously disputed by the United States. With Chile it has been the nationalization of large U.S. companies, principally those engaged in copper mining. Simply put, the general climate of relations between these countries and the United States has been something less than ideal since the mid-1960's.

* Clem Cohen. "Venezuela Preparing to Enter Andean Group." *Andean Air Mail and Peruvian Times,* Dec. 3, 1971, p. 6.

Not surprisingly, then, the matter of formulating foreign-investment and trade policies was accorded the highest priority by ANCOM officials.

In late 1970, the five member nations met for the avowed purpose of fabricating a functional code for foreign investment and brought to the surface one of the sharpest dichotomies within the "family," namely, the ideological gap between the "soft-liners" and the "hard-liners." Without question, each country has a strong sense of nationalism, but some are more protectionist than others. While all five agreed that some diminution of U.S. influence was desirable, Peru, Bolivia, and Chile favored a stiff code for alien interests. Colombia and Ecuador were less convinced. These positions were easily reasoned. During the last decade Colombia has been the Andean country in receipt of the largest amount of private foreign investment in manufacturing industries, most of which are designed to supply the local market. Therefore it was only to be expected that it would espouse a rather lenient attitude in the matter. Conversely, Peru, Chile, and Bolivia were predictably tough when it came to mining policy.

Unable to reach a policy decision acceptable to all participants, the initial negotiations became bogged down as the rift between Peru, Bolivia, and Chile, on the one hand, and Ecuador and Colombia, on the other, became manifest. Realizing that the quandary cast a gloomy shadow over integrationist efforts, the ANCOM commission called a new meeting a month later. Only through the aid of conciliatory gestures on the part of everyone was the crisis resolved, as each member agreed to some dilution of its original proposals. This conquest of a major structural obstacle ought not to be dismissed lightly, for it is testimony to the strong political will of the ANCOM partners and augurs well for their determination to make integration work to the benefit of all.

As a result of ANCOM's negotiations on foreign investment, several policies are couched in more moderate terms than those originally pro- posed. Foremost is the regulation compelling foreign-owned companies that wish to participate in the newly created and expanded Andean market to sign an agreement within three years to become joint ventures (com- panias mixtas). Such agreements necessitate the handing over of at least 51 per cent of their share of capital to nationals through a process that has now come to be known as the "Andeanization" of foreign interests. In Peru, Chile, and Colombia a period of fifteen years is allowed for the transfer of stock; in Bolivia and Ecuador the time allotment is twenty years. Not all companies are obliged to seek authorization in the common- market framework. But those foreign companies not wishing to avail themselves of the ANCOM setup must still relinquish 15 per cent of their capital shares to nationals within three years. Limitations have also been imposed on the mining operations of foreigners. Although non-Andean companies can still enter the field of mining prior to 1980, it is now stipulated that no such concession be granted for a term in excess of twenty years. The strictest prohibitions are those against foreigners who had hoped to invest in enterprises such as commercial banking, insurance, publicity, radio, and television. Under the new policy this incursion of out-side capital is not allowed.

Although perhaps not explicitly stated, the tenor of such policy is directed at lessening the U.S. hold on Andean development, while hopefully fostering fresh avenues for extra-American investment and trade. Rather surprisingly, the impact of this new Andean stance was immediately felt. Upon learning of the new investment regulations, the Council of the Americas, comprising over 200 U.S. firms, which account for more than three quarters of the U.S. private investment in all of South America, announced the postponement of 84 investment projects in the Andean countries.

In a very real sense, the potential role of foreign investment in the sub-region has been diminished by what can only be regarded as an unfortunate accident of history. To be more explicit, while the common market was being formalized, its development was shadowed by the parallel manifestation of rather intense nationalism. As one observer has sagely noted, "If ANCOM had been created five years earlier or five or ten years later, the restrictions on foreign companies would probably not have seen the light of day." * Instead, what has happened is that antiforeign economic nationalism, which has become a hard fact of life in Andean states, has surfaced in the dictums of ANCOM, and only time will tell just how difficult it will be for United States private business to live with these economic realities.

Reorientation of External Trade

Attendant to its role as major investor in the Andean bloc is the status of the United States as chief trading partner. As mentioned earlier, the Andean states have become heavily dependent on the United States for

* Ralph A. Diaz, "The Andean Common Market: Challenge to Foreign Investors." *Columbia Journal of World Business*, VI, no. 4 (1971), p. 23.

their commercial exchanges. In 1970 the Andean group bought $970 million worth of imports (38 per cent of the total) from the United States; their exports were valued at $848 million (29 per cent of the total). The continuance of this dependence is much in question, and most Andean governments apparently think that a diversification of the trade relations would be a healthy change.

Consonant with this belief, the Andean group has begun assiduously seeking augmented trade relations with other parts of the world. Japan is always an eager prospect. As the European Economic Community's best customer in South America (about $490 million per year) the Andean bloc hopes to further this economic relationship. But at present the political geographer, as well as the economic geographer, is likely to focus his attention on the relationship between the Andean countries and the Soviet Union. Soviet trade in this part of the world is nothing new. In fact, for some years now the Soviets have been buying and selling in several South American markets. True, the amount of trade is minuscule when compared to the yearly exchange between the United States and South America, but nonetheless the mere Soviet presence in the area carries with it some provocative long-range political and economic overtones. The current Soviet policy in this part of the globe seems to be directed toward developing friendly relations. That is, mutual commercial interests are used to form ties with the existing governments, in line with a peaceful pursuit of "coexistence with capitalism." Generally, the Soviets seem determined to avoid jeopardizing their foothold in the area.

Unlike the United States, the Soviet Union usually maintains a balance of trade in favor of the Andean countries. Their strategy has heretofore been well planned and executed. In 1968 Quito and Moscow signed an agreement for reciprocal import-export trade. Following that, a Colombo-Soviet commercial accord was reached which called for trade exchanges reaching $25 million a year. Peru has already exchanged commercial representatives with the U.S.S.R. and in 1970 Bolivia exported more than $3 million in ores to that country. Furthermore, the Soviets recently negotiated contracts for the exploitation of non-ferrous metals, mostly zinc and tin, and for prospection of oil and gas in the Bolivian Highlands. In return, Bolivia is to receive $27 million worth of Soviet machinery and equipment. But more significant than these independently initiated agreements is the fact that in 1971 an official delegation of the Andean Development Corporation traveled to Moscow in quest of new avenues of economic cooperation. Chile, which now has a Marxist government, pushed for this contact as it is especially interested in furthering trade with the Soviets, envisioning a healthy export market for its canned fish and seafood, wines, textiles, and footwear. The politico-economic implications of these developments are uncertain. The long-range results could well be a major re-shaping of things in the six Andean countries as we have known them. But the short-term impact is likely to be minimal, for it is only realistic to assume that during the next decade or so the United States, for good or ill, will continue to be the major trading partner of the Andean nations.

Political Realities

It is judicious to remember that the shaping of six nations into a single bloc transcends the simple addition of people and resources. In any quest for regional integration, the economic and political are inextricably linked. Amiable relations not traditionally considered a characteristic of the Andean neighbors will be required. This is not to say that there are any insoluble problems, but a glance at the region's history reveals more strife than cooperation, and clashes between old rivals have left a residue of grievances and distrust not easily forgotten, even in the present desire for mutual betterment. For example, since the War of the Pacific in the 1880's, both Peru and Bolivia have been politically at odds with Chile. Resentment persists over Chile's expansion at the expense of their territory. The fact that Bolivia, to this day, finds itself landlocked causes considerable economic frustration. And to these past differences new ones may be added. Illustrative of this point was the recent political dispute between Chile and Bolivia over water rights on the Lauca River. There is also potentially inflammatory bickering between Colombia and Venezuela over the oil-rich but ill-defined frontier along the Gulf of Venezuela, where an already sensitive situation is compounded by the continued and unauthorized migration of Colombians into Venezuela.

The road to economic cooperation in the Andean region is a long and arduous one, strewn with obstacles similar to those that beleaguer nations sophisticated in the ways of commerce and industrialization. But the emergence of the Andean Common Market is unmistakable evidence that the member states believe that their alliance offers a more rational basis for cooperation than does the Latin American Free Trade Association. The members of ANCOM are so dedicated to this principle that LAFTA, within whose orbit the Andean Common Market is really supposed to be operating, has virtually become a secondary consideration. This has been manifested at recent LAFTA conferences in Montevideo in which the Andean countries behave as mere observers, making no contribution to the discussions on tariff cuts within the parent organization.

Peru's Minister of Economic Affairs and Finance, Francisco Bermudez, voiced the sentiments of all ANCOM nations when he stated:

> We believe that integration is a historic requirement in a realistic policy of survival that seeks joint action as an external mechanism for achieving development, respects the sovereign will of states, decreases the heavy dependence on industrialized countries, and encourages the formation of a new style of international community, implementing new, more equitable and more humanistic formulas of cooperation that define a true "development strategy" for reducing today's growing imbalances and correcting the injustices it entails.*

The reference to "survival," "international community," and "humanistic formulas" reveals the scope and spirit of the pact. The Andean Common Market is in an embryonic stage; therefore, it would be premature to conjecture as to its ultimate success or failure. What may be said, however, is that this cooperative endeavor seems to offer the best opportunity in South America to thoroughly test the most fundamental tenets of integrationist theory. And, one might add, if the Andean scheme fails, economic cooperative efforts elsewhere on the continent are not likely to succeed.

* *Proceedings of the Eleventh Meeting of the Board of Governors*, Inter-American Development Bank, Punta del Este, April, 1970, pp. 103–4.

Suggested Readings for Part I

ARRIAGA, EDUARDO E., and KINGSLEY DAVIS. "The Pattern of Mortality Change in Latin America." *Demography,* VI, no. 3 (August, 1969), pp. 223–42. Data developed by the authors show that the rate of mortality decline in Latin America is greater than had been assumed. This has less to do with economic development than with improved public health care.

BARRACLOUGH, SOLON. "Employment Problems Affecting Latin American Development." *Monthly Bulletin of Agricultural Economics and Statistics.* Food and Agricultural Organization of the United Nations, Rome, XVIII, nos. 7–8 (July–August, 1969), pp. 1–11. Examines programs for economic development in terms of labor utilization; argues that a nation's natural resources and population constitute the basis for development planning, and that the goals of development include, not only economic growth, but national integration and independence.

BEYER, GLENN H., ed. *The Urban Explosion in Latin America.* Ithaca, N.Y.: Cornell University Press, 1967. Discusses the role of the Latin American city in the modernization process, and tries to suggest how the advantages of urbanization can be enjoyed while its penalties are minimized.

BOGUE, DONALD J., ed. "Progress and Problems of Fertility Control Around the World." *Demography,* V, no. 2 (May, 1968), pp. 539–1001. An excellent collection containing nine articles on family planning, and nine case studies of Latin America and other regions of the world.

BURNELL, ELAINE H., ed. *One Spark from Holocaust—The Crisis in Latin America.* Santa Barbara, California: The Center for the Study of Democratic Institutions/The Fund for the Republic, 1972. An ever-increasing number of impoverished South Americans are becoming insistent on immediate change and reform. Seventeen experts, including Raúl Prebisch, discuss such problems as agrarian reform and economic integration, control of inflation, full employment, tax reform, and population growth.

Business International Corporation. *Andean Common Market: Research Report.* New York, 1970. Probably the most comprehensive analysis available on the Andean Common Market, its prospects and investment potentials.

COLE, J. P. *Latin America: An Economic and Social Geography.* London: Butterworths, 1970 (rev. ed.). A useful general survey of the continent.

DORNER, PETER, ed. *Land Reform in Latin America: Issues and Cases. Monograph Series No. 3.* Madison: published by *Land Economics* for the Land Tenure Center at the University of Wisconsin, 1971. A collection of articles dealing with development policy, employment and development, and peasant organizations as a vehicle of reform; also contains case studies of three nations.

Food and Agriculture Organization of the United Nations. *Provisional Indicative World Plan for Agricultural Development.* I (August, 1969). An analysis of the major issues facing world agriculture in the 1970's, with suggestions regarding the directions in which efforts must be made, especially in the economically less-developed nations.

FURTADO, CELSO. *Economic Development of Latin America: A Survey from Colonial Times to the Cuban Revolution. Cambridge Latin American Studies, No. 8.* Cambridge: The University Press, 1970. A socio-economic profile of the region. The author suggests that in Latin America, more than in any other important area, obstacles to development are mainly institutional in nature.

GEYER, GEORGIE ANNE. *The New Latins: Fateful Change in South and Central America.* Garden City, New York: Doubleday, 1970. A study of changing continental attitudes toward, among other things, the Catholic Church, authoritarianism, and the military.

GONZALES, ALFONSO. "Population Growth and Socio-Economic Development: The Latin American Experience." *Journal of Geography,* LXX (January, 1970), pp. 36–46. Argues the need for much greater attention to population policy and program implementation, since population control will be a slow process; very rapid growth is expected to continue for at least one or two decades.

JAMES, PRESTON E. *Latin America.* New York: Odyssey Press, 1969 (fourth ed.); London: Cassell, 1955 (third ed.). The classic regional geography of Latin America.

JENKS, WILFRED P. "The World Employment Program." Report of the Director General to the International Labour Conference, Geneva, 1971.

KRAUSE, WALTER, and F. JOHN MATHIS. *Latin America and Economic Integration: Regional Planning for Development.* Iowa City: University of Iowa Press, 1970. A study of the move toward a Latin American Common Market.

LEVINSON, JEROME, and JUAN DE ONÍS. *The Alliance That Lost Its Way: A Critical Report on the Alliance for Progress. A Twentieth Century Fund Study.* Chicago: Quadrangle Books, 1970. Far from having improved relations between the United States and Latin America, this important channel of inter-American relations threatens to increase resentment and misunderstandings between the peoples of the Americas. The authors suggest ways of improving the effectiveness of the Alliance.

NISBET, CHARLES T., ed. *Latin America: Problems in Economic Development*. New York: The Free Press, 1969. A collection of articles analyzing such issues as the economic consequences of population growth, agrarian structure, export problems, and causes of inflation.

PREBISCH, RAÚL. *Change and Development—Latin America's Greatest Task. Report Submitted to the Inter-American Development Bank.* New York and London: Praeger, 1971. Deals with such problems as the external factors hampering development, insufficient dynamism, and the high rate of population growth.

RABINOWITZ, FRANCINE F., and FELICITY M. TRUEBLOOD, eds. *Latin American Urban Research.* Beverly Hills, California: Sage Publications, 1971, 1972, two vols. Discusses urban migration, changing cultural patterns, and other factors affecting regional and urban development.

United Nations Economic Commission for Latin America. *Development Problems in Latin America.* Austin: Published for the Institute of Latin American Studies by the University of Texas Press, 1970. A synthesis and evaluation of the Commission's labors over the past twenty years.

————. "Economic Bulletin for Latin America." XVI, no. 1 (first half of 1971). Articles dealing with the significance of and potential for development of public enterprises, population trends, and policy alternatives, and the Commission's activities in connection with the development of Latin America's water resources.

U.S. Department of State. *Latin American Free Trade Association: Progress, Problems, Prospects.* Washington, D.C.: Office of External Research, 1969. An indispensable publication for serious students of LAFTA. Comprehensive analysis, including statistics and excellent bibliography. Attention is also given to the Andean Subregional Pact.

See also *Américas, Ceres, Demography, Inter-American Economic Affairs, International Development Review, International Migration Review, Journal of Developing Areas, Journal of Inter-American Studies and World Affairs, Journal of Latin American Studies, Latin American Digest, Latin American Report Newsletter,* and *Latin American Research Review.*

II NATIONS OF SOUTH AMERICA

6 VENEZUELA

Raymond E. Crist and Edward P. Leahy

Historical Highlights • Ranchers and Slash-and-Burn Farmers • Settled Farmers and Their Rising Expectations • Petroleum and Other Mineral Riches • Industrialization, Diversification, and New Cities • Future Trends

Venezuela, long ruled by a small, rich, and powerful élite, has embarked on a "revolution" designed to bring a greater number and variety of opportunities for material and cultural change to an increasing proportion of its inhabitants, at the same time assuring a greater degree of political participation. It was the discovery of petroleum and the profits from petroleum, coupled with new government policies, that permitted Venezuela to "modernize" at a pace unusual among the economically less-developed nations of the world.

Before the oil era began, in the 1920's and 1930's, more than 70 per cent of the people were illiterate village dwellers with little or no chance to get an education, change occupation, or influence the governing élite. As exploitation of the oil increased, new job opportunities attracted a large number of farmers to work in the petroleum fields and processing centers. Many others left the land to seek jobs in the new industries established with profits from petroleum, most of which were located in the few large northern cities, and especially in Caracas. Within a few decades, large numbers of rural dwellers thus became city dwellers. This massive migration from the country to the cities has brought the urban population to 70 per cent of the total, about the same percentage as in the United States. It has created a greatly increased desire for better education and health facilities and better jobs. Government attempts to provide these services have met

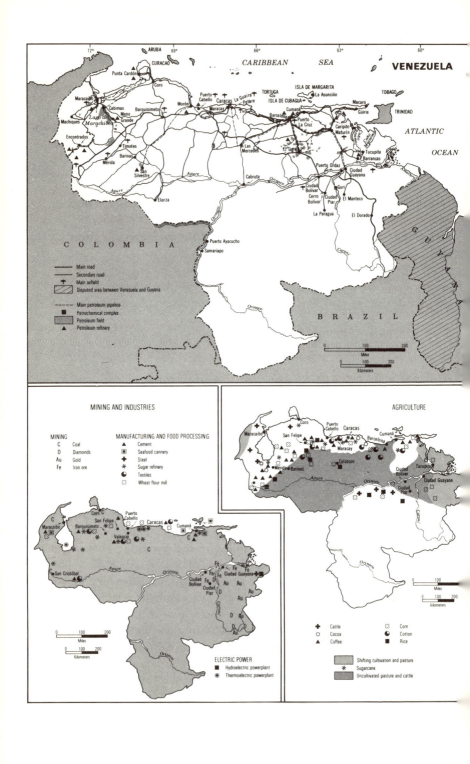

VENEZUELA

CARIBBEAN SEA

ATLANTIC OCEAN

COLOMBIA

BRAZIL

Main road
Secondary road
Main airfield
Disputed area between Venezuela and Guyana

Main petroleum pipeline
Petrochemical complex
Petroleum field
Petroleum refinery

MINING AND INDUSTRIES

MINING
C   Coal
D   Diamonds
Au   Gold
Fe   Iron ore

MANUFACTURING AND FOOD PROCESSING
▲ Cement
▥ Seafood cannery
✛ Steel
✳ Sugar refinery
☾ Textiles
✿ Wheat flour mill

ELECTRIC POWER
■ Hydroelectric powerplant
● Thermoelectric powerplant

AGRICULTURE

✛ Cattle   ✿ Corn
○ Cocoa   ☾ Cotton
▲ Coffee   ■ Rice

Shifting cultivation and pasture
✳ Sugarcane
Uncultivated pasture and cattle

with some success, but there is still much to be done. In and around Caracas, for example, where about one third of Venezuela's total population of 11.1 million (1971 estimate) now lives, roughly one third of the people live in improvised housing, much of it without proper water and sewage facilities. Here, as in other South American nations, the cities are the chief initiators of dynamic social and political changes, and the urbanites are largely responsible for ambitious plans to diversify the national economy so as to reduce dependence on petroleum. They are also seeking a better regional distribution of both industries and people through the creation of new communities such as Ciudad Guayana (discussed on pages 76–77).

Historical Highlights

The first Spanish settlement in South America was Nueva Cádiz on Cubagua Island, established about 1507 to exploit the pearl fisheries. From Cubagua and another settlement established soon after on Margarita Island, the Spanish immigrants gradually took over the coast, the mountains, and the *llanos* (the great plains of the Orinoco Basin), enslaving the Indians, incorporating them into towns and missions, or exporting them to other Spanish colonies which were clamoring for laborers. Indian women frequently became wives or concubines of the Spaniards. Together with nearby Colombia, the coastal towns of Coro and Cumaná (founded in 1521 and 1523) became take-off points for a series of expeditions in search of El Dorado. But no gold was found, and by the end of the next century the city of Caracas, laid out in 1567, had grown to only about 300 Spaniards with five or six times as many Indians, Negroes, and mixed-breeds, both free and slave. Trade in maize (corn) and wheat, grown in the mountains, was, however, increasing. Cacao and tobacco, grown on large plantations operated by slave labor, were shipped to Spain, as were hides from the large cattle ranches of the Orinoco *llanos*. Sun-dried meat, called *tasajo* or *charqui*—from which the North American term "jerky," or "jerked beef," was derived—was also produced on these ranches.

In the 1730's new crops, such as coffee, cotton, and *añil* (indigo), were introduced and helped to create a thriving agricultural industry, while the cattle population of the *llanos* grew rapidly. Hides, lard, hams, cotton cloth, sugar, and cacao were shipped to the Antilles, Cartagena, and Spain. There was also a brisk smuggling trade with the British and Dutch islands of the Antilles. The independence movement that got under way in the early 1800's under the leadership of Simón Bolívar, a Venezuelan aristocrat, was sparked by the desire of the Venezuelan-born business leaders to have a larger share of the profits as well as to govern without interference from Spain.

After the destruction of the colonial system, Venezuela went through an era of government by force, which lasted over a century, until the death of Juan Vicente Gómez in 1935. The country that Gómez took over in 1908 was agricultural, poor, debt-ridden, and dominated by the owners of large estates. Gómez ran the country ruthlessly for the benefit of the few rich, but he also instituted an "open door policy" that allowed powerful foreign oil companies to discover and extract oil, thereby transforming Venezuela from a poor producer of agricultural products into a rich producer of petroleum.

Since 1935 Venezuela has endured several other upheavals and further periods of despotic rule, but under three elected presidents—Betancourt, Leoni, and Caldera—in the 1960's and early 1970's the civilian and democratic elements established and have successfully maintained a slightly left-of-center course.

Ranchers and Slash-and-Burn Farmers

Venezuela's landscape ranges from snow-capped peaks to arid mountain slopes to hot humid jungles. It consists in the main of four regions: highlands in the north and west with towering peaks south of Lake Maracaibo; lowlands immediately around Lake Maracaibo; the vast central Orinoco *llanos;* and the Guiana Highlands in the southeast, which make up about half the nation's land area. Parts of the first two of these regions are relatively thickly settled; large parts of the *llanos* and Guiana Highlands are very sparsely populated. All four have rich untapped agricultural and mineral resources.

There is considerable grazing and dairying on intensively managed pastures in the crescent west and south of Lake Maracaibo, but most of the 6.7 million cattle in Venezuela live in the Orinoco *llanos,* although this large plain roughly 200 miles wide by 600 miles long, is not especially well suited for ranching. This is a land of tall, coarse grass, with here and there clumps of palms and shallow ponds. Numerous streams both large and small meander across it; long serpentine strips of broad-leaf evergreen forest border the main rivers. Vast areas are flooded during the rainy season, between June and October, and parched during the dry months of January through March or April. Until recently, cattle had to be moved on the hoof to high ground as rivers overflowed and back on the hoof to low ground when the water receded. In places in the north the tall grasses turn brown during the dry months and become inedible so that the cattle had to be moved, again on the hoof, to the more humid areas far to the south around the Orinoco River. During the long hard trek to market, the animals lost so much weight that they had to be fattened again on holding pastures. In recent decades, however, a network of roads has made it possible to transport animals by truck. Lately, too, airplanes have carried increasing amounts of beef to market, the cattle having been slaughtered, butchered, and frozen near their points of origin: The ranchers have discovered that the cost of such transportation more than offsets the value of the weight loss sustained when driving the animals to market on the hoof. If these pasture lands were improved, they could provide huge quantities of additional meat and milk for hungry people in other parts of the Third World.

The slash-and-burn farmers have long constituted one of the nation's most serious agricultural problems. Thousands of these people live a hand-to-mouth existence on tiny clearings in the forest. They move from place to place and occupy plots called *conucos* or *rozas* (subsistence farms of 2.5 to 5.0 acres in size), barely large enough to provide for single families. They clear the land and work it by primitive means, often with no tools except a machete and a digging stick. After the land is cleared, the trees and brush are burned, and crops (corn, potatoes, plantains, manioc, and a few vegetables) are grown for a few seasons. When the plots become choked with weeds or brush, or the soil loses its fertility, or the pest population builds up, the fields are abandoned, and the semi-nomadic farmers go farther into the forest and clear another plot. Thus fields are rotated instead of crops. If they live near roads, the farmers sell a portion of their crops in order to purchase other necessities, but few of them have the means to transport their produce to distant markets. There is no accurate census of these seminomadic farmers, who either squat on unused parts of large estates or occupy public lands. They live virtually outside the money economy of the nation, demanding little from it and producing little for it. One of the many aims of the agrarian reform program has been to settle them, together with the many renters and sharecroppers, on lands and in permanent homes of their own, to bring better health and educational services to them, and to help them to become settled agricultural producers.

Settled Farmers and Their Rising Expectations

An Agrarian Reform Law was passed in 1958 which enabled the government to expropriate privately owned lands that were (1) not worked or worked inefficiently, (2) worked by renters or sharecroppers, or (3) suitable for cultivation but used as pasture for livestock. Payment for expropriated lands is partly in cash, partly in government bonds. By the early 1970's, over 165,000 farming families had been settled on 11.2 million acres of land formerly held privately or by the government.

Along with land redistribution, the government has been active, especially on the *llanos,* in the construction of irrigation works. During the 1960's, almost 150,000 acres were brought under irrigation, and many new projects are in progress. Furthermore, land redistribution and irrigation works are not going forward in a vacuum. New settlers benefit from the nationwide government programs of agricultural extension work and the organization of rural cooperatives. The government makes fertilizers and improved seeds available, farm subsidies are made, and marketing methods improved. The government also continues to improve and strengthen the infrastructure. More than 6,000 miles of new roads were built during the 1960's and more than 11,000 miles of old roads were paved. During the same period, the number of people served with electricity in their homes more than doubled, as did the number of pupils in elementary schools, the number of schools, and the number of teachers. Attendance and instruction in institutions of higher learning experienced a corresponding increase. Thus, not only is land being made available to poor people, but they are being provided with means for making optimal use of it.

In the program for agrarian reform, the country's leaders have tried to give the people themselves an ever greater voice in planning the details of their new ventures. Local leadership is encouraged in community-development programs. Hundreds of rural schools, community centers, recreation grounds, and dispensaries have been built under the community program, as have many aqueducts to bring pure water to rural communities. About a third of the cost of these programs is contributed in the form of labor by the people served.

Petroleum and Other Mineral Riches

During the 1930's and 1940's Venezuela changed from a primarily agricultural and pastoral economy, producing most of its own food, to one dominated by the extraction of petroleum. Prices skyrocketed and agricultural production fell off as rural migrants flocked to the oil fields and the cities. More and more food had to be imported, even sugar and canned tropical fruits, formerly produced domestically. Little of the enormous wealth derived from oil was expended internally on aspects of the infrastructure necessary to a modern nation.

Since that time, the production of crude oil continued to rise dramatically, from less than 53,400 tons in 1918 to over 198 million tons in 1971. Up to 1960, production was in the hands of foreign companies. The nation's leaders sensed the danger of overemphasis on one extractive industry, with no provision made to plow profits back into the national economy. In 1960 a government entity, the Venezuelan Petroleum Corporation, was established to produce, refine, and distribute petroleum products in competition with private industry. It was also decreed that no further private concessions would be granted. In 1971, as increased nationalism swept through the oil industry, a law was passed that transfers foreign control to the government when the concessions expire, which, for many, is in 1983.

There are three major oil fields, or oil-producing centers: the Lake Maracaibo area; eastern Venezuela, north of the lower Orinoco; and the Apure-Barinas area, in the *llanos* of western Venezuela. The last of these fields began production in 1957. Crude oil was originally shipped out of Lake Maracaibo in shallow-draft tankers to refineries on the Dutch islands of Aruba and Curaçao. The Lake Maracaibo channel has now been dredged so that Maracaibo is a deep-water port, connected by bridge to the rest of the country. New refineries have been built in Venezuela itself, and today more than a third of its crude oil is refined domestically into gasoline, kerosene, fuel oil, lubricating oil, and asphalt. Almost half the total petroleum exports go to the United States.

Natural gas, now widely distributed via pipelines, is increasingly used in thermoelectric power plants, in the new petrochemical industry, and in the manufacture of liquid gas for export as well as for domestic consumption. Vast quantities of gas are reinjected into the ground to increase and maintain the pressure that pushes crude oil to the surface, thus lengthening the life of the field.

The volume of reserves and the cost of production per ton will determine the impact of the recent Alaskan discoveries on the future of Venezuelan exports to the United States. There has already been a substantial slowdown in the growth of Venezuela's real gross national product due to the decline in the petroleum industry. Petroleum output rose by

Courtesy United Nations

A dramatic contrast between *barrio* shacks and luxury housing in Caracas. In Venezuela as in other South American nations, rapid urbanization has created severe problems of congestion, social disorganization, and unemployment. The government, with the help of the United Nations, is trying to ease these problems by investing heavily in housing, sanitation, water supplies, and roads.

only 3.7 per cent during the period 1966–68, whereas world output rose at an annual rate of 7 per cent. Since the government policy of granting only service contracts instead of concessions was initiated in 1959, foreign companies have rolled back their programs of explorations and operations in new areas in Venezuela. The ratio of reserves to production has steadily fallen since that year, whereas world reserves have increased greatly. Further, Venezuela's share of United States imports of crude oil has dropped sharply, from 60 per cent in 1950 to only 28 per cent in the early 1970's.

In general, the Venezuelan petroleum industry is at a disadvantage *vis-à-vis* some other producers, such as the Middle East, Libya, Indonesia, and the Soviet Union, because their production costs are lower.

When reserves of high-grade iron ore in the Mesabi Range of the United States began to run low at the end of World War II (1945), steel companies looked elsewhere for their supplies. The first major discovery in Venezuela was made at El Pao in 1941, but it required ten years to develop because of its inaccessible location. Later, in 1954, after much preliminary work, Cerro Bolívar, the world's largest known single iron-ore deposit, came into production by the Orinoco Mining Company, a subsidiary of the United States Steel Corporation. A railroad was built to Puerto Ordaz, and the Orinoco River was dredged to accommodate ocean-going ore carriers. The Venezuelan government has entered the iron-mining field. The government organization known as the Venezuelan Iron Corporation (CVH) started mining a deposit at San Isidro near Cerro Bolívar that has estimated reserves of 650 million tons, and it established a steel mill at Puerto Ordaz. The quantity of iron ore produced rose from some 200,000 tons in 1950 to nearly 20 million tons a year in the early 1970's, and plans are under way for further expansion. At present Venezuela produces only 5 per cent of the world's iron-ore requirements, but it could produce much more since reserves are estimated to be very large and will last well over a century at the current rate of production. Venezuela also mines significant quantities of gold, diamonds, coal, copper, nickel, manganese, sulphur, asbestos, and gypsum.

Industrialization, Diversification, and New Cities

More than a decade ago, Venezuelan leaders began to see the advantages of an integrated approach to mining, industrial development, and planned settlement. The Morón industrial complex, located near Puerto Cabello, about 100 miles west of Caracas, is typical of Venezuela's program of industrial development and diversification. It is now turning out caustic soda, fertilizers, insecticides, explosives, and organic chemicals, especially those derived from petroleum. Enough phosphates and nitrates are already produced to meet domestic requirements. Synthetic rubber, plastics, and detergents are also being produced. The establishment of meat-packing plants as well as plants for processing fish, fruit, and vegetables reflects the rising production of foodstuffs. With the increase in dairying comes increased production of powdered milk and ice cream. Sesame, cottonseed, and coconuts are processed for their oils, and oleomargarine is another important industrial product. Rice-, wheat-, and corn-processing mills are on the increase. More paper, cotton cloth, automobile tires, cement, electrical equipment, and pharmaceuticals are being produced domestically, and the government is striving to "decentralize" the process of industrialization.

In the first century of the republican era, the political colonialism that existed under Spain became economic colonialism: National strong men, given huge sums for oil, business, and mining concessions, were able to prevent or impede political, economic, and social change. But no more. As Venezuela has become more independent and self-governing, the process of industrialization and land reform, in its broadest sense, has proceeded apace. To be sure, some ugly corollaries of modern industrialization can be found. Garish, neon-lighted billboards proclaim the efficacy of liver pills, aspirin tablets, soft drinks, and the like. But these are minor matters. Of greater significance is the fact that there is not a sharp line but a broad zone between the private and public sectors of the economy, and in this zone capital expenditure and generation are taking place on a mammoth scale. The nation also invites and welcomes private foreign capital as long as private enterprise fits into government programs and policies designed to increase local participation in the profits.

Industrialization and diversification are helping the nation to achieve economic self-sufficiency and raise standards of living, and this in turn is strengthening the democratic regime. Venezuelan leaders, recognizing the interdependence of the modern world, are planning to work closely with the other members of the Latin American Free Trade Association, and Venezuela has now joined the Andean Common Market (see pp. 47–60).

As part of its effort to relieve the acute congestion in the major northern cities, the Ministry of Public Works plans to establish two new cities, one in the Tuy Valley south of Caracas, the other in the oil-producing area of Zulia across the lake from Maracaibo. A third regional-development center is already well under way. In 1960, the Venezuelan Guayana Corporation (CVG) was established to coordinate and promote the over-all development of the region within a 200-mile radius of Ciudad Guayana, where coal, petroleum, natural gas, iron ore, limestone, manganese, refractory clays, and many other raw materials are to be found. The urban complex growing up at the confluence of the Orinoco and Caroní rivers already has a population of well over 100,000 and is expected to have 600,000 people by 1980. Job opportunities increase as housing, health, and recreational facilities become available. The educational system is oriented toward advanced vocational training that will create a skilled labor force for existing and planned industries. The great Guri power station and dam, eventually to become the world's largest hydroelectric plant, is being built in three stages, as the demand for power increases in the nation or in neighboring nations. The low-cost electricity will be utilized for smelting iron and steel, aluminum, and other products of the Guayana industrial complex. A new pipeline already brings natural gas to Ciudad Guayana from the oil fields north of the Orinoco, to be used for household purposes as well as in the electrochemical industry.

Detailed studies of the soils of the Delta Amacuro made by the CVG indicated that they are suitable for growing sugar cane, bananas, sesame, peanuts, cotton, artificial pasture grasses, and so on, which would help solve the problem of producing enough foodstuffs domestically. A two-phase project was decided on: (1) construction of a dam across the Caño Mánamo, (completed in 1966), connected by road to Ciudad Guayana, and (2) construction of retaining walls along the natural levees of Caño Macareo to prevent the annual flooding by the Orinoco of potentially valuable crop land. Drainage and irrigation canals, highways, and planned settlements are also being built to reclaim some 2.5 million acres of land for productive agriculture, which should help to meet the growing demand in Ciudad Guayana and environs for agricultural produce. Roads are being built to make this produce accessible to the tremendous market being generated by the industrial complex. Automobiles and trucks can now roll from Caracas over good paved or graveled roads to Ciudad Bolívar, Ciudad Guayana, the Delta country, and on to the Brazilian border. Since the dredging of the Orinoco River, Ciudad Guayana is a deep-water port capable of docking ocean steamers with capacities of up to 60,000 tons.

Future Trends

Venezuelan leaders are well aware that every effort must be made to achieve national cohesion, for the threat is ever present that Venezuelan crude oil will come under a steadily tightening squeeze in the world markets because of its cost and big sulphur content (sulphur is a pollutant, and many areas ban the use of high-sulphur oil). Also, competition from new sources of oil elsewhere, such as Alaska, is increasing. If a period of financial stringency is in the offing for Venezuela, it will inevitably reduce President Caldera's chances of effecting new, or expanding old, programs with which to bring a more equitable distribution of the national income. At present, a large part of the government budget is spent on public works and to support agricultural, industrial, educational, and health programs and sponsor social security, the cooperative movement, and the organized labor movement. The general attitude of the government, as expressed by former President Leoni, will probably not change much in the foreseeable future:

> We are . . . building the foundations of a democracy which is conscious of its social mission. We place emphasis on the social content of our regime because without it all efforts to achieve dynamic change would be in vain. . . . Though we may have made a late entrance into the twentieth century, we now live in the serene conviction that we will arrive on time at the threshold of the twenty-first.[*]

An ever increasing proportion of the great wealth extracted from the subsoil of Venezuela is being plowed back into agriculture and industry. Increased purchasing power in the hands of the consumer, both rural and urban, good roads on which the farmer can move his produce to market, and a decreased "take" for the middleman have acted as a stimulus to the producers of food. Generally, as purchasing power increases, economic development increases, standards of living rise, and exchanges between regions become more active and varied. The construction of a national network of good roads, the establishment of industries, and price supports for agriculture are reducing unemployment and underemployment. General economic growth, in turn, goes a long way toward creating a more cohesive society with greater geographical, economic, and social mobility and with a growing concern with the development of arts and crafts, science, and higher education generally. And this evolution may help to maintain the nation firmly on that middle ground between the far left and the far right.

Suggested Readings

American University. *Area Handbook for Venezuela*. Washington, D.C.: U.S. Government Printing Office, 1971. A comprehensive analysis of social, economic, and political aspects of the country.
CRIST, RAYMOND E., and EDWARD P. LEAHY. *Venezuela: Search for a Middle Ground*. New York: Van Nostrand Reinhold, 1969. An analysis of

[*] Raúl Leoni. "View from Caracas." *Foreign Affairs*, XLIII, no. 4 (July, 1965), p. 646.

Venezuela in terms of its natural setting, its people, and its political, social, and economic development. Includes profiles of four representative Venezuelans.

FRIEDMANN, JOHN. *Regional Development Policy: A Case Study of Venezuela.* Cambridge, Mass: M.I.T. Press, 1966. Discusses a strategy for national development in a country that has embarked on a course of industrialization. Special emphasis is given to the program in the Guayana area of Venezuela.

HEATON, LOUIS E. *The Agricultural Development of Venezuela.* New York: Praeger, 1969. A detailed analysis of the agricultural scene, particularly of the government's attempts to create a viable agriculture in the face of inflationary tendencies.

PEATTIE, LISA REDFIELD. *The View from the Barrio.* Ann Arbor: The University of Michigan Press, 1968. A study of a neighborhood in the planned city of Ciudad Guayana, focusing on the adjustment of rural immigrants to urban life.

PENFOLD, ANTHONY. "Caracas: Urban Growth and Transportation." *Town Planning Review,* XLII, no. 2 (April, 1970), pp. 103–20. Discusses the urbanization process, aspects of the transportation problem, and the plans for the highway system.

SCHUYLER, GEORGE W., and DIETER K. ZSCHOCK. "Venezuelan Progress Reconsidered." *Current History,* LX, no. 354 (February, 1971), pp. 95–101, 118. For decades Venezuela's economic situation was better than that of most other South American nations. The authors suggest that, in the coming decades, Venezuela must place increasing emphasis on solving problems of unemployment and poverty.

Venezuela Up-to-Date. A quarterly publication which deals informatively with significant national and international topics. (Available free from the Embassy of Venezuela Information Service, 2437 California Street N.W., Washington, D.C. 20008).

WILGUS, A. CURTIS, ed. *The Caribbean: Venezuelan Development—A Case Study.* Gainesville: University of Florida Press, 1963. A collection of penetrating and perceptive papers, most of them by Venezuelans, on the country's historical and physical background, education, agrarian reform, and the public and private sectors of the economy.

See also Suggested Readings for Part I, pp. 61–63.

7 GUYANA

James W. Vining

Historical Background • The Six Peoples • The Physical Environment • Agriculture and Land-Development Projects • Mining, Manufacturing, Trade, and Transportation • A Viable Future? • focus *on Environmental Problems and Land Development*

British Guiana, which became the sovereign state of Guyana on May 26, 1966, was one of the last British colonies to be given its freedom. The developments that delayed independence stemmed mainly from the racial and political dichotomy of the population. Despite the fact that the country has long been called the "land of the six peoples," it is primarily a land of *two* peoples: East Indians and Negroes. Deep-rooted racial discord and the establishment of political parties along racial lines resulted in greater and greater unrest. In the early 1960's, demonstrations, strikes, and riots accompanied, or led, almost every political event and, in 1964, the ever increasing violence came close to civil war. Because it seemed that the Guyanese people might become irrevocably split, the British government was unwilling to relinquish its control until 1966, when some semblance of stability returned to the troubled country.

Historical Background

During his third voyage to the Americas, in 1498, Columbus sailed along the coast of Guyana, and in 1499 the first Spanish sailors set foot on

Guyana's shores. Yet Guyana did not become part of the Spanish domain, perhaps because the mangrove-lined shores of this wild coast did not seem inviting. The first settlement was established by the Dutch, on the Pomeroon River, in 1581. In 1595 Sir Walter Raleigh explored the coast and the rivers in search, so the legend goes, of the mythical city of El Dorado. Settlement was consolidated in the 1620's by the Dutch West India Company.

The early Dutch settlers created a plantation economy based on a profitable European market for such crops as tobacco, cotton, coffee, and cacao. They cultivated the lands along the banks of the rivers for many miles upstream, for these were much easier to bring into cultivation than the swamps of the coast. Before long, the need for increased labor to work the plantations began to be felt. As in the rest of the Americas, this need for labor was met by the importation of thousands of African slaves, which made possible the construction of the sea-defense, drainage, and irrigation systems without which the fertile coastlands could not be worked. As the hydraulic works made coastal settlement feasible, there was a gradual move from the river banks to the coast during the early part of the eighteenth century. Sugar cultivation, which had become important on the banks of the Pomeroon during the last decades of the seventeenth century, became extensive with the move to the coast, and sugar soon became the major export of the Dutch colony.

With the outbreak of the American Revolutionary War, Guyana was occupied first by the English and then by the French. In 1796 the British captured the coastal settlements again, and, except for a brief return of Dutch rule in 1802–3, retained control for 170 years. From about 1810 on, British Guiana was a significant exporter of sugar on a world scale. The nature of the export economy did not alter with the abolition of slavery in 1833, although the transition from a slave system to a free society did involve far-reaching changes in the structure of Guianese society. As the Negroes moved out of the confining and regimented system of the plantations, other workers were brought in. These were indentured immigrants brought to British Guiana to work out labor contracts, usually for five-year periods.

From 1834 to 1928, contract laborers came mainly from India, China, the West Indies, and Europe. Of approximately 350,000 who migrated to British Guiana during this period, about 240,000 were East Indians, both Hindu and Muslim. Of all the indentured servants, the East Indians proved to be the most effective plantation laborers.

The Six Peoples

In descending order of numerical importance, the "six peoples" of Guyana are East Indians, Negroes, Amerindians, Portuguese, Chinese, and British. The estimated population at the end of 1971 was 800,000.

East Indians, descendants of indentured servants, comprise about half the total population, and they have a higher birth rate than any other ethnic group. Most of them are either rice farmers, cultivating miniature farms usually on leased land, or wage laborers on the sugar plantations. Many divide their time between their farms and regular jobs. Although many East Indians were converted to Christianity, about 33 per cent of Guyana's total population is still Hindu and about 9 per cent Muslim. Like everyone else in Guyana, except some of the Amerindians, all East Indians speak English.

Guyanese of African descent comprise about 31 per cent of the population. Most of them are descendants of former slaves who set up their own villages upon emancipation and became small farmers or moved to the major towns. Today there arc a few villages still consisting primarily of Negro farmers, but most of the African population are urban dwellers. They predominate in the capital, Georgetown (which has 168,000 inhabitants), in Mackenzie (30,000), and in New Amsterdam (15,000). Most Guyanese Negroes are Christians.

Amerindians, who comprise about 5 per cent of the population, are in little evidence on the coastal plain, where 90 per cent of Guyana's population lives. Most of the 30,000 Amerindians live in vast reservations in the interior, where they practice subsistence agriculture. The government is now developing a special program for their economic and social assimilation. It has installed two-way radios in some twenty-five villages and undertaken the construction of new roads.

Today there are a few thousand Portuguese and Chinese, largely shopkeepers and merchants. The least numerous of the six peoples are the British. There were never very many Englishmen in British Guiana, and their numbers have dwindled since independence, but, throughout the British colonial period, they were at the top of the social scale. The few who remain are mostly overseers or engineers on the sugar estates, missionaries in the interior, or advisers to the Guyanese government.

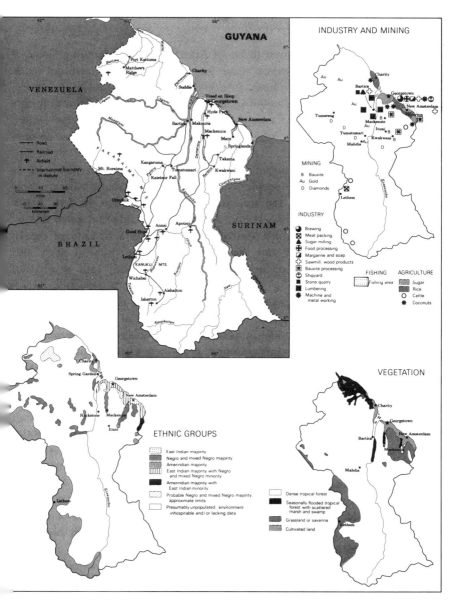

GUYANA

VENEZUELA

BRAZIL

SURINAM

Borima
Port Kaituma
Matthew's Ridge
Charity
Suddie
Vreed en Hoop
Georgetown
Hyde Park
New Amsterdam
Bartica
Makouria
Mackenzie
Mara
Springlands
Takama
Kangaruma
Kwakwani
Mt. Roraima
Tunatumari
Kaieteur Fall
Orinduk
Good Hope
Annai
Apoteri
Lethem
KANUKU MTS
Wichabai
Aishalton
Isherton

Road
Railroad
Airfield
International boundary in dispute

miles
0   40   80
kilometers
0   40   80

PAKARAIMA

INDUSTRY AND MINING

Au
Au
Charity
Bartica
Georgetown
New Amsterdam
Mackenzie
Tumereng
Ituni
D
Tumatumari
Kwakwani
Mahdia
Au
B
D
B

MINING
B   Bauxite
Au Gold
D   Diamonds

Lethem

INDUSTRY
◐ Brewing
▦ Meat packing
▲ Sugar milling
⊕ Food processing
✚ Margarine and soap
✛ Sawmill, wood products
▩ Bauxite processing
◉ Shipyard
■ Stone quarry
✦ Lumbering
✳ Machine and metal working

FISHING
▦ Fishing area

AGRICULTURE
▨ Sugar
○ Rice
○ Cattle
✳ Coconuts

ETHNIC GROUPS

Charity
Spring Garden
Georgetown
New Amsterdam
Rockstone
Mackenzie
Ituni
Lethem

▦ East Indian majority
▦ Negro and mixed Negro majority
▦ Amerindian majority
▥ East Indian majority with Negro and mixed Negro minority
▦ Amerindian majority with East Indian minority
▢ Probable Negro and mixed Negro majority, approximate limits
□ Presumably unpopulated, environment inhospitable and/or lacking data

VEGETATION

Charity
Georgetown
New Amsterdam
Bartica
Mackenzie
Mahdia
Lethem

□ Dense tropical forest
■ Seasonally flooded tropical forest with scattered marsh and swamp
▦ Grassland or savanna
▦ Cultivated land

The Physical Environment

The word "Guyana" is said to be an Amerindian term meaning "land of waters." It is an appropriate name for a country that receives so much rainfall and has such enormous rivers and such serious hydrologic problems. Three great rivers, the Essequibo, Demerara, and Berbice, drain Guyana's five natural regions: the coastal plain, the white sand and clay region, the Rupununi savanna, the Pakaraima Mountains, and the forested highlands.

By far the most important natural region is the coastal plain, for it is here that most of the people live. The ten- to forty-mile-wide area was largely reclaimed from the sea, and the coastlands are, in fact, below sea level at high tide. This region was made habitable and cultivable by the construction of complex and costly sea defenses and drainage canals. The soils of the coastal zone are silty clays, pegasse (tropical peat), and sand. Agriculture is restricted largely to the silty clay soils within ten miles of the sea.

South of the coastal plain is the white sand and clay region, covering nearly one fourth of Guyana. Much of the surface of this region consists of white quartz sands, highly permeable and inherently infertile, and the rest is impermeable clays on which swampy conditions usually prevail. Although the soils are unsuitable for agriculture, this area has two valuable resources: hardwood forests and metallic minerals, the most important of which is bauxite.

Guyana's climate is characterized by high but variable rainfall, high humidity, and rather small annual and diurnal temperature ranges. Rainfall on the coastal plain averages about 90 inches per year, but a variation between 60 and 120 inches is common. Usually there is a long rainy season lasting from mid-April to mid-August and a short rainy season from mid-November to mid-February. The rainiest part of the country is the Pakaraima Mountains, parts of which get as much as 140 inches of precipitation annually. The white sand and clay region and forested highlands get considerably less, generally 60 to 90 inches a year, while much of the Rupununi area gets only 40 to 60 inches. Average annual temperatures in Guyana are high, and so is the mean relative humidity. Georgetown has an average temperature of 80.4° F., with only a three-degree annual range and a diurnal variation of about fifteen degrees, and its relative humidity is 79 per cent. But immediately along the coast the steady sea breezes tend to lower perceptible temperatures.

Agriculture and Land-Development Projects

Only about 1 per cent of the total land area of Guyana is under cultivation, and almost all the cultivated land is on the coastal plain. More than 75 per cent of the farms are less than 10 acres in size; only 2 per cent are over 100 acres. All the farms together occupy about three fourths of the cultivated land; the rest is in sugar plantations, 13 in all, which vary in size from 784 to 15,844 acres. The government is the great landholder. Less than 2 per cent of the total area of the country is under freehold titles. Practically all the freehold land is on the coastal plain. Government-owned agricultural lands are leased to small farmers for long-term periods. The second largest landholder is Bookers' Sugar Estates Ltd, a subsidiary of a British company, which owns eleven of Guyana's sugar plantations. Some plantation land is also leased to small farmers.

Guyana has often been described as a sugar island, bounded by sea and jungle. In terms of value of production, sugar cane is, and has been for more than a century and a half, the most important crop. Annual production now averages over 300,000 tons. Approximately 100,000 acres of cane are harvested each year from large estates, and another 9,000 acres are cultivated by small farmers.

Until very recently, sugar was Guyana's main export. Although it has lost its predominant position in the national economy, it is still a vital industry and is highly dependent upon foreign markets. The United Kingdom takes nearly 55 per cent of the production and the United States over 25 per cent, both at preferential prices. Canada buys some 8 per cent, and around 10 per cent is consumed in Guyana. One of the most serious problems that threaten Guyana is the prospect that the United Kingdom may not continue to buy Guyanese sugar at supported prices.

While sugar production is a highly mechanized and centralized agricultural industry, the production of rice involves a large number of producers and relatively little central control. Both sugar and rice are big employers of labor and both are export industries, but there the similarities end. Rice is grown on small farms rather than large estates. Over 90 per cent of Guyana's rice farms are less than 16 acres in size, and nearly a fourth of the total are less than two acres each. Rice contributes directly to the livelihood of an estimated one third of the population, and more than twice as much land is devoted to rice as to sugar cane. The average production of rice is about 154,000 tons a year on 300,000 acres; about one third of this acreage is harvested twice a year. Paddy (wet rice) yields generally exceed those of most Asian nations, though the average yield has been slowly declining for many years. Problems contributing to this unfortunate development have been soil depletion in the long-cultivated areas, the poorer quality of land recently placed under cultivation, inadequate water control on some of the new rice lands, and, above all, the fact that increasing mechanization has led to the widespread practice of direct sowing instead of transplanting. All but about a fifth of the rice harvest is exported, mainly to the Caribbean area.

Sugar and rice are the only crops with any substantial export market. Most other agricultural production is for local consumption. Rice is the basic food in the coastal belt, but other subsistence crops include cassava, plantains, bananas, and coconuts. Livestock of various kinds contribute to the local economy, and many farmers keep a few cattle, sheep, goats, pigs, or poultry as a source of subsidiary income. In the Rupununi savanna there are a few large ranches which produce cattle for meat.

One of the major developments in Guyanese agriculture since World War II has been the opening up of new lands for agricultural utilization and settlement. This was brought about because of the increasing number of people on the coastal plain and the desire of the government to provide land for landless farmers. The land-development projects have involved clearing land, establishing drainage and irrigation works, laying out the land into cultivation and house lots, and leasing it on easy terms to tenants. At present there are 13 more or less active land-development projects in operation. They encompass nearly 90,000 acres and support about 4,500 families.

Guyana's economic prospects are closely linked to developments in agriculture, for it employs over half the population and produces almost half the gross national product. Yet, as is true of many other tropical American nations, Guyana's economy is dependent upon too few export products, and there is still much underemployment of farm labor.

Mining, Manufacturing, Trade, and Transportation

The product that recently replaced sugar as Guyana's main export is bauxite. Bauxite production, which began in 1914, now totals over 3 million tons per year, making Guyana one of the world's leading producers. The largest-producing company, the Demerara Bauxite Company (a subsidiary of Alcan Aluminium, Ltd, of Canada), was nationalized by the Guyanese government in 1971. The new government-owned "Guybau" mines, which yield over 90 per cent of Guyana's annual production, are located mostly

Courtesy Surinam Tourist Bureau
Rivers are the principal transportation routes in both Guyana and Surinam, and in the skillfully crafted dugout canoes of the Bush Negroes they are navigable far into the interior. Because the lower courses of many rivers are deep and wide enough to accommodate ocean-going vessels during the rainy season, most freight is moved by water.

around Mackenzie, 65 miles up the Demerara River. The only other producing company is Reynolds Metals Company, whose mines are near Kwakwani, about 100 miles up the Berbice River. All of Guyana's bauxite mines are in the white sand and clay region. A thick overburden of sand and clay adds to the cost of the open-pit mining process. Further expansion and development of the bauxite industry is one of Guyana's greatest hopes for the future.

From 1960 to 1968 manganese, found in small quantities in many areas of the country, was the nation's second-largest mining industry. The most valuable deposits are in the northwest around Matthew's Ridge. The ore moved by rail to Port Kaituma on the Kaituma River, where it was loaded onto seagoing ore boats for transport to Trinidad and then trans-shipment to North American buyers. Operations ceased in 1968 because of unfavorable market conditions for the Guyanese ore. In order to make use of the large infrastructure investments, the government subsequently undertook an enormous agricultural land-development project in the Matthew's Ridge–Port Kaituma area.

The manufacturing base of the Guyanese economy is still quite narrow. The secondary industries are mainly the manufacture and processing of food products, such as rum, molasses, beer, preserves, and shrimp. The milling of sugar and rice accounts for two thirds of all industrial production. There are also numerous nonfood industries, such as paints, medicines, and clothing, serving the small domestic market. Many consumer goods, however, must be imported, including some food products such as wheat flour and milk.

During recent years, Guyana has had a foreign-trade surplus; that is, total exports have had a higher value than total imports. The major recipients of exports are the United States (25.3 per cent), the United Kingdom (24.4 per cent), and Canada (18.2 per cent). In order of value, the leading exports are bauxite and alumina, sugar, and rice. The main sources of Guyana's imports are the United Kingdom (31.5 per cent) and the United States (21.5 per cent). In addition, nearly 14 per cent of Guyana's total trade is with the other Caribbean Free Trade Association (CARIFTA) nations. A small portion of the imports are from Communist countries, and recently Guyana began selling its export products to members of the Communist bloc. Although the gross national product has slowly been increasing in recent years, Guyana remains one of South America's poorer nations. In 1971 the average per capita income was $340 compared with $950 in Venezuela, $820 in Argentina, and $480 in Chile.

One of Guyana's most critical problems is its wholly inadequate transportation network. Road building and maintenance are very difficult on the low coastlands where most of the people live, for roads must be made to follow the sea-defense dams. Although over half a million people occupy the coastal area, this region has only about 400 miles of roads, only some 150 miles of which are paved. The main road is the Public Road, which extends from Springlands, on the Courantyne, to Charity, on the Pomeroon. This surfaced road is broken by estuaries of the Berbice, Demerara, and Essequibo, and large ferry boats carry people and goods across these river mouths. Unsurfaced roads often become sheer mud during the rainy seasons and are sometimes impassable by any type of motor vehicle. The ancient custom of placing wooden poles across the muddy roads, called "corduroying," is still practiced.

Although Guyana has the distinction of having had the first railroad on the South American continent, there are only 48 miles of public railroads in the country, and the rolling stock is outmoded. In addition, the Demerara Bauxite Company has some 80 miles of track to bring bauxite from the mines to the plants at Mackenzie. There are approximately 3,700 miles of inland waterways. The Demerara River is navigable to Mackenzie by ocean steamers, and ferry boats and small craft ply the other rivers. There is one modern airport, Timehri International Airport, located about twenty-five miles south of Georgetown. Guyana's own airlines, Guyana Airways, offers domestic service.

A Viable Future?

As a newly emerged nation, Guyana has yet to prove that it can survive economically and politically. The indications are, however, that it has both the natural and human resources needed. Certainly, it is better equipped for independence than many other newly independent nations. Social and economic progress will be slow, however, unless certain problems are solved in the near future. The transportation system must be improved so as to facilitate the flow of people, goods, and services. The educational system must be improved and expanded to provide for more secondary and higher education. And, perhaps most important, *all* the people must learn to think of themselves as *Guyanese* first and only second as East Indians or Negroes or members of other ethnic groups.

focus *on Environmental Problems and Land Development*

There are few countries where water control is more important than in Guyana. Major hydrologic problems on the coastal plain arise from the lowness of the land and the surcharge of water, which accrues not only from plentiful rainfall but also from the overflow of the many rivers that traverse it. For five miles inland, the coast is below the level of the high tides, and the extensive river systems have such low gradients and interfluves that a downpour often brings widespread floods. Water runoff is slow and natural drainage poor. The entire history of settlement in the coastal zone, where over 90 per cent of the Guyanese people live, can be viewed as a struggle against water, involving three aspects: sea defense, drainage, and irrigation.

The sea defenses that have been built along the coast serve to protect the sea coast and river banks from erosion by wave action and to prevent the inundation of the coastal belt.

By 1860 it had become obvious that responsibility for sea defense could not be left to independent proprietors of estates and, in 1874, it was decided to build a long coastal wall to protect Georgetown and adjacent areas. The wall was completed in 1882, and the following year the colonial government assumed the authority to order any estate proprietor to carry out at his own expense any sea-defense works thought necessary for the protection of British Guiana's coast. In 1933, a Sea Defense Board was established by the government to be responsible for the construction, maintenance, and management of all sea-defense works.

Sea defense was the first step in reclaiming the coastlands from the sea, but keeping the sea out was not enough. Excessive rainfall behind the defenses made drainage a necessary second step in producing a modified physical environment suitable for agricultural utilization. The basic principle employed by the Dutch planters was simple. The land was laid out in rectangular strips running inland from the coast. A front dam was constructed to keep out the sea and a back dam at the southern end of the plantation to keep back the excess swamp water. Then major drainage ditches, called "side line trenches," were dug to drain surplus rainwater to the sea. Where each drainage ditch crossed the sea dam, a wooden gate, called a sluice, or *koker,* was erected. The *kokers* were opened at low tide to let out surplus water and thus prevent the encroachment of the sea upon the coastlands at high tide. Most often it was necessary to dig secondary drainage ditches, usually perpendicular to the main trenches, to accommodate excess water until the *kokers* could be opened.

Since drainage through a *koker* could be accomplished only when the tide was low, there was bound to be a flood whenever there was very heavy rainfall and the tide was high. Further, in times of coastal erosion, drainage into the ocean was feasible; but during times of accretion the *kokers* silted up. Excess water accumulated at high tide and during periods of accretion could be eliminated only by pumping over the sea dam; the first steam pumps were introduced during the 1860's. The basic drainage system begun by the Dutch is still used today. It has been calculated that each square mile of sugar-cane land on the Guyanese coastal plain has an average of forty-nine miles of drainage ditches.

In addition to sea-defense and drainage facilities, the establishment of irrigation works is also a requisite for the reclamation of the coastal zone. It might seem peculiar that there should be a need for irrigation in Guyana, where the average yearly rainfall is about 90 inches, but rainfall distribution is seasonal. Because of the great loss of moisture by evapotranspiration, there is often insufficient moisture for optimum crop-growth conditions during the dry season, from mid-August to mid-November, and the farmers and estates must use water collected behind the back dams during the rainy season. The scope of the drainage and irrigation problem on the coastal plain can be appreciated when one considers that an average of sixty-five miles of drainage and irrigation ditches is necessary for each square mile of cane land, and that the hundreds of original sugar plantations encompassed thousands of square miles. It has been estimated that the original construction of the sugar plantations required the removal of approximately 100 million tons of earth—this labor being performed by slaves. Today, the larger trenches are usually dug and maintained by draglines, although much hand labor is still needed for maintenance.

Behind the back dams are reservoirs of fresh water in shallow lakes and swamps made by damming small streams. These conservancies are the source of irrigation water for the sugar-cane and rice lands of the coastal belt. Some conservancy water must travel as much as forty or fifty miles before it serves its vital purpose. In some places, canals have been cut through the conservancy swampland to facilitate the movement of water when it is needed, while in other places this is still accomplished simply by opening the *kokers* in the back dam: gravity moves the water into the irrigation channels. Enormous pumps are also used to transport the water from the reservoirs. A very careful watch has to be kept on the water level in the conservancies so that during periods of drought enough water will be provided for the needs of the plantations and small farmers. During times of very heavy rainfall, excess water is drained off through outlets called "relief sluices."

Among the most significant recent developments in Guyana has been the opening up of new lands, the responsibility of the Land Development Division of the Ministry of Agriculture and Natural Resources. After the site of each new project has been cleared and the hydraulic works have been provided, the area is laid out into cultivation and house lots and leased to tenant farmers.

Because the government has been eager to settle landless small farmers in its new land-development projects, settlement has sometimes occurred prior to the completion of the hydrologic works. But, in most cases, adequate hydraulic facilities are available and provide optimal agricultural conditions. The largest project, located north of the Canje Conservancy and provided with irrigation water by it, is the Black Bush Polder, which supports about 1,400 families on its 31,000 acres. The smallest of the land-development projects, on the Essequibo coast, encompasses only 170 acres laid out into thirty-five plots. Currently, the Guyanese government is investigating the possible establishment·of seven additional projects which would provide 135,000 acres of new land for the livelihood of over 4,000 families.

Large portions of Guyana's coastlands have population densities exceeding 200 people per square mile, and the population is growing at a rate of 2.9 per cent per year. It seems clear that this growing population must continue to consist largely of farm families because Guyana, for a long time to come, will continue to have an economy based on agriculture and mining. It is doubtful whether there is any possibility of bringing about sudden and significant increases in the agricultural productivity of the already settled portions of the coastlands by the use of better seeds and farming techniques, including a greater use of fertilizers. This is particularly so in the case of rice, where intensive methods and double-cropping are already practiced. Even if the productivity of these areas could be significantly increased, they would not necessarily be able to support a significantly larger population, certainly not at a significantly higher standard of living. It seems necessary, therefore, that new lands be opened up to provide for the extension of farming. It is one of the premises of present agricultural policy that the rapidly increasing population will be settled on small family farms; it is further assumed that there is and will continue to be a shortage of agricultural land, despite the fact that vast areas of the coastal plain are virgin swamp and marshland. The problem is that the clearing of new land and the establishment of hydrologic facilities are very expensive. In some of the land-development projects, for example, it has cost the government more than $500 per acre to prepare the land for settlement. In addition to the original cost, there are annually recurrent maintenance costs. Because Guyana is a relatively poor country, progress in the extension of farming into new lands is necessarily slow, even though it is recognized as essential.

Suggested Readings

American University. *Area Handbook for Guyana*. Washington, D.C.: U.S. Government Printing Office, 1969. A comprehensive review of social, political, and economic aspects of the nation.

DAVID, WILFRED L. *The Economic Development of Guyana, 1953–1964*. Oxford: Clarendon Press, 1969. A comprehensive analysis of some of the more important development problems facing a small and dependent economy.

HENFREY, COLIN. "Guayana." In *Latin America and the Caribbean: A Handbook*. Edited by Claudio Véliz. New York: Praeger, 1968; London: Anthony Blond, 1968, pp. 279–90. A resumé of Guyana's political history and economy.

LOWENTHAL, DAVID. "Population Contrasts in the Guianas." *Geographical Review*, L, no. 1 (January, 1960), pp. 41–58. A comparison of the three areas, with an explanation of how the differences came about.

NEWMAN, PETER. *British Guiana: Problems of Cohesion in an Immigrant Society*. London and New York: Oxford University Press, 1964. This book, published for the Institute of Race Relations, distinguishes the long-run forces that have shaped today's Guyanese society from more recent economic and political trends.

SMITH, RAYMOND T. *British Guiana*. New York: Oxford University Press, 1962. A classic text on the natural resources, history, economy, and social and political structure of Guyana, written by a sociologist.

See also Suggested Readings for Part I, pp. 61–63.

8 SURINAM

Ranjit Tirtha and Cornelius Loeser

Physical Setting • Historical Background • A Mixture of Peoples • The Economy • focus on *Aluminum: Key to Industrialization*

Although the area formerly called the Guianas is part of South America and peripheral to the Caribbean, its cultural framework is distinctive in several significant respects. Unlike the rest of South America, the Guianas lack a heritage of feudal land ownership, with its typical attendant problems: vast areas of good land held by a small minority and a high degree of social immobility. Historically, the economies of the area have been associated with the plantation complex of the Caribbean, but the three nations are less overpopulated with respect to their resource base than are the Caribbean islands.

Surinam (formerly Dutch Guiana) is located west of French Guiana and east of Guyana (formerly British Guiana). In economic evolution it occupies a median position. All three began their modern histories as colonies of Western nations, developed for the export of raw materials: minerals, timber, and especially plantation crops. In French Guiana, plantations failed early and were never successfully reestablished. In Guyana they succeeded and still play a dominant role in the economy. The plantations of Surinam ultimately failed after a long period of struggle—but not completely. The resulting compromises and accommodations gave rise to a distinctive society.

Physical Setting

Northern Surinam consists of a coastal plain, 50 miles wide in the west and 10 miles wide in the east. It is flat except for a series of low sandy beach ridges. Vast areas of swamp lie below sea level. Soils are generally heavy clays and tropical peat, lateritic and acidic, but they are capable of sustaining continuous cultivation when properly drained, and they support most of the nation's 400,000 people.

In the chief agricultural lands, which are concentrated on the coastal plain along the lower portions of the rivers, the tidal range is about four feet. The fields have to be empoldered—that is, reclaimed from the sea and drained by the opening of sluices at low tide, methods introduced by the Dutch. The maintenance of dikes and canals is critical for irrigation as well as for handling surplus water. Water applications are necessary to extend the growing season and to control the quality of the water, because swamp water becomes excessively acid and salt water encroaches from the sea during the dry season.

Inland from the coastal plain is a gently rolling, slightly elevated plain from 30 to 40 miles wide, much of it forested. Covered subsequent to formation by a thin layer of alluvial wash from the interior, the plain's soils are older and less fertile than those of the coastal plain. In isolated stretches between the south-to-north flowing rivers, the soils are nearly pure quartz sand. Although this soil is not good for cultivation it supports an open, grassy savanna. Grazing and dairying have been moderately successful here, but the principal economic activity is bauxite mining. Extensive deposits are being exploited; some of these cap low hills, others are beneath 30 feet of overburden, making extraction difficult in this area of heavy rainfall and a high water table.

Still farther inland is a vast hilly region rising gradually in elevation to the highest peak in the Wilhelmina Mountains (4,200 feet). Much of this region is blanketed with tall, closed-canopy rain forest which contains a wealth of timber, one of Surinam's chief resources. Extensive bauxite deposits and lateritic iron deposits have been discovered in this highland area but they have not as yet been exploited, although several small air strips and advance base camps have been established in a development-oriented exploration plan called "Operation Grasshopper." Also, a new north–south road is being built to facilitate exploitation of the interior forest and mineral resources. This road is the first serious attempt to create a national road network. Most of the 800 miles of all-weather roads are in the densely peopled coastal area, where swamps make it extremely difficult to build and maintain roads or railways.

Along the coast, strong ocean currents coupled with trade winds, both moving from east to west, have created sandbars which deflect the lower

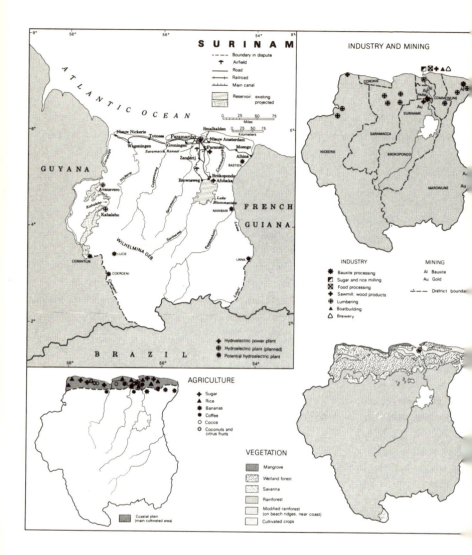

SURINAM

--- Boundary in dispute
✝ Airfield
── Road
┤├ Railroad
┼┼┼ Main canal
▒ Reservoir existing
projected

INDUSTRY AND MINING

ATLANTIC OCEAN

GUYANA

FRENCH GUIANA

BRAZIL

Nisuw Nickerie · Totness · Paramaribo · Smalkalden · Nisuw Amsterdam
Wageningen · Groningen · Paranam · Moengo
Saramacca Kanaal · Zanderij · Albina · BASTIEN
Brokopondo · Afobaka
Browneweg · Lake Blommestein · MANBARI
Avanavero
Kabalebo
Kabalebo
WILHELMINA GEB.
CORANTIIN · LUCIE · COEROENI · LAWA

INDUSTRY
✳ Bauxite processing
▣ Sugar and rice milling
⊠ Food processing
✚ Sawmill, wood products
⊕ Lumbering
▲ Boatbuilding
△ Brewery

MINING
Al Bauxite
Au Gold
--- District boundary

✚ Hydroelectric power plant
⊕ Hydroelectric plant (planned)
✳ Potential hydroelectric plant

AGRICULTURE
✚ Sugar
▲ Rice
✳ Bananas
● Coffee
○ Cocoa
✿ Coconuts and citrus fruits

VEGETATION
▨ Mangrove
▦ Wetland forest
░ Savanna
▒ Rainforest
░ Modified rainforest (on beach ridges, near coast)
□ Cultivated crops

Coastal plain (main cultivated area)

courses of the rivers and partially block their mouths. Siltation of the
river mouths restricts their use to small ocean-going vessels and has limited
the size of bauxite-ore boats. However, the deflected portions of the rivers
and the Saramacca Canal provide a complete east–west inland artery for
boat traffic through the populated coastal plain.

The innumerable wandering rivers and streams that crisscross the country have traditionally served as highways. Many are navigable for barges

and other shallow craft all year and for larger ships in the rainy season. Inland, the rivers and streams are generally deep in proportion to their width and carry very low sediment loads, but they are obstructed by numerous waterfalls and rapids, especially where they pass from the harder crystalline rocks of the interior onto the older alluvial surface. They could be made navigable far into the interior by the construction of dams and locks, which at the same time could tap their enormous hydroelectric potential. Control of these rivers would provide greater access to the interior, more power, and drainage control and irrigation water to improve the agricultural potential of the country.

Historical Background

In Surinam, as in many other parts of the world, European colonization was motivated by the desire first for raw materials and later for export crops raised by native and imported labor. The English and the French were the first to establish small plantation settlements in Surinam, between 1630 and 1640. Then, in 1667, in the course of an Anglo-Dutch war, the Dutch succeeded in conquering the territory near Paramaribo along the Suriname River and began rejuvenating the old plantations and creating new ones with the help of immigrant Jews who had been driven out of Brazil and Cayenne (French Guiana). The Dutch established courts of justice, built canals, empoldered the coast, introduced new commercial crops like cacao, and improved the existing sugar-cane, cotton, and coffee plantations. The displaced indigenous Indians, however, constantly pillaged the settlements, and the badly treated Negro slaves imported from Africa sporadically escaped to the interior, known as the Bush country, where they banded together in small villages. Dense forest and swamps made the task of recapturing the runaways unending and often fruitless.

With the British abolition of the slave trade in 1807, the supply of slave labor from Africa ceased. Also, the Dutch were again embroiled in European wars (the British held Surinam for almost the entire period between 1796 and 1814). Dutch interests began to focus more on East Asia. Dutch capital went elsewhere. The development of Surinam suffered, and it became a deficit item for the Dutch exchequer. In addition, the introduction of beet sugar in Anglo-America reduced the value of sugar cane in the world market. In 1863 the slaves were emancipated, and most of them soon left the remaining plantations. Between 1830 and 1875, the plantation labor force was reduced by one third; the cultivated area in plantations shrank by one half. Facing an acute labor shortage, the Dutch recruited indentured laborers from British India on a contract basis. Soon after, they also began recruiting in Java, then under Dutch rule. At the expiration of their contracts (five years), most Asian immigrants declined repatriation and either remained on the estates or became small farmers.

In 1947 Surinam became an integrated territory of the Netherlands, but the Surinamese still were greatly dissatisfied with Dutch administration. World War II further estranged them, and postwar negotiations finally gave Surinam complete autonomy in internal affairs in 1954. The Netherlands government, however, retained control of defense and foreign affairs.

Following internal independence, the Surinamese elected representatives in the legislative, executive, and ministerial branches of the government and organized many political parties, mainly along ethnic lines.

A Mixture of Peoples

With a population of 400,000 and an area of 62,500 square miles, Surinam has the very low gross density of 6.5 persons per square mile. But the density per cultivated square mile, a little over 1,000 persons, is high, almost as high as in the Netherlands (but only half the density on cultivated land in, for instance, the United Arab Republic). Furthermore, the crude birth rate of 4.6 per cent per year is among the highest in the world, and the annual mortality rate of only 0.9 per cent is among the lowest. And since almost half the population is under fifteen years of age, the present rate of population increase (3.7 per cent per year) is not likely to decrease for some time to come. At this extremely high annual rate of increase, Surinam will have more than 1.2 million people by the end of the century. Despite some underemployment at present, the anticipated increase in manpower could well be an asset rather than a burden, as in so many other parts of the world. In the first place, the populace enjoys a high degree of literacy (76 per cent) and fairly good health. With proper planning, the large and growing manpower reserve can be utilized for the country's economic development, particularly for increased exploitation of mineral resources, industrialization, transport improvements, and expansion of agriculture.

Surinam's population is richly diversified in ethnic composition, and the various groups live together harmoniously, although each adheres to some extent to its own culture, religion, and language. Minor friction between culture groups over political and economic issues is greatly eased by the government's conscious effort to promote universal racial equality. For example, the government, although largely controlled by Hindustanis (an East Indian group), recently invited the former creole office holders to form a coalition government, offering them greater participation in the administration.

Following the colonization of 1650, thousands of native Amerindians were driven from the areas along the rivers and near the coast into the interior, where their descendants (about 2 per cent of the present population) make a living by hunting, fishing, and shifting agriculture, and by such handicrafts as basket-making and rope-making.

Many of the Africans brought in by the Dutch perished on the plantations under very repressive conditions or succumbed to diseases. The Bush Negroes, descendants of those who escaped from slavery into the interior, now live in isolated, self-reliant settlements where the principal occupations are hunting, fishing, and lumbering. Government efforts to draw the Bush Negroes (about 9 per cent of the present population) into the general culture are only slowly, if at all, yielding success, for the Negroes are keenly conscious of their history of self-liberation.

After the emancipation of the slaves in 1863, large numbers of Hindustanis and Javanese came as indentured laborers. The Hindustani immigration came to a halt in 1918 under the pressure of nationalist sentiment in India, and World War II almost entirely stopped the Javanese influx. The Hindustanis (about 35 per cent of the population) are mostly engaged in farming, chiefly sugar cane and rice. One quarter of them reside in Paramaribo, where they work in commercial enterprises or as teachers, lawyers, and doctors. Like the Hindustanis, the Javanese (15 per cent of the population) are engaged in small-scale commercial enterprises. Recently both the Hindustanis and the Javanese have been moving into the cities in increasing numbers in search of greater economic opportunities.

The creoles, descendants of the freed African slaves, now form 35 per cent of the population. With the demise of the larger coffee, cacao, and sugar-cane plantations after 1870, many of them drifted to Paramaribo. Today, the creoles are the most westernized, urbanized, and politically active of the various groups. Many of them are employed in administrative positions in Paramaribo. A few still work on farms in the rural areas, where they raise coconuts and subsistence crops.

The Europeans, primarily Dutch, are concentrated chiefly in the capital. They are occupied in administrative, advisory, and consultative capacities and serve a managerial role on a few estates. The Chinese, who arrived between 1853 and 1872, now represent 2 per cent of the population. Most of them are retail traders and are scattered about in various settlements. They have intermarried with other groups to a great extent and may possibly become absorbed in other communities to the point of losing their group identity.

Paramaribo, the capital and chief port of the country, lies on the Suriname River. Despite the diverse ethnic composition of its 150,000 inhabitants, it is distinctively Dutch in architecture and layout. Nieuw Nickerie, Albina, Moengo, and Paranam are other locally important towns. A new major port is planned in the west for development in the near future.

The Economy

The people of Surinam are predominantly independent rice farmers. Three quarters of all cultivated land is in rice; it is the main staple of the diet and the leading export crop.

Land is in ample supply but can be made productive only if the forest is cleared and kept back and the land is drained and supplied with irrigation water. Rice needs a great deal of water. The average rainfall is about 80 inches a year, but most of it comes between April and August or between November and February, and during dry spells unirrigated crops tend to dry up. Irrigation is also needed to counteract the periodic encroachment of salty water from the sea. At present most of the clearing, draining, and irrigating is done by individual hand labor, which brings poor returns for very hard work. Much of the productive area is operating with the dikes and canals built by the now-defunct plantations, and these are not being satisfactorily maintained. These ditches cut up the land into small plots, averaging 30 by 30 feet, making mechanization difficult. Although the temperature regime (usually between 70° and 90° F.) would permit the continuous production of rice, only one crop a year is grown, and the cultivated area is intensively planted with nursery seedlings by hand labor. Rotation of crops is minimal.

The government has been investing in many land-clearing and pilot farm projects, leasing and transferring land to small farmers as quickly as it can be made available, and animal husbandry is slowly developing.

Government experimental farms have been working for twenty years to upgrade domestic cattle, for much of the population suffers from a lack of protein in the diet. Sanitary milk and meat processing and distribution systems are well organized within Paramaribo, but the supply of meat and milk is far from adequate. Farmers place much more emphasis on rice than on animals and see little point in clearing land for growing grass when it could be used for rice. When the fields are in rice there is little room for cattle, and many are sent out into the swamps, an environment to which they are poorly adapted. Many suffer from diseases and split hooves and, since most calves are born in the swamps, calf losses are high. The substitution of water buffalo for these cattle is being given serious consideration.

There are plenty of fish in the rivers and drainage ditches and in the coastal waters, and efforts are being made to increase the catch as an additional source of protein and also as a source of foreign revenue. Shrimp, processed in new packing plants, are becoming a valuable export.

A few sugar, coffee, and cacao plantations have survived and continue to contribute modestly to the economy. Efforts to upgrade them through disease control and mechanization continue, and promising newer crops (pineapples, citrus fruits, and especially bananas) are being introduced. Only two crops—rice and coconuts—offer much potential, however, within the chronically depressed world market for tropical crops.

In 1949, the Foundation for the Development of Mechanized Agriculture in Surinam was created and the Wegeningen poldered rice farm was established, partly with the aim of settling Dutch farmers in Surinam. It failed to attract such immigrants but proved an outstanding economic success. The Foundation cleared some 16,000 acres of swamp forest with chemicals, controlled water levels with modern pumps, sowed and dusted the crops by airplane, and introduced scientifically selected seed. Fields started to yield excellent returns: 2,470 pounds per acre, as compared with a world average of 1,600. Double-cropping has been introduced, and if the new faster-growing varieties of rice are planted, three crops a year can be expected. Production could be tripled if projected water-control schemes are effected. The Coronie area, where this expansion would take place, is also being considered as a possible locale for modernizing and expanding coconut production. Authorities feel that the potential for coconut crops along the coast here is exceptionally promising. Coconuts could supply the domestic market with badly needed vegetable oil and animal feed, and they have a firmer long-range overseas market than rice.

The Paranam complex of the Surinam Aluminum Company (Suralco) is one of the first facilities to combine mining, alumina refining, and aluminum smelting in a single location. The refining plant and smelter are powered by the generators at Afobaka Dam, 45 miles away. Bauxite (aluminum ore) is important also to the economy of Guyana and French Guiana, where there are large, as yet unexploited, reserves of bauxite.

The lumbering industry is rapidly being modernized and expanded. Round lumber, cut by Bush Negroes in the vast forests in the interior and floated down the main streams, is still exported, but about half is now processed into sawed lumber for export, and a small but growing amount is manufactured into plywood, particle board, parquet flooring, and prefabricated houses. The potential for pulp production is being tested in an eighteen-year stand of experimentally planted pines. The inaccessibility of much of the forest at present and the variety of species per acre are major handicaps in the further development of the industry.

Small-scale manufacture of such items as garments, shoes, beer, sausages, matches, and bricks provides low-wage-level employment in the cities and supplies the small domestic market. The limited size of the local market has not encouraged foreign investment in industries geared to local needs, although some American capital has gone into lumber, plywood, and bottling plants. But Surinam is an autonomous part of the Kingdom of the Netherlands and an Associate Member of the European Economic Community; hence it enjoys preferential treatment for its exports to EEC nations. This, plus a relatively stable and democratic government, a stable currency, a pool of inexpensive labor, and rich, untapped forestry and mineral resources, has attracted sizable amounts of foreign capital in industries geared to exportable items. International Telephone and Telegraph, for instance, has built an assembly plant for the production of telecommunications equipment to be sold to the EEC and in the Caribbean area. But to develop a modern nation commensurate with its enormous potential, Surinam will need to generate much more local capital. For this, the government is looking to its resources of bauxite ore and its hydroelectric potential.

focus *on Aluminum: Key to Industrialization*

Surinam has one of the world's richest deposits of bauxite (aluminum ore); its average annual output of some 5.6 million tons gives it second rank in world production, after Jamaica.

At present, bauxite processing is confined to two areas: at Moengo and around Paranam, which together yield 4.7 million tons of bauxite yearly. Most of this bauxite is exported. In the past, the shallow depths at the mouth of the Suriname River hindered shipping operations: small vessels had to deliver the ore to a collection station on the island of Trinidad, where it was loaded onto larger ships. To avoid the expense of dredging a channel, the Surinam government organized a scheme using double-hulled ships which, when confined to a tightly restricted path across the mud flats, scoured a channel with their bottoms. The effective depth was increased, and now boats can carry a load of bauxite directly to the United States or Europe.

The Surinam government would like to export less bauxite and manufacture more aluminum, however. As in many newly independent and developing nations, industrialization is held to be the key to higher standards of living. And the key to industrialization here is aluminum. Abundant supplies of bauxite are available: besides the ones already being exploited, vast new reserves—400 million tons—have been discovered in the west, in the Kabalebo area. And the nation's hydroelectric potential is estimated at over 2 million kilowatts, more than enough for the most ambitious plans.

Proximity to markets has never been a decisive factor in locating aluminum-processing industries in the past: both Canada and Norway export 90 per cent of their output, France exports 15 per cent, and a plant is being built in Iceland. The aluminum industry provides a classic illustration of how the traditional precepts concerning plant location, proximity of physical resources, and availability of markets can be overridden by considerations of capital control. Surinam hopes to be the site of a significant breach in the established framework, perhaps a model for other economically less-developed nations that have impressive sources of bauxite and the hydroelectric power needed to produce aluminum. The reduction from ore to metal brings a thirteen-fold increase in value. In the past this profit has gone into already highly industrialized countries, such as Canada and the United States. Surinam's aim is to refine and smelt and also manufacture aluminum products locally, so that greater profits will become available for local use. This is an aim shared by many less-developed nations that are rich in mineral resources and power but lack capital for projects that could hasten economic and social evolution.

A large step toward this goal was the construction at Paranam of the world's first complex combining mining, refining, and smelting. The refining plant has a capacity of 800,000 tons; production in the late 1960's was just over 400,000 tons per year. The smelter has a capacity of 60,000 tons of aluminum; 1970 production was over half that. Power for these plants is supplied by the recently built government hydroelectric station at Afobaka, which has a capacity of 180,000 kilowatts and currently generates 150,000.

The present limiting physical factor for aluminum smelting in the Paranam-Afobaka area is the supply of electric power. The Afobaka Dam proved temporarily disappointing, since its completion was followed by a long drought, and impounded Lake Blommestein took a long time to reach an adequate level. Water supply, not storage capacity, is limited. The government has proposed that the Saramacca River be diverted by a canal to sustain the lake's level. The estimated increase in capacity at Afobaka would be enough to increase aluminum production tenfold. The ore in this area is substantially controlled by Alcoa, however, and since it is committed to already existing smelters in the United States, the company has not shown interest in this scheme.

The government has made extensive feasibility studies for the development of smelting and power facilities in the Kabalebo area. According to present plans, it intends to build a plant to smelt a large proportion of the ore in this area into pure aluminum. The Coeroenie River is to be diverted into a reservoir and then returned to the Corantijn River by way of the Kabalebo River. Two dams and power stations planned for Kabalebo and nearby Avanavero would generate 850,000 kilowatts of electric power. In addition, the dams would regulate the flow of the Corantijn downstream, thus extending navigation inland nearly 200 miles and making the whole area and its resources more accessible.

The Surinam government would own the power plants and lease mineral deposits. It would obtain capital for the plants through long-term commitments by customers to buy power, as it did at Afobaka. Alcoa and Billiton have requested concessions to explore for and perhaps develop deposits near Kabalebo, in return for which they will "consider" purchase of power. The government has invited other aluminum companies to make counteroffers, in the hope of obtaining the firm commitments that would make it possible to construct the planned dams. Such projects are crucial if Surinam is to develop industrially.

Other phases of the current development plan involve efforts to raise productivity in agriculture, improve education and health facilities, extend and improve transportation, carry out further geological surveys, and diversify industry. One indication of the results achieved is a nearly 200 per cent increase in manufacturing output during the last ten years. Another is the growth in the gross national product, which has outstripped the growth in population; hence the standard of living of the population has gone up, whereas in many newly independent and less-developed nations the reverse is true. In Surinam five years ago the per capita GNP was $444; it is now $540, well above the average in South America.

Suggested Readings

DE BRUIJNE, G. A. "Surinam in Regional Geography. An Alternative to Preston James' Latin America." *Geografisch Tijdschrift*, V, no. 3 (June, 1971), pp. 228–31 (in English). A brief description of the country, by a Dutch geographer.

————. "Surinam and the Netherlands Antilles: Their Place in the World." *Geografisch Tijdschrift*, V, no. 4 (September, 1971), pp. 517–24 (in English). A discussion of the area's potential, in terms of its geography.

LOWENTHAL, DAVID. "Population Contrasts in the Guianas." *Geographical Review*, L, no. 1 (January, 1960), pp. 41–58. A comparison of the three areas, explaining how their differences came about.

U.S. Bureau of International Commerce. "Basic Data on the Economy of Surinam." *Overseas Business Reports, OBR 67–51*, (August, 1967). A brief analysis of the nation's economy.

See also Suggested Readings for Part I, pp. 61–63.

9 FRENCH GUIANA

Historical Background · Environment and People · The Economy ·
Problems of Economic Development

French Guiana has much closer ties with France than nearby Guyana, for example, does with Great Britain, or Surinam with the Netherlands, their former colonial rulers. These ties are based on the fact that France supplies virtually all of French Guiana's revenues and the majority of its inhabitants enjoy their country's relationship with France and consciously seek a French identity.

In French Guiana, uninterruptedly French since the seventeenth century, one is in France, though perhaps France of 1900 rather than 1970. The marks are evident everywhere: café life, school curricula, books and journals, French bread baked in even the most remote settlement. Wine, champagne, and liqueurs are not merely articles of commerce, they are sacrosanct emblems of Gallic culture.*

As a result of the money France provides, educational and health facilities are better than in many other parts of South America, and civil-service jobs are plentiful. French money also helps to pay for the food imports needed to supplement local supplies. The benefits to France are perhaps more psychological than financial: the feeling of still having a foothold in South America and the prestige of the rocket-launching site recently built at Kourou. But there are also forest and mineral resources that await further economic development.

* David Lowenthal, *West Indian Societies*. London: Oxford University Press, 1972, pp. 266–67.

Historical Background

In 1635 the French established a small colony on the Ile de Cayenne and in the 1760's some 14,000 French emigrants, recruited by misleading propaganda to enlarge the colony, were landed on the Korou River. They had no provisions. Within two years, 11,000 of them died of fever, and 2,000 returned to France. The few remaining colonists established plantations worked by slaves imported from Africa.

When slavery was abolished, England and Holland began to bring into their neighboring colonies large numbers of indentured servants from Asia; France was unable to attract such labor to French Guiana because of the small number of its plantations and its already malodorous reputation as a penal colony. The French government had decided in 1852 to reinvigorate the plantations by developing a penal colony in this area, forcing the convicts to work in the fields—a permanent indentured servitude. The most important installations were at St. Laurent and on the Îles du Salut, a group of islands off the northern coast. The name of one of this group, Devil's Island, came to be applied to the whole penal colony, perhaps because several famous political prisoners, Captain Alfred Dreyfus among them, were incarcerated there. Accounts of the starvation diets and inhuman treatment of prisoners continued until the penal institution was closed in 1947. At about that time, after years of neglect on the part of the French government, French Guiana voted to become an Overseas Department of France.

Environment and People

Located on the northern coast of South America between Surinam on the west and Brazil on the east and south, French Guiana covers 35,135 square miles including its rocky offshore islands. Mainland French Guiana is divided into two regions: the coastal lowlands, which extend inland ten to thirty miles, and the interior plateau, which rises in many levels, forming a mass of low, steep hills, to the Tumucumaque Mountains. The lush, green interior plateau is part of the Amazon tropical forest. The main rivers—Maroni, Mana, Sinnamary, Approuague, and Oyapock—are the principal means of access to the interior.

The climate of French Guiana is subequatorial. Temperatures average around 80° F.; humidity is high, despite cool offshore winds. Heavy rains, falling from December through January and from April to July, bring an average of 110 inches annually, but French Guiana is outside the path of tropical storms.

Of the approximately 45,000 inhabitants, 90 per cent are creole (a mixture of African, Asian, and Caucasian); the rest are French, Indian, or of other nationalities. Some 20,000 people live in the capital, Cayenne, or along the coast in the other larger towns. The creoles are mainly farmers; the French are active in government service and business; the Chinese dominate the retail trade. Syrians and Lebanese manufacture cloth and clothes.

The indigenous Indians of the interior live at a subsistence level, hunting, fishing, and cultivating the land until the soil no longer produces sufficient food, when they move to another area. These Indians —Roucouyennes, Emerillons, and Oyampis—have no inclination to become citizens; indeed, France rigorously guards them against assimiliation. Until recently, indiscriminate contacts with creoles and tourists were decimating some tribal groups and corrupting others. Creole gold panners, for example, introduced malaria, tuberculosis, prostitution, and alcoholism among the Emerillon Indians. In 1962 the French government restricted visits to tribal areas.

Another group living in the interior consists of descendants of rebel slaves—members of the Boni, Bosch, and Saramaca tribes in Africa—who managed to escape and re-create their tribal life styles there. They make their living transporting supplies into the interior by canoe. Official recognition by the government is given to their chief, "The Grand Man."

The Indians of the coast—Galibis, Arawaks, Palikours, and Amerindians— have the option to become French citizens, but there is no pressure on them to alter their traditional ways of life. Whether citizens or not, the Indians do not have to submit to many French laws: they live according to their customs, under a chief who is recognized by the administration. In addition, they are not required to serve in the military, pay taxes, or perform other obligations usually associated with citizenship.

The Economy

One of the great unexploited resources of French Guiana is the forest, which covers nine tenths of its area. Exploitation is difficult because the varieties of trees are intermixed and the lumberer thus has to travel farther from tree to tree than in forests of pure stands. Another problem is poor transportation: lumber is processed only at cutting sites near the coast or a river, because of the lack of roads and tracks. Marketable forest products include essential oil from rosewood, gum from balata trees (used, among other things, for making golf balls), and timber. Teak, mahogany, and Caribbean pine have been planted in special groves for the future extraction of hardwood and pulp.

Most food must be imported, and costs are high. Agriculture hardly exists beyond the subsistence level. The reason for this is the same in the 1970's as it was in the 1770's: it hardly seems worth the trouble. Nearly nine tenths of the farms are subsistence-level slash-and-burn enterprises. Products include manioc, bananas, potatoes, and yams. Produced on a smaller scale are pineapples, watermelons, maize, and citrus fruits. Sugar cane, the only cash crop, is cultivated mainly around Cayenne and St. Laurent. In addition, experiments with rice growing are under way.

Along the fresh-water rivers and streams, small farmers and interior tribesmen fish for their own consumption or to sell at local markets. Shrimp is the major catch from the Atlantic Ocean. Other types of shellfish, turtles, tuna, and swordfish are also caught.

Industry is chiefly food processing and wood processing. There are two soft-drink factories, a brewery, a few rosewood-essence factories, and a sugar plant, which makes rum. Rice, cocoa, and pineapples are also processed. The main food-processing industry, employing about 400 people, is shrimp packaging and freezing; the industry was developed with American capital, and most of the shrimp goes to the United States. Fifteen sawmills and several wood-peeling and veneering companies process forest products.

Local handicrafts also bring in some income. Pottery, baskets, and woven hammocks are made for the tourist trade.

French Guiana has large bauxite deposits near Kaw, about thirty miles from Cayenne. Reserves are estimated at about 50 million tons; the Péchiney-Alcoa Company has an option for bauxite extraction, but mining is slated for some indefinite time in the future. There are also limited deposits of tantalite, lithium, uranium, lead, and beryl.

In 1964, when Algeria won its prolonged struggle for independence from France, the French had to abandon their space center in Hamaguir and sought an alternative site. Kourou seemed an ideal location for launching rockets for scientific and commercial use. Proximity to the equator (between 2° and 5° north latitude) enables satellites to be sent into numerous orbits, from polar to equatorial. Its coastal location offered advantages for transportation, the savanna vegetation required little leveling, and relatively few people lived in the area.

The space center includes the launching complex, a technological center, equipment for trajectory analysis and telemetry, an industrial zone and port, and an urban area for expansion of the town of Kourou. The complex was built by France at a cost of $100 million and has a yearly operating budget of $20 million. This huge investment has created some new jobs but it has also increased still further the imbalance between imports and exports and has sparked an increase in both wages and prices. In 1968 the first rocket was launched and since then more have gone up. Although the base is available for use by other nations, interest has waned in recent years.

Problems of Economic Development

The transport system of French Guiana is slowly penetrating into the less populous interior plateau, but it must be greatly upgraded before the resources of this area can be used more profitably. The heavy annual rainfall presents a problem for road building, since flooding is a constant hazard. There are only 125 miles of paved roads, 45 miles of nonpaved roads, 218 miles of interior paths, and 125 miles of roads that can be traversed by jeep. The main road follows the coastline from Cayenne to St. Laurent.

A large proportion of French Guiana's imports come in by sea, mainly to the port at Cayenne, and are then transshipped to St. Laurent and Kourou. Freight costs are high: entering ships are frequently half empty when they leave because of the lack of exportable items.

Air transport is also beginning to be used to connect isolated places in the interior with the rest of the country, but it is too expensive for most goods. There are no railroads.

Another obstacle to development is the distribution of the limited working population. Most people live along the coast and work in service industries in the towns; few people are available or have the desire to work in the interior to develop forest and mineral resources because living conditions there are so primitive.

Differential pay scales also have been a source of trouble. Since French Guiana is an Overseas Department of France, government workers receive salaries based on the French minimum wage scale, which is well above the local average. In recent years, some creoles have shown their dissatisfaction with the differential by staging strikes for increases in wages of as much as 40 per cent. If these demands are granted, they are likely to cause further disequilibrium in the economy.

On the other hand, industry and agriculture are so rudimentary that the society is not split between a mass of farm workers and a few great land-holders, a serious problem in many areas in South America. Also, French Guiana is not troubled by the racial and ethnic disharmony that charac-terizes so many South American nations, and no large-scale importation of labor to develop resources is being considered, mainly because of the fear that such antagonisms might develop.

So the goal of economic development and the goal of preserving ethnic harmony are to some degree antipathetic. As far as one can tell at present, French Guiana's reciprocal relationship with France will continue to the satisfaction of both.

Suggested Readings

GRITZNER, CHARLES F., JR. "French Guiana Penal Colony: Its Role in Colonial Development." *Journal of Geography*, LXIII, no. 7 (October, 1964), pp. 314–19. Argues that French Guiana's underdevelopment is a direct result of France's attempt to colonize the area with its own "human refuse."

LOWENTHAL, DAVID. "Population Contrasts in the Guianas." *Geographical Review*, L, no. 1 (January, 1960), pp. 41–58. A comparison of the three areas, explaining how their differences came about.

———. "French Guiana: Myths and Realities." *Transactions of the New York Academy of Sciences*, Ser. II, Vol. XXII, no. 7 (May, 1960), pp. 528–40. An excellent description of the realities of life in French Guiana.

U.S. Bureau of International Commerce. "Basic Data on the Economy of French Guiana." *Overseas Business Reports, OBR 68–112* (December, 1968). A brief report on the nation's economy.

U.S. Department of State. "French Guiana: Background Notes." (May, 1971), 3 pp. A brief review, containing some useful information.

See also Suggested Readings for Part I, pp. 61–63.

10 COLOMBIA

James J. Parsons

Highland and Lowland People • *Coffee and Bananas* • *Minerals, Energy, and Industry* • *Transportation* • focus *on Attitudes Toward Innovation and the Process of Industrialization*

Few places on earth have such striking physical contrasts as Colombia. Its rugged, broken topography, together with a location near the equator, creates an extraordinary diversity of climate, vegetation, and agricultural crops. Here, in close juxtaposition, are desert wastes, dripping rain forests, temperate valleys, barren, wind-swept plains, and towering snow-covered mountains.

Two great river valleys, the Magdalena and the Cauca, provide avenues from the Caribbean coastal lowlands into the heart of the Colombian Andes, which flare out northward from the Ecuador frontier in three distinct ranges. Lowest and least populous of these north–south spurs is the Cordillera Occidental (Western Cordillera), which blocks off the Cauca Valley from the rain-drenched Pacific coast. Loftiest is the Cordillera Central, with its towering volcanoes and permanent snow fields, until recently an almost insuperable barrier to the east-west movement of bulky goods; to the north, in Antioquia, this range continues as an older, stable, crystalline highland. The valley of the Magdalena River separates the Cordillera Central from the massive Cordillera Oriental (Eastern Cordillera), whose broad, treeless plains and high, intermontane savannas and plateaus have been the traditional centers of Chibcha, Spanish, and Colombian culture and government.

Beyond the Cordillera Oriental, great piedmont plains stretch unbroken toward the Orinoco and Amazon rivers. These warm, wet lowlands occupy

60 per cent of Colombia's 440,000 square miles but contain less than 2 per cent of its 22.1 million people.

The Andean highland area with its extension northward to the Caribbean coastal lowlands is the Colombia that counts, the Colombia of history, of coffee and oil, of textile mills and cities. A small but distinctive subunit consists of the Chocó on the Pacific coast, a world of Negroid river dwellers and miners, which probably has the highest annual rainfall in the New World.

Unlike the Andean nations to the south, Colombia is almost entirely a white and *mestizo* country. The replacement of the Indian language and culture by Spanish was curiously abrupt and complete. Yet pre-Columbian New Granada had supported a dense Indian population of considerable wealth and cultural attainment. The Chibcha, the Quimbaya, the Sinú, and the Tairona were peoples of relatively high culture, although without the political sophistication of the Aztecs and the Incas.

In much of the land west of the Magdalena River, the Indian population seems to have been nearly exterminated within a few years of the Spanish contact, by wars, epidemics, or forced exile. In the Cordillera Oriental and in the Department of Nariño the Indians survived in larger numbers, but extensive intermarriage with Spaniards and the absence of large tribal groups and linguistic unity led to an early and general acculturation and the adoption of the Spanish language as the lingua franca.

Highland and Lowland People

Climate, mineral wealth, and the presence of a potential Indian labor force first attracted the Spaniards to the interior highlands. Today, after more than four hundred years, the highlands are still the center of political and economic power in Colombia. Here live three fourths of the nation's population, and here are the three largest cities: Bogotá (elevation, 8,700 feet), Medellín (5,100 feet), and Cali (3,300 feet).

In Antioquia, where gold mining attracted the first Spanish settlers, there arose in semi-isolation a peculiarly energetic and cohesive cultural group. During the nineteenth century it overflowed from the barren highlands of Antioquia onto the steep but fertile volcanic-ash slopes to the south, in what has become the rich coffee region of Caldas and northern Tolima. The zone of Antioqueño colonization now extends southward on the deeply dissected flanks of the Cordilleras Central and Occidental to the latitude of Cali and even beyond.

These proud and frugal "Yankees of South America," with their aggressive colonizing genius and high birth rate, are today the dominant and most clearly defined population element in Colombia. They have been the most important single force behind the economic growth and development of the nation during the past half century. Their family-size farms produce more than 70 per cent of Colombia's coffee crop. Medellín is the home office for many of the largest banks, industries, and transportation companies.

Bogotá, the capital and largest metropolitan center (2.5 million population), is the focal point of economic activity for the mountains east of the Magdalena River. Its growth rate, close to 9 per cent per year, shows no signs of abating. Here, as elsewhere, urbanization seems an irreversible phenomenon, a reflection as much of the limited economic opportunities in most rural areas as of the jobs and social benefits that cities may offer. Every Colombian city has its *tugurios,* or squatter communities, collections of makeshift shelters of temporary materials and of ingenious architecture, usually lacking public services of any kind. Although the slums located conspicuously close to the city centers have been eradicated in recent years, their inhabitants have often resettled in public-housing developments, and other slums have proliferated spontaneously on the urban periphery. These communities of newly arrived migrants in many cases manifest a powerful creative dynamism and spirit of cooperation, leading to their gradual evolution as stable urban communities. In others, adaptation to city life has been slow and social disorganization has persisted.

Not all parts of the highlands are participating in the economic and social revolution now surging through urban, commercial Colombia. In many parts of the Cordillera Oriental, in particular, and in the Department of Nariño, one finds extreme rural poverty—farmers growing potatoes, wheat, barley, *haba* beans, and the lesser Andean root crops on *minifundios* (excessively small or fragmented holdings) or under an oppressive system of tenancy inherited from the colonial era.

The preferred lands in Colombia have been the midslopes and high plateaus of the Andean region, but as these become crowded, the future must lie increasingly in the warmer lowlands. In the upper valley of the Magdalena River, aridity has restricted agriculture, but government-sponsored irrigation projects have recently been opening new lands for colonization, as on the Coello River near Ibagué. Fields of cotton, rice, sesame, and improved pasture grasses have been the result.

The Cauca Valley, centering on the city of Cali, is, by contrast, well

COLOMBIA

Main road
Secondary road
Projected road
Railroad
Airfield

0   100   200
       Miles

0   100   200
     Kilometers

INDUSTRY

Textiles
Food and beverage
Metallurgy
Steel mill
Refinery

Hydroelectric power plant
Thermoelectric power plant

INDUSTRIES AND MINING

MINING

Fe   Iron
C   Coal
P   Oilfield
Au   Gold
E   Emeralds

Oil or natural gas pipeline

NATURAL REGIONS

Amazonia
Orinoquia
Caribbean Lowland
Andean region
Pacific region

POLITICAL AND NATURAL
REGIONS

watered. This 120-mile-long valley is an old inter-Andean lake bed that contains some of the best farming land in the country. Once given over to great cattle and sugar estates, it is gradually becoming an area of intensive diversified farming as the floods that used to plague it are brought under control.

The Caribbean coastal plain, containing some 20 per cent of Colombia's population, has been traditionally oriented to stock raising. In recent years, however, field crops such as cotton, rice, and sesame have been extensively planted to meet the demands of the growing domestic market. This has been especially the case in the valley of the Sinú River near Montería and in the upper valley of the César River in the vicinity of Valledupar. In Atlántico, between the port cities of Barranquilla and Cartagena, the older pattern of smallholders raising cattle or growing yuca and maize has persisted, although neither the soil nor the drier climate is particularly propitious for farming. South of Santa Marta, in the Department of Magdalena, bananas and *potreros* (pastures) of introduced African grasses are irrigated by water from streams descending from the snow-capped Sierra Nevada de Santa Marta (elevation, 18,947 feet).

Coffee and Bananas

The spirit of nationalism created by the successful termination of the Wars for Independence (1810–21) made it imperative that new exportable commodities be found to supplement the products of the gold mines of Antioquia and the Chocó, which had been the principal support of the colonial economy. More foreign exchange was necessary to pay for increasing imports of manufactured goods.

Aided by steam navigation on the Magdalena River, Colombia experienced a series of wildly speculative booms in export crops during the mid-nineteenth century. Cinchona (a tree whose bark contains quinine), rubber, indigo, cotton, and tobacco in turn provided shortlived bonanzas, only to lose out as other producing countries captured the world market.

Coffee was late in coming to Colombia. It was first established on a modest scale as a plantation crop in the Cordillera Oriental after 1850 and did not become a significant export until the 1880's. Then, with the opening of the railroad from the Magdalena River to Medellín, the volcanic slopes of southwestern Antioquia and the new lands of what is today the Department of Caldas began to be converted into coffee plantations. These

Hand labor is extremely important in Colombia's coffee production. Because a coffee tree may bear both ripe and unripe fruit at the same time, no machine can replace people in harvesting the crop. Nearly two thousand cherries must be picked to provide enough beans for one pound of roasted coffee. After the coffee beans have been separated from the surrounding pulp of the cherry, they are washed and spread to dry on a platform. These workers will rake the beans for hours to ensure uniform drying.

deep, rich ash soils were admirably suited to the crop, and as the Antioqueño homesteading frontier pushed southward, Colombia's coffee exports rose. The rolling hill lands of the Quindio region, which has been separated from Caldas as a new department, proved particularly favorable for coffee growing. Centering on the city of Armenia, it is today one of the most productive tracts of farmland in the country. Cundinamarca, Santander, and Norte de Santander are also significant coffee-producing areas.

But all is not well with coffee. Fragmented holdings, inadequate agricultural credit, and the endemic intestinal diseases associated with the damp plantation environment have increasingly concerned government planning agencies. Much of the coffee is still carried by muleback for at least part of the distance to local markets, for in many places the topography virtually prohibits construction of feeder roads. Only a valuable crop can stand the freight charges.

The high quality of Colombian coffee is due partly to the fact that the plants are shade-grown and the ripening period is therefore prolonged, and partly to the practice of hand-harvesting the beans, which ensures that each is picked at its peak of maturity. These factors, together with a special technique for washing and drying, probably account for the premium prices that Colombian "milds" have brought over Brazilian grades in the world coffee market.

For many decades bananas were the second most valuable agricultural export crop; they are now the fourth, after coffee, cotton, and sugar. The main banana-producing center has shifted from Santa Marta to the area south of Turbo in Antioquia, where irrigation is unnecessary and the threat of both blow-downs and disease is much reduced. Colombia's banana exports, some 20 million stems a year, place it among the world's three or four top suppliers. Most of the fruit moves to European markets.

Minerals, Energy, and Industry

During the seventeenth and eighteenth centuries, New Granada was one of the world's principal gold-producing regions. Colombia's gold today comes chiefly from the auriferous gravels of the Chocó and the Cauca River, which are worked by several giant floating dredges. Production in the early 1970's was 207,000 ounces per year, a decline of 50 per cent from ten years earlier. On the other hand, emerald production, from mines in Boyacá, has increased sharply, and Colombia is now the chief source of emeralds in the world. Platinum and silver are also mined, but in smaller quantities than formerly. Iron reserves are estimated at over 100 million tons, although only some 20 million have been proven.

The availability of cheap and abundant hydroelectric power and mineral fuels has greatly facilitated the growth of industries in Colombia. Hydroelectric power is widely used in the interior. Generating capacity at present is over 1.5 million kilowatts, and it is increasing.

Three regional corporations similar to the United States' Tennessee Valley Authority—the Cauca Valley (CVC), the Sabana de Bogotá-Ubate and Chiquinquira (CAR), and the Magdalena and Sinú Valley (CMV)—have brought major economic changes in their respective areas by making hydroelectric power available. Agricultural land has been increased through associated land-reclamation and flood-control projects and cities have expanded with the influx of industries. The CVC, for example, increased the valley's electric-generating power by 356 per cent in the 1950's and 1960's. It made possible a commercial and industrial boom in Cali that led to an increase in its population from 243,000 in 1950 to 920,000 in 1970. Among the new industries are a cement plant, a rolling mill for finished aluminum products, a cable manufacturing plant, a citric and acetic acid plant, and a small steel foundry.

Substantial coal deposits are known to exist, but most have not been exploited because of their difficult location. Good coal is available near Cali, however, and also in the Cordillera Oriental, near the nation's only integrated iron and steel plant at Paz de Río, some 100 miles north of Bogotá. Established in 1956, the plant is now undergoing an expansion program which will double its capacity to 500,000 tons by 1975. It is soon expected to produce 70 per cent of the nation's needs for steel and steel products, but substantial protection from foreign competition is necessary. Paz de Río employs 7,000 workers, 2,500 of them in the iron, coal, and limestone mines, all within 20 miles of the blast furnace and connected with it by an electric railroad network. Despite an oxygen problem (the plant lies at an elevation of nearly two miles above sea level and is the world's highest iron and steel unit). the installation is an efficient one, but transportation problems make the costs to most of the market areas very high.

Although petroleum has never quite lived up to the high hopes held for it, the oil fields of the middle Magdalena Valley and the Catatumbo Basin area have produced exportable surpluses for more than forty years. Domestically produced petroleum fuels the steam-generating plants of the middle Magdalena Valley and the port cities of Cartagena and Barranquilla. New discoveries of oil were made in 1966. A major petroleum-producing province, Putumayo, adjacent to the Ecuador border, was opened up, and a pipeline built to the Pacific coastal port of Tumaco. In 1970 Colombia's output was some 11 million tons of crude oil. Petroleum exports rank second to coffee with 9 per cent of the value of all exports although rising domestic demand has recently caused a drop in exports.

There are two major petrochemical and refining centers, at Barrancabermeja and at Mamonal, near Cartagena, where oil and natural gas pipelines from the interior converge and where imported phosphate rock and potassium chloride are readily available. Although the chemical industry employs relatively few people, its potential contribution to the economy is great. Already, the chemical industry is the fourth largest in South America and membership in the Andean Common Market should bring greater opportunities for development (see pp. 47–60).

With a population roughly equivalent to that of California, Colombia has a domestic market large enough to support a wide range of consumer industries, such as textiles, processed foods, and leather goods. Medellín, despite its mountainous location and relatively poor distribution facilities, has been the traditional manufacturing center, but Bogotá, Barranquilla, and Cali are today challenging its leadership.

Transportation

Air transport has played a special role in Colombia ever since SCADTA (a company founded and run by German and Austrian pilots) began operations in the valley of the Magdalena River in 1920. Much cargo that would move by land in other countries moves by air in Colombia, mainly by AVIANCA, Aerovías Nacionales de Colombia, successor to SCADTA. The availability of superior air service has undoubtedly delayed the development of an adequate overland transport network. The 35-minute flight between Bogotá and Medellín costs little more than the 24-hour truck trip over one of the most tortuous mountain roads on the continent.

The early history of Colombian transport was largely that of river navigation. The lower Magdalena, navigable for 615 miles from the mouth to the rapids at La Dorada, has been the lifeline linking the interior with the coast and the outer world. From river ports such as Puerto Wilches, Gamarra, Puerto Berrío, La Dorada, and Honda, railroads, aerial cables, and truck roads have been built to the principal highland centers. Until the opening of the Cali–Buenaventura rail and motor route, even the Cauca Valley trade and the coffee of Caldas moved out by the Magdalena. Today the river route is little used as a result of increased competition from highway, pipeline, and railroad.

In recent years, Buenaventura has become the leading port. Through it move almost all Colombia's coffee exports. With the improvement of truck and rail transport, Bogotá and the middle and upper Magdalena Valley have come to depend increasingly on Buenaventura for a coastal port. Over the Quindio Pass (10,800 feet) between Ibagué and Armenia, formerly a major barrier and bottleneck to travel, several thousand vehicles now pass daily. The opening of the Medellín–Cartagena highway in 1955 brought about a significant reorientation of trade and led to the virtual abandonment of the rail-and-river route through Puerto Berrío to the coast. Likewise, the completion of the Magdalena railroad linking Bogotá with the Caribbean coast at Santa Marta has drained off some trade that formerly moved through La Dorada and down the Magdalena River. A modernized and interconnected truck and rail network has top priority in Colombian economic planning, and the World Bank has made substantial loans to this end.

Improved transportation may also help to solve the problem of overcrowding in the highlands. There are extensive empty areas available for agriculture, and they are rapidly being made accessible by new roads built down from the Andes. The resistance of the highland small farmer to any suggestion that he move downhill seems to be gradually lessening, owing in large measure to the success of malarial-control projects in the tropical lowlands. The capacity of the soils of these areas of high rainfall and high temperature to support a permanent intensive agriculture remains to be proved, however.

focus *on Attitudes Toward Innovation and the Process of Industrialization*

In Colombia, as elsewhere in South America, hopes and aspirations for a better life are closely tied to industrialization. Colombia is still an agrarian nation, although the relative role of manufacturing and service industries in the economy is increasing. There are four principal poles of development: Bogotá, Cali, Barranquilla-Cartagena, and Medellín. Each competes with the others vigorously for industrial and commercial leadership. Together they account for four fifths of the country's manufacturing capacity. But it is Medellín, the Antioqueño capital in the mile-high valley of Medellín, that is in many ways the most significant as well as the most interesting of the developing industrial nodes of Colombia. It was here, despite handicaps imposed by physical isolation and rugged terrain, that the successful transformation from craft industry to modern corporate enterprise was first achieved. Industry has continued to thrive, fed by domestic capital and the entrepreneurial talents of the Antioqueños. The special case of Medellín has recently attracted much attention from students of economic development as an example of the successful early industrialization of a predominantly agricultural society.

Medellín has the oldest industrial tradition in Colombia. The early development of commercial and banking institutions, the technologic background associated with nineteenth-century gold mining, and the contacts with foreign tradesmen and engineers that these induced, all helped to establish the necessary conditions under which the new manufacturing ventures might flourish. These were supported, at the appropriate time, by a protective tariff policy. Most important, they were reinforced by the distinctive Antioqueño way of life, fostered and sharpened by experience in mining ventures and relative success in extending coffee plantings.

The Antioqueños' vigor and business acumen and their attitudes toward innovation, risk-taking, and capital accumulation brought out a not quite anticipated response to a certain set of circumstances. Although only a few persons, who thought it a good thing to industrialize, actively participated in the movement, it had the collaboration of many others. This attitude toward industry led first to small successes and then to larger ones, as the local and regional markets expanded. Capital accumulated in gold mining had made some of the Antioqueños the richest men in the nation, and they controlled the capital market, the export tobacco industry, and much of the nation's trade and commerce.

In this early industrial development, it was cotton textiles that played the pre-eminent role. Modern textile manufacturing dates from 1902 with the founding of the Compañía Antioqueño de Tejidos by Pedro Nel Ospina, who had studied the industry in Mexico and Lancashire. The first plant was established at Bello, a few miles downvalley from Medellín, thus setting a pattern of decentralization toward the small towns of the metropolitan fringe, which has continued to the present. The heavy textile machinery was all brought in by muleback from the railhead some 50 miles away, with much loss and damage from breakage that almost wrecked the project. After a series of reorganizations and combinations, the Bello mills emerged in 1939 as the modern Fabricato, the second largest textile concern in Colombia.

Of the Big Three that today dominate Colombian textiles, the largest is the aggressive Compañía Colombiana de Tejidos (Coltejer), one of the richest corporations in South America. Established in 1907 on a ravine in the upper part of Medellín by a wealthy coffee merchant, Alejandro Echavarría, the first plant was patterned closely after Bello. Real expansion did not get under way until the depression years of the 1930's, which saw the beginning of many of Antioquia's major industrial concerns. By the late 1960's it was operating some 233,000 spindles and 4,800 looms, employing 8,500 persons at four plants (Medellín, Itagüi, Envigado, Rionegro), and an additional 800 in related machine and parts shops and starch mills. Annual sales are close to $50 million. More than 37,000 stockholders hold a stake in the company, one of the most broadly held corporations in all South America.

Coltejer and Fabricato are the pacesetters among the 460 mills that constitute Colombia's textile industry, the most efficient and modern in South America. Its gross product is equivalent to 15 per cent of the total output of all Colombian manufacture, exceeded only by foodstuffs. In terms of spindles—the accepted manner of judging textile capacity—Colombia, with one million spindles, is second only to Brazil in South America. Four fifths of these are in the Medellín area.

The related garment industry employs two thirds as many persons as textiles, but only 20 per cent of this labor force is found in Medellín. Textiles (including woolens and synthetics) and garment making combined account for one out of every three persons employed in manufacturing in Colombia.

At an earlier time, young girls from the country provided the most important reservoir of cheap labor to operate the looms and spindles of Medellín. As late as 1945, half the textile workers in Antioquia were women and 65 per cent of them were from rural sections of the department. Today the proportion of women is much reduced.

A kind of benevolent paternalism still marks the relations between employer and employee in the large textile companies. At Bello, Fabricato maintains a dormitory under the supervision of nuns, where single girls are given board and lodging on a payroll-deduction plan. Within the well-kept building are a chapel, dining hall, auditorium, library, and lounge. Schooling is provided to all workers who desire it. The company maintains a modern clinic. Coltejer has long provided married workers with low-cost rental housing in company *barrios* near the mills, but in recent years these have been sold to workers, on very favorable terms. More than three quarters of the married workers at both Fabricato and Coltejer now own their own homes. Job stability is accordingly high.

Twenty years ago Antioquia's textile industry was supplied largely by imported raw materials, but today it is close to self-sufficiency. Raw cotton comes from the Sinú and César valleys on the north coast, either by truck or rail, and by truck from the Tolima plains. Caustic soda, soda ash, dyestuffs, sulphuric acid, and polyester fibers come from factories in Cali, Bogotá, and Barranquilla, as well as in Medellín. Wool, part of it imported, plays a relatively minor role. A German-Swiss consortium and the Dutch-owned Enka have both constructed major facilities in outlying communities near Medellín to supply polyester fibers and plastic resins to the local industry. Coltejer has its own polyester fiber plant at Itagüí, near Medellín, the pioneer producer of synthetic yarns in Colombia. Celanese operates a similar plant in Bogotá.

Apart from textiles, Medellín's chief industries include building materials, tanneries, plastic and light metal goods, sulphuric acid, chemical fertilizers, rubber goods, cigarettes, patent medicines, beverages, and foodstuffs. According to the Associación Nacional de Industrias (ANDI), Medellín in a recent year produced the following percentages of total Colombian output: cotton cloth, 90; phonograph records, 80; aluminum ware, hardware, and cutlery, 70; woolens, 63; electrical apparatus, 56;

industrial machinery, 51; sulphuric acid, 50; glass, 47; ceramics, 42; leather goods, 40. The Empresa Siderúrgica produces structural steel and bars for Medellín industry from scrap iron.

The stepped-up tempo of manufacturing has been accompanied by an increasing urban congestion, both in Medellín and in such satellite valley communities as Bello, Itagüi, América, Sabaneta, and Envigado, today merged into one metropolis. The most recent census shows the population of greater Medellín (the capital and its five suburban valley *municipios*) to have reached more than 1 million or 40 per cent of the population of the entire Department of Antioquia. This represents an increase of more than 100 per cent since the 1951 census, or an annual growth rate of better than 9 per cent. The largest share of this growth must be attributed to the influx of farmers and farm workers from outlying districts, attracted largely by new industrial employment, educational opportunities, and welfare.

As the Medellín Valley has filled up, attention has been directed increasingly to the need for decentralization of future industrial expansion. To this end, two major new plants have recently been built some 12 miles down the valley at Girardot (Mancesa, Enka de Colombia), and production of women's wear has been initiated near Rionegro, in branch plants of Coltejer and Pepalfa.

The relatively low level of foreign investment in Medellín industry as compared with Bogotá, Cali, or Barranquilla has been a source of pride in Antioquia. Recently it has also been a cause for concern, however, as the area has lost its early lead in industry. New plant investment in the 1960's did not keep pace with the earlier growth rate, nor with that in rival centers. Between the 1945 and 1964 industrial census, Antioquia's share of the country's manufacturing employment dropped from 25 per cent to 16 per cent; its value added, from 25 to 22.4 per cent. To some extent this is inevitable, as other centers and other industries, starting later, catch up with Medellín and textiles. But it is also possible that Medellín's reputation for closed, inner-oriented society had much to do with the reluctance of foreign firms to locate major facilities there. Today a move is afoot to change this image.

Suggested Readings

American University. *Area Handbook for Colombia*. Washington, D.C.: U.S. Government Printing Office, 1970. A comprehensive analysis of social, economic, and political aspects of the area.

BREWER, THOMAS K. "Basic Data on the Economy of Colombia." U.S. Bureau of International Commerce, *Overseas Business Report, OBR 71–048* (December, 1971). A brief analysis of the economic structure of the nation.

Colombia Today. New York: Colombia Information Service, Colombian Center. A monthly publication, each issue of which deals with a particular aspect of Colombia's economy: e.g., the expansion of the rail and road network, the petrochemical industry, autonomous regional corporations. Informative and up-to-date.

Development Digest. "Toward Full Employment in Colombia." VIX, no. 1 (January, 1971), pp. 114–24. (Excerpted from *Towards Full Employment.* Geneva: International Labour Office, 1970). Suggests that Colombia must expand its agricultural sector; major efforts should be devoted to land reform, in order to create employment.

DOW, J. KAMAL. *Colombia's Foreign Trade and Economic Integration in Latin America. Latin American Monographs, Second Series, No. 9.* Gainesville: University of Florida Press, 1971. A study of Colombia's relationship to both LAFTA and the Andean Common Market, assessing the relative value of the two organizations to Colombia's economy.

DUFF, ERNEST A. *Agrarian Reform in Colombia.* New York: Praeger, 1968. Agrarian reform in Colombia, in the light of social, economic, and political obstacles. Discusses arguments for and against such reform, as well as the role of the United States and international institutions in supporting reform efforts.

FLINN, WILLIAM L., and JAMES W. CONVERSE. "Eight Assumptions Concerning Rural-Urban Migration in Colombia: A Three Shantytowns Test." *Land Economics,* XLVI, no. 4 (November, 1970), pp. 456–66. A study of three types of shantytowns in Colombia: (1) illegal and clandestine subdivisions of land sold without official permits; (2) squatter settlements on public and private land; and (3) legal subdivisions designed according to city specifications and provided with some public services. Contrasts commonly held ideas about these settlements with the actualities.

MCGREEVEY, WILLIAM PAUL. *An Economic History of Colombia, 1845–1930. Cambridge Latin American Studies, No. 9.* Cambridge: The University Press, 1971. Asserts that the external sector has been a major influence on the process of economic change in Latin America, using Colombia as an example.

PARSONS, JAMES J. *Antioqueño Colonization in Western Colombia.* Berkeley and Los Angeles: The University of California Press, 1968. A study of the historical and modern development of the "Antioqueño country," which includes not only the Department of Antioquia but lands colonized by Antioqueños. Describes the natural setting, population patterns, role of agriculture, transportation, and the emergence of modern industry.

SCHOUTZ, LARS. "Urbanization and Changing Voting Patterns: Colombia, 1946–1970." *Political Science Quarterly*, LXXXVII, no. 1 (March, 1972), pp. 22–45. An examination of the potential effect of increasing urbanization on Colombia's political structure.

WIERER, KARL. "Analysis of Agrarian Structure and Agrarian Reform in Colombia." *Land Reform; Land Settlement and Cooperatives.* No. 1 (1969), Food and Agricultural Organization of the United Nations, pp. 29–41. A study of progress in agrarian reform since its institution in Colombia in 1961.

See also Suggested Readings for Part I, pp. 61–63.

11 ECUADOR*

*Political Instability • Cultural and Environmental Problems •
Plans and Reforms • The Indian and the Highlands • The
Oriente • The Coastal Region • Social Conflicts • focus on a
Community-Development Project,* by Joseph B. Kelley

For centuries the Quechua-speaking Indians of Ecuador have been sub-
jected to powerful and often ruthless rulers who have been more interested
in their labor than their welfare. About the middle of the fifteenth century,
they were conquered by the Incas, who established colonies and military
outposts in their midst. In 1533, Atahualpa, who had assumed control of
the Inca Empire, was captured, held for ransom, and ultimately murdered
by Francisco Pizarro, a Spanish conqueror who claimed the kingdom of
Quito. This episode was followed by several small wars and assassinations
among rival *conquistadores* bent on seizing power, until Quito became an
audiencia under the Viceroyalty of Peru.

During the whole period of Spanish rule, which lasted for nearly three
hundred years, the Indians were abused and exploited. They supplied the
food and labor necessary for the operation of gold and silver mines in the
mountains. They also raised sugar, cacao, cattle, and mules in the hot
country along the coast, especially near Guayaquil, which had the best
harbor on the Pacific and enjoyed a large volume of trade in hemp, lumber,
leather, and cacao.

Political Instability

When the Ecuadorians finally won their independence, in 1830, the Spanish
privileged class was replaced by the privileged creole caste; the majority of

* Parts of this chapter were adapted from a 1967 issue of *focus*.

the population continued to live like serfs, having almost no contact with modern education and culture. In fact, the Indian population was perhaps worse off after independence, because the Spanish Crown had tried, however ineffectively, to curb the rapacity of its representatives.

In the years following independence, the national government virtually collapsed. The economy had been ruined by years of war, the country was divided into hostile factions, and there was growing civilian resentment against government by the military. In 1861, Gabriel García Moreno was elected president. Directly or indirectly, he was the dominant force in the nation for the next fifteen years. He planned roads and railway systems, including a link between Guayaquil and Quito, to diminish the regionalism so damaging to national cohesion, worked to improve education, and attempted to stimulate agriculture and foreign trade. But growing opposition arose and he was assassinated in 1875.

After his death, the country relapsed into chaos until 1914. The following decade was politically peaceful, but inflation and the high cost of living provoked widespread unrest, and in 1925 the military seized power. For the next twenty-three years political chaos prevailed once again, until 1948, when Galo Plaza Lasso, a moderate, was elected president. He was one of the few Ecuadorian leaders who actually ruled in accordance with the existing constitution. Another important achievement of his regime was the stabilization of the economy. Galo Plaza showed real interest in improving the standard of living in the country. But lack of funds, lack of time, and a series of natural disasters prevented him from accomplishing most of his goals. (Another of Galo Plaza's accomplishments, perhaps the most startling, was that he became the first freely elected president in over twenty-five years to serve out his full term.)

Galo Plaza's successor is a man who has continued to figure in Ecuadorian politics until very recently—José María Velasco Ibarra. Velasco Ibarra has tremendous personal magnetism and has had a huge following among the Ecuadorian populace. A favorite saying of his was "Give me a balcony and Ecuador is mine." He was first elected president in 1934 and served on and off until 1961, when the economic situation was rapidly deteriorating, and strikes, demonstrations, and riots occurred almost daily. A military junta then took over the country, decreed martial law, suspended the constitution, and banned the Communist Party. In 1968, in the first election held in seven years, Velasco Ibarra was elected for the fifth time. As in his earlier presidencies, the nation was in a state of growing economic and social unrest; the liberal faction again became disenchanted with his gov-

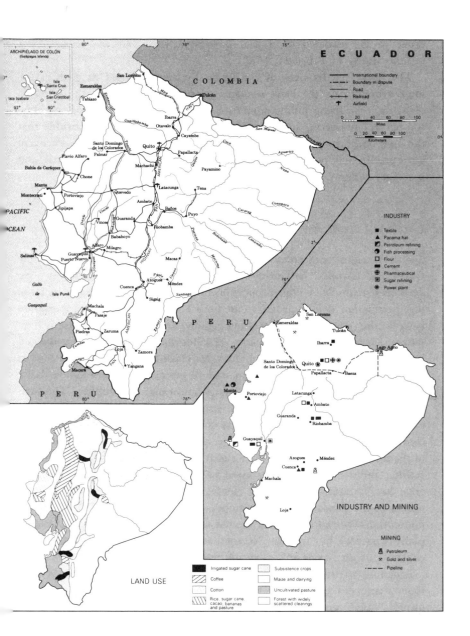

ARCHIPIÉLAGO DE COLÓN
(Galápagos Islands)

Isla Santa Cruz
Isla San Cristóbal
Isla Isabela

E C U A D O R

COLOMBIA

San Lorenzo
Esmeraldas
Tabiazo
Tulcán
Ibarra
Otavalo
Cayambe
Santo Domingo de los Colorados
Quito
Papallacta
Flavio Alfaro
Palmar
Payamino
Machachi
Bahía de Caráquez
Chone
Manta
Portoviejo
Montecristi
Jipijapa
Quevedo
Latacunga
Tena
Ambato
Baños
Puyo
Guaranda
Riobamba
Vinces
Babahoyo
Macas
Alfaro
Guayaquil
Milagro
Puerto Nuevo
Salinas
Golfo de Guayaquil
Isla Puná
Azogues
Méndez
Cuenca
Sigsig
Santiago
Machala
Pasaje
Piedras
Zaruma
Loja
Zamora
Macará
Yangana

PACIFIC OCEAN

P E R U

— International boundary
—·—·— Boundary in dispute
———— Road
+++++ Railroad
✈ Airfield

0 20 40 60 80 100
Miles
0 20 40 60 80 100
Kilometers

INDUSTRY

■ Textile
▲ Panama hat
◪ Petroleum refining
◕ Fish processing
□ Flour
▤ Cement
✦ Pharmaceutical
⊞ Sugar refining
⊕ Power plant

San Lorenzo
Esmeraldas
Tulcán
Ibarra
Lago Agrio
Santo Domingo de los Colorados
Quito
Papallacta
Baeza
Manta
Portoviejo
Latacunga
Ambato
Guaranda
Riobamba
Guayaquil
Azogues
Méndez
Cuenca
Machala
Loja

INDUSTRY AND MINING

MINING

◮ Petroleum
✳ Gold and silver
—·—·— Pipeline

LAND USE

▨ Irrigated sugar cane
▨ Coffee
☐ Cotton
▨ Rice, sugar cane, cacao, bananas and pasture
☐ Subsistence crops
☐ Maize and dairying
▨ Uncultivated pasture
☐ Forest with widely scattered clearings

ernment. He assumed dictatorial powers in 1970 and was ousted by a military junta in February, 1972.

The junta, led by General Guillermo Rodríguez, stated its goals as follows: reorganizing the basic structure of the nation, raising the standard of living, expediting public administration, improving education, developing natural resources, and respecting human rights. It seems possible that the new military government may follow the example of the Peruvian government, making serious attempts to institute agrarian, educational, and monetary reforms.

Cultural and Environmental Problems

Today, Ecuador, with an estimated population of 6.3 million (including the Galápagos Islands), has many characteristics of the economically less-developed nations: A high proportion of the people are engaged in farming, production is low, primitive methods keep prices high, transportation is weak, the population is increasing rapidly, and the illiteracy rate is high (about 35 per cent). Furthermore, Ecuador has to cope with a divided people: 10 per cent of its population are classed as white, 41 per cent as mestizo, 39 per cent as pure Indian, and 10 per cent as Negro and mulatto. It is also divided physically, in climate, landscape, and culture. The massive cool-to-cold Andean cordilleras, strewn with volcanoes, most of them extinct, and the intermontane valleys contain all the important towns (except Guayaquil) and 51 per cent of the country's people, the great majority of them Indians who cling to their cloistered way of life, have little national feeling, and are largely uninterested in commerce. East of the Andes, the great hot, forested plain of the Oriente, through which meander the headwaters of the Amazon, is nearly empty, with only 2 per cent of Ecuador's population. West of the Andes, the hot and generally low and damp coastal plain is peopled by Indians, Negroes, and mestizos, who grow most of the country's export crops and carry on most of its commerce.

Ecuador's natural wealth was until recently mainly agricultural; yet less than 5 per cent of the land was cultivated, and 1 per cent of the landowners held 40 per cent of the land by value; 92 per cent held only 32 per cent of it. Some 73 per cent of all holdings were less than 12 acres in size, comprising only 7 per cent of the area in farms; 0.2 per cent of the holdings were 2,500 acres or more in size but included 37 per cent of the area in farms. The great estates (*latifundios*) belonging to the few rich, mostly urban dwellers, are market-oriented, but little of the income seeps down to the laborers. The crops grown on the thousands of tiny *minifundios* of the poor villagers are generally consumed by the producers.

Plans and Reforms

Ecuador initiated a ten-year national development plan in 1964. Two of its most important aims were to increase agricultural production and to institute agrarian reforms. It was hoped that by 1973 171,000 families would receive title to government land they already occupied, and 68,000 would receive land for new colonization. The average size of the farms was to be fifty acres.

There were other objectives, too: the average diet was to be raised from 1,830 to 2,280 calories per day, and improved nutritionally. Literacy was to be raised from 65 to 80 per cent; life expectancy at birth was to be increased by at least five years and infant mortality reduced by 27 per cent. An attempt was to be made to extend social-security coverage to artisans, agricultural workers, and domestic servants.

Perhaps the key to the success of the plan was increasing agricultural production. More than half the population is engaged in agriculture, but agriculture contributes only about 31 per cent of the gross national product. A healthier agriculture is needed in order to expand domestic industry and service industries.

But unfortunately, few goals of the 1964–68 portion of the plan were met. Agricultural production, for example, increased by only one fourth of the planned rate—a rate lower than the rate of population increase. Since agricultural exports increased during the period, the decline in domestic supplies was even greater. Therefore, nutritional levels actually declined during the period. Meanwhile imports grew at almost twice the planned rate. One of the reasons for this is that, despite its importance to the economy, agriculture was given low priority in the budget: it received only 8 per cent of the total annual expenditure. Another reason is the inffective-ness of the land-reform program.

Some gains were made in improving the lot of the poorest people: the *huasipungo* system—the system by which a tenant farmer labors for a land-owner in return for food, lodging, and perhaps a minute amount of cash—was abolished, and by 1967 farm laborers in the sierra (high central plateaus) were earning five sucres per day (in 1971, U.S. $1.00 equaled 25.25

sucres). Many people were resettled on land of their own; some 25,000 families were resettled on about 561,000 acres of land. Over 7,500 families obtained clear titles to nearly 677,000 acres, and 7,000 families colonized some 1.3 million acres. These figures seem impressive, but they are overshadowed by one unfortunate fact: much of the land on which these people were resettled was poorer than the land they had farmed as serfs. Therefore, many were worse off than they had been before the land reforms.

Two other factors contribute to the weakness of the land-reform act. In the first place, large landholders on the coast and in the sierra had a great deal of influence in the drafting of the law and were naturally not in favor of radical reform. In the second place, a relatively large legal maximum landholding was permitted. Whenever a more equal distribution of land has been attempted or even proposed, those in power have given the stereotyped reply: there's plenty of land in the Oriente for those who want it. This attitude has justified the practice of the great landholders of keeping unproductive thousands of acres, both in the uplands and in the warm coastal region. Actually, of course, before settlers can move into the Oriente, a reasonable network of roads is needed. So far, despite a fever of road building or improvement from the mountain centers of Quito, Latacunga, Ambato, Cuenca, and Loja, road money has been spent in a rather haphazard manner, more often for the benefit of absentee landowners than of the nation as a whole, and seldom for the benefit of the Oriente.

Increase in agricultural production is essential to the health of Ecuador's economy. This increase depends on redistribution of good land, adequate provision of water for irrigation, technical assistance, a fair credit system, and an efficient means of marketing produce. Some progress was made in tax reform under the national development plan: The number of individual income-tax returns filed increased from 7,000 in 1962 to 60,000 in 1965. But property owners, both rural and urban, rarely pay taxes.

The plan greatly underestimated the growth of imports and, as a corollary, the growth of exports needed to stimulate economic growth. In fact, one of the principal weaknesses of the plan, and a chief reason most of its goals were not achieved, was that Ecuador relied on import substitution and restriction of imports rather than trying to develop a dynamic export market. Another weakness stems from the government's apparent failure to take into account the very high rate of population growth: 3.4 per cent per year. Such a yearly increment in population requires not only a constantly rising output of food and other agricultural products, but more jobs, more schools and teachers, more doctors. Also, in Ecuador, as elsewhere in South America, a large percentage of the population is young. The youth and rising tide of people place a heavy burden on an adult population already struggling to improve their own economic and social conditions. There are, however, some signs that Ecuador's leaders will at least consider ways of coordinating population and economic growth.

Perhaps Ecuador's economy will be helped by the nation's membership in the Andean Common Market. Ecuador and Bolivia, the poorest members of the group, will receive special preferences in trade and tariff exemptions and so will receive a relatively equal share of the benefits of the Andean Common Market (see pp. 47–60).

Of more immediate help, perhaps, is the fact that the nation has become the second largest producer of petroleum in South America (after Venezuela). An estimated 12 million tons per year of high-grade oil has begun to travel from the Lago Agrio district in northeastern Ecuador through a 318-mile pipeline over the Andes to the port of Esmeraldas. The prospect of a petroleum boom has created complications, however. The new military government has stated that it plans to review existing contracts with the Texaco and Gulf Oil companies, whose investment made the extraction of petroleum possible. This "review" is expected to be costly to the U.S. companies and may make other prospective investors cautious. There is also a good deal of quarreling within the government about the distribution of petroleum revenues. Even the prospect of an oil boom has caused prices to rise, triggering unrest among the impoverished groups. It is to be hoped that Ecuador's prospective new wealth will be used to raise the standards of living of its many poor.

The Indian and the Highlands

At least three quarters of the highland people are hard-working Indians. They perform most of the agricultural and construction labor and also work in factories and make up the servant class in city homes.

Maize is the basic food of the country, and most of it comes from the highlands; potatoes run a close second. In response to the wider use of fertilizers, more than enough potatoes are being grown (over 300,000 tons a year). Wheat and barley also do well in these cool lands; undoubtedly enough wheat to meet current needs could be raised if more modern methods were instituted, especially rotation of crops to maintain soil fertility. Higher up, above the upper limit of cultivation, hundreds of

Most of Ecuador's Indians live in extreme poverty; an exception is the population of the community of Otavalo. These frugal and industrious people devote their spare time to crafts. Their beautiful woven shawls, leatherwork, and pottery bring in appreciable supplementary income. Here a weaver works at his loom.

thousands of sheep and a few cattle graze on the rough grasslands known as the *páramo.* Besides sheep, most Indians keep pigs, chickens, and guinea pigs, the flesh of which is a delicacy to be eaten on great feast days.

In the warmer intermontane basins, adequate rains from December to April ensure good crops of corn, peas, lima beans, lentils, onions, cabbages, lettuce, asparagus, celery, and a variety of other vegetables and such fruits as peaches, apples, pears, plums, strawberries, and cherries, which are consumed locally or sent to city markets. Several crops almost unknown outside the Andean area are also cultivated, notably *oca, melluco, jícama,* lupine seed, and *quinoa,* the seed of the giant pigweed. Much of the irrigated land in the drier basins has been made into fine pastures of alfalfa, rye grass, and clover, which support a growing dairy industry.

In the foothills of the Andes it is warm enough to grow such subtropical crops as sugar cane, avocados, tomatoes, mangoes, lemons, grapes, and coffee in the fertile, irrigable river valleys.

Nearly three quarters of Ecuador is forest-covered, and in its Andean trees the country has one of its greatest potential resources. If properly managed, these could be a perpetual source of building timber, pulpwood, and other raw materials for industries operated by hydroelectric power drawn from the many local mountain streams.

Quito, the chief city of the Andean region and capital of the nation, with a population of about 463,000, lies at an altitude of 9,340 feet. Consequently, although it is close to the equator, the average temperature is definitely cool. And because it is equatorial, the yearly range is small: an average of 55° F. in the hottest months (February and September) and 54° in the coldest months (April and November). Night temperatures in the high central plateau are often only slightly above freezing, and heavy woolen clothing, warm bed blankets, and large meals are indicated. Hence the Indians, in many cases poorly housed, inadequately clothed, and undernourished, would not subscribe to the frequently expressed view that highland Ecuador has a climate of perpetual spring.

Quito has lost little of its colonial flavor. The huge wooden doors, barred windows, and geranium-festooned balconies remind one of the hill towns of southern Spain, as indeed do the monumental churches, chapels, and monasteries filled with fabulous collections of art objects. The streets of the old city are narrow and tortuous, many of them so steep that they can be used only by pedestrians or pack animals. The shops of silversmiths, wood carvers, and tailors in the old section are tiny, dark holes in the thick walls of old colonial houses. In the industrial district, poorly paid laborers toil in the textile mills, shoe factories, soap and pharmaceutical plants, and a brewery. So low is their pay, as almost everywhere in this pre-industrial country, that they have almost no purchasing power, and the economy as a whole benefits little from their activities. Underemployment of a vast segment of the population is another problem, for it means that there can be virtually no accumulation of capital to be invested in land, labor, and equipment and thus increase production.

There are, however, a few places in the highlands where the people have managed to accumulate enough capital to buy small tracts of land and achieve a certain amount of independence and prosperity. Such a community is Otavalo, with a population of 8,600, nestling at the foot of an extinct volcano near picturesque Lake San Pablo. In the villages all around the lake, the Indians' dress and customs have remained almost unchanged for centuries, but these frugal and industrious people are now devoting their free time to crafts. Their beautiful shawls and other fabrics, their leatherwork, and their pottery are bringing in appreciable supplementary income and, incidentally, have made the colorful Otavalo market world-famous.

The Oriente

Apart from the few thousand settlers who have come from the highlands, only wild, nomadic Indian tribes inhabit the immemorial forests of the Oriente, and they resist the outside world today as they resisted the armies of the Incas and the Spaniards, and later the cruelty of the slavers and the greed of the rubber gatherers and explorers searching for gold or quinine. Only the Catholic missionaries have been able to maintain a few spiritual outposts or fortresses.

Not a few of the highland settlers, notably two or three thousand from Cuenca, imbued with a desire for adventure, or merely tired of trying to live on the pittance to be earned making Panama, or Jipijapa, hats, have come to the Oriente to search for gold in the Upano River valley near Méndez. Here, in spite of very hard work, they seldom make more than a bare living, but they are noticeably better off than they were in the uplands. Loans have been approved for the government's Upano River project, in which 15,000 squatters and 1,150 settlers will receive 420,000 acres of farmland; another 3,000 families will be settled later on 570,000 acres.

It is here, on the right bank of the San Miguel River in the northeast Oriente, that the first military colonization project in the Amazon Basin —Palma Roja—began, in 1962. The colony, now containing a population of 250, foresees for itself an increasing role in the Oriente's development due to the planned Interoceanic Route: It is to become not only the terminus of a trans-Andean highway from coastal San Lorenzo, but also a transshipment point to the Atlantic via the Putumayo and Amazon rivers.

A logical project for the government would be completion of the road from Quito to Papallacta, into the Quijos Valley, then on to Payamino, which is on a navigable stream that flows into the Napo River. The countryside here is covered for many miles with a deep layer of volcanic ash and is extremely fertile; the soil should be ideal for coffee. This could be a rich area if it were linked to Quito by a good road, and if land were made available for small farmers. Indeed, roads are proposed throughout the Oriente which will, if constructed, connect Ecuador with Colombia, Peru, and Bolivia.

The Coastal Region

The 27,000-odd square miles of coastal Ecuador produce a large exportable surplus of bananas, coffee, cacao, and rice, along with sugar, cotton, citrus fruits, and pineapples. In fact, this is the most fertile part of the country —and one of the most promising rainy-tropics lowlands in the Western Hemisphere—provided, again, that transport facilities are improved. Thousands of acres of these forest lands are well suited to crops and pastures.

An example of what can be done in this respect is the vast new area opened up for agriculture by completion of the road from Quito to Santo Domingo de los Colorados in 1947 and beyond to Esmeraldas in 1949. The soils are fertile, average temperatures range between 75° and 79°, rainfall is between 60 and 80 inches a year, and there is no dry season. Here bananas, cacao, and coffee are grown for the domestic market in Quito. Thousands of independent banana farms, mostly small holdings of 10 to 30 acres, many of them owned by Negroes, now line this road northward from Santo Domingo to Esmeraldas.

Despite a spreading and serious epidemic of Sigatoka leaf blight, rapidly rising production from this area and others in the coastal plain, particularly around Chone, in the northern part of the Guayas Basin, and inland from Machala, has brought Ecuador in a few years to the rank of top exporter of bananas in the world. Bananas bring in more than 50 per cent of the foreign-exchange revenue. Another 16 per cent is derived from coffee, 12 per cent from cacao, and 5 per cent from sugar. These exports, together with rice, Panama hats, castor beans, shrimp, pyrethrum, and timber (chiefly balsa wood, prized for its lightness), pay for the necessary imports of textiles, chemicals, vehicles, machinery, foodstuffs, and the high-grade cotton needed to blend with the rather low-grade local varieties for the country's textile industry, the only one of any magnitude. The small family workshop is still the provider of most household and farm equipment.

The chief coffee zones are east and south of Portoviejo, northeast of Zaruma, and in the hills east of Santo Domingo. Efforts are being made to improve the quality for export, for the Ecuadorians are not coffee addicts.

Guayaquil, larger than Quito, with a population of more than 680,000, is the chief seaport and commercial city. It lies on an all-important commercial artery, the Guayas River, and is connected by rail with Quito and other highland centers and with the coast at Salinas. This railroad has helped to open the interior to foreign trade and lessen regional strife between the coastal and mountain factions. The completion of Guayaquil's new deep-water seaport now provides a modern marine terminal that handles about 90 per cent of the nations' imports and 70 per cent of its exports. Here, as elsewhere in Ecuador, the local industries—textile mills, flour mills, sawmills, foundries, machine shops, cement factories, and breweries— are hampered by lack of power. Some coal has apparently been discovered in the south, but it is not yet exploited, and the hydroelectric potential has been scarcely touched, although generating capacity has been growing at a rate of 10 per cent per year.

The extensive rich alluvial soils of the flatlands around Guayaquil, in the Guayas Delta, are used for rice and sugar cane, and thriving cattle ranches occupy the higher ground. Much of the labor performed on these coastal farms and ranches, and also much of the gathering of the products that grow wild in the great forests, such as rubber, vegetable ivory (the endosperm of the ivory nut; it takes a high polish and is used as a substitute for ivory), balsa wood, and lignum vitae, is performed by the *montuvios*, persons of mixed white, Negro, and Indian blood.

In 1956, the railroad from Quito thirty miles beyond Ibarra was extended to the port of San Lorenzo, opening the northern coastal region, with its forest and manganese resources. The lack of a comprehensive colonization and development plan, however, has thus far not only maintained the relatively scarce settlers as subsistence agriculturists but also has dimmed somewhat San Lorenzo's dream of being a competitor to Guayaquil.

Social Conflicts

Ecuador possesses unique advantages in its hot, humid, and fertile low lands and its cool highlands, which produce crops complementary to each other. Economically, it is not a poor country but an underdeveloped one. The nation is, however, torn by the widely differing interests of its citizens. About 10 and 2 per cent of the people, respectively, can be classfied as members of middle- and upper-income groups. Few of these appreciate the aspirations of the 88 per cent in the lowest income group.

A great gap also exists between the population of the sierra and that of the coast. At the time of the conquest, the Spaniards settled almost exclusively in the intermontane valleys of the sierra, where there was a stable and docile native population to provide them with labor. The descendants of the Spaniards are even today somewhat rigid and conservative. These members of the highland élite have stoutly maintained that their culture is more deeply rooted than that of the *costeños* (coastal people), and they have been able to prove this to their own satisfaction by retaining most of the political power. This has had a repressive influence on the uplands, particularly on the migration of upland people to the potentially rich and sparsely peopled lowlands. Those in political and economic control do not wish to lose their labor force. Hence the Indians are encouraged to retain their identity as Indians, and this retention of "Indianism" acts as a further brake on migration and a better-rounded development of the nation as a whole.

Before modern medical methods were introduced, the hot and humid coastal region was unhealthy, and it tended to attract adventurers and would-be entrepreneurs. After independence, contact with world markets increased, and the coastal society grew in size, power, and complexity. The pleasure-loving yet practical and outward-looking *costeños* have made Guayaquil the economic capital of the nation, center of a rich agricultural region.

Another societal division exists between the hispanic (including *mestizo*) group and the Indians. The former places a high value on individuality and the expression of it. The Indians, on the other hand, are passive and circumspect. They frown on aggressiveness—indeed, on any strong expression of individuality. They have, at least so far, seen little value in merging with the dominant society. In fact, the Indian's loyalty is often narrowly focused on his own relatives and community, and even Indians outside this community are regarded with suspicion. This phenomenon is perhaps most clearly expressed by the absence in rural areas of widespread Indian rebellion.

The government has tended to lump all the Indian societies together for the purposes of legislation and administration of aid, discounting ethnic and regional differences. This insensitivity has hindered implementation of social and economic reforms. And the reforms themselves show that the government regards the Indians as a depressed group rather than as a people with a distinctive and viable way of life.

A basic problem in Ecuador is how to achieve the economic union of its various cultural groups, without destroying the values by which they have lived for centuries.

focus *on a Community-Development Project,*
by Joseph B. Kelley

Although slightly more than half of Ecuador's population now lives in urban areas, there is no national urban program, so that each city must deal with its own problems. One of the cities that is beginning to look toward the future is Quito, the national capital and second largest city (after Guayaquil, the teeming coastal port). For about two years I was associated with a community-development project in a section known as La Colmena, or "beehive," on the south side of Quito. The project sought to identify existing problems at the *barrio,* or neighborhood, level and to develop and implement solutions to them. It was sponsored by the School of Social Work of the Catholic University of Ecuador and the Ecuadorian Institute of Planning for Social Development, a private research organization, with support from St. Louis University and the U.S. Agency for International Development.

La Colmena is as representative as any neighborhood can be of emerging urban life in the Andean range, which has the major part of the nation's population. According to the results of our house-to-house survey, 75 per cent of the residents had total family incomes of less than $50.00 per month; 85 per cent lived in only one or two rooms (although the average number of children per family was slightly over four); only about 20 per cent had water and toilet facilities in their own homes, and 15 per cent had no access whatsoever to any type of toilet facility; 22 per cent of those over age fifteen were unable to read or write; over two thirds of the births occurred at home without medical attention.

What to do in the face of such an array of problems? In the initial survey, the residents stated as their major concern additions to or construction of churches and schools, extension or improvement of streets and sewage lines, and housing improvement. A majority of the residents said they thought most of these improvements should be effected through a neighborhood organization rather than through municipal or national government, although this judgment may reflect their view of the realities of severely limited municipal and national budgets.

The formation and strengthening of such self-help organizations became the first project and was, in fact, carried on simultaneously with the survey itself. The approach taken by the professional social workers-in-training was that the community being served should determine the objectives to be sought and the ways in which they were to be attained.

Two major projects combined the residents' interests in street improvement and sewage/health. The first of these was the pick-and-shovel improvement of the streets through work projects of thirty to sixty residents. Previously, delivery trucks and carts could not pass in many streets; it was difficult for many people to walk to their homes, especially during the rainy season; and, even more serious, the sewage ran in open ditches in which the children played and which often overflowed. The personal satisfaction the people derived from solving these problems—and improving the appearance of their house fronts—was clearly very important to them. Four streets of three blocks each were changed from quasi-pathways surrounded by high embankments to passable thoroughfares. Laying these streets was a requirement for receiving assistance from the city in developing a sewer system.

This project also had intangible benefits in terms of fostering community spirit and strengthening the self-help organization. Anyone who wanted to help—men, women, and children—could and did work, and the project had the advantage of clear visibility—everyone could see and know that it had been a success.

A second, related project was the filling in of a canyon, using as part of the fill the extra soil obtained by knocking down the embankments in the street project. After clarification of the legal status of the land, one section of a canyon one block long and thirty feet wide and deep, was filled. The dirt was moved several blocks by wheelbarrow and loaded onto city trucks, loaned for use on weekends. The installation of sewage lines for twenty houses which discharged sewage into the canyon was planned as well as the filling in of the remainder of the canyon, which ran the full length of the community. Recreational facilities were planned for the improved land. This project did not require money—only borrowed tools and hand labor—and therefore was under the control of the residents. AID provided only the salary of one consultant—no other financial support.

A third project involved vocational education. Arrangements were made to change various requirements so as to allow a special group of sixty young men from this community to take a series of courses in a school which conferred the title of Journeyman of Electricity and Mechanics. Very few men from the neighborhood had ever attended this school because they lacked the academic preparation and grades usually required for entrance. The men were selected through interviews, meetings, and home visits. The chief criteria were their need for work and their motivation. The objective of the experiment was to determine what success a group of previously excluded young men could have when carefully selected at the neighborhood level and assisted during the training course by back-up services (conferences, tutorial assistance, minor financial aid related to transportation, etc., and discussions with instructors to foster progress). After completing the first cycle of three months, all but a few men, who failed the course, expressed enthusiasm to continue. The experiment gave a boost to *barrio* morale and to the young men chosen, who felt that they "represented" the *barrio*. Unfortunately, it was not possible to continue the back-up services or to follow the progress of the group to the planned termination of the course.

A fourth project was a pilot plan involving the improvement of housing for six or seven low-income families. The improvements included adding a room, installing windows and doors, building a floor, dividing rooms, painting, constructing a laundry, and installing water. These improvements were achieved through self-help and neighborhood work groups with the assistance of a budget from the British-North America Women's Group. Although this project was on a very small scale in relation to housing needs in the *barrio,* it was hoped that it might develop into a cooperative that would include housing improvement as one of its programs or that the National Housing Program would aid in the project. Neither of these goals had materialized by the time this phase of the project ended.

The four projects described above can be thought of as long-term self-help projects. There were also petitions and short-term self-help projects. In petitions the activity of the residents is restricted to gathering facts about a situation and requesting that the appropriate public or private entity furnish the facility or service to provide for this need. Petitions are typical activities of new organizations because they are clearly understood and generally respond to urgently felt needs. A number of petitions in Quito brought results, including the installation of public street lighting and improved bus transportation.

In general, our experience indicates that it is preferable for a group to develop a mixture of long- and short-term projects, of petitions and self-help activities, of simple and complex programs. In this way, the residents can achieve small successes regularly at the same time that they are seeking more difficult goals. If the most important business of a meeting consists in a report by a committee chairman that "we are still waiting" on such and such a long-term project, many of those in attendance will not return to another meeting. If, on the other hand, a committee chairman is able to report that "we were able to clear another block last week," he may succeed in enlisting volunteers to work on another street.

The deep involvement of a number of people in the community, a characteristic of the approach used, has a number of advantages. First, it utilizes their efforts as part of a total national effort. Visible results provide personal satisfaction for individuals and foster their identification with an organization and with national development. A second advantage seems to be integration at the local level, which can strengthen a sense of community. Third, the mix mentioned earlier seems to maximize the development of positive motivation, and the achievement of improvements. Finally, in the Quito projects, we were concerned with the training of professional social-work students, who were learning to work with local leaders so as to stimulate their motivation and improve their capacity to plan and carry out projects.

There were, however, some disadvantages in the program. One was that it lacked a link to a strong national program with more extensive resources, and this restricted it to relatively limited achievements. Among the objectives of community development are the incorporation of the aspirations and efforts of all citizens and the "integration of all groups of citizens into the life of the nation." * These objectives do seem to have been furthered in this case.

A danger of the community-level approach is that the program may become involved in partisan politics, which may detract from the organization's ability to effect badly needed improvements. This problem was not encountered in a serious way during the period described.

Suggested Readings

American University. *Area Handbook for Ecuador*. Washington, D.C.: U.S. Government Printing Office, 1966. A comprehensive analysis of social, economic, and political aspects of the nation.

Andean Indian Community Research and Development Project, Department of Anthropolgy, Cornell University. *Indians in Misery. A Preliminary Report on the Colta Lake Zone, Chimborazo, Ecuador*. A report prepared for and in collaboration with the Ecuadorian Institute of Agrarian Reform and Colonization. *Contract No. AID la-206* (Regional). Ithaca: Cornell University Department of Anthropology, 1965.

* United Nations Economic and Social Council, *Community Development and Related Services*. New York: United Nations, 1964, p. 9.

GIBSON, CHARLES R. *Foreign Trade in the Economic Development of Small Nations: The Case of Ecuador.* New York: Praeger, 1971. A study of the relation of international trade theory and economic development theory as they pertain to Ecuador.

MINNIES, MALACHY T. "Basic Data on the Economy of Ecuador." U.S. Bureau of International Commerce, *Overseas Business Report, OBR 68–52* (July, 1968). A brief analysis of the nation's economy.

PRESTON, D. A. "Negro, Mestizo, and Indian in an Andean Environment." *Geographical Journal,* CXXXI, pt. 2 (June, 1965), pp. 220–34. A study of environmental and social aspects of the settlements of these groups in Ecuador.

WATKINS, RALPH J. *Expanding Ecuador's Exports. A Commodity by Commodity Study with Projections to 1973.* New York: Praeger, 1967.

WILSON, JACQUES M. P. *The Development of Education in Ecuador. Hispanic-American Studies No. 24.* Coral Gables, Florida: University of Miami Press, 1970. Outlines the development of education in Ecuador since colonial times, stressing a problem prevalent in many less-developed nations: the marked preference for the humanities and law, although what are needed are more experts in engineering, agriculture, medicine, and education itself.

ZUVEKAS, CLARENCE, JR. "Economic Planning in Ecuador: An Evaluation." *Inter-American Economic Affairs,* XXV, no. 4 (spring, 1972), pp. 39–69. An analysis of the success of various economic plans from 1933 until the Velasco Ibarra regime. Argues that, on the whole, Ecuador's economic policies have not succeeded because of a lack of long-range planning and that, unless a more rational decision-making process is adopted, most of Ecuador's new petroleum wealth may be dissipated among relatively unproductive activities.

See also Suggested Readings for Part I, pp. 61–63.

12 PERU*

Historical Highlights · The Isolated Indian · Land Reform · Economic Troubles and the Move to the City · The Coastal Desert · The Sierra · The Selva · The Search for Creative Leadership

The mere mention of Peru evokes images of fabulous Inca treasure, Spanish galleons loaded to the gunwales with gold and silver bars, curious-looking animals—alpaca, vicuña, llama—and vast mountain chains rising to snow-clad heights. To the west of the mountains are dry, rolling deserts cut by fan-shaped cultivated oases along the silt-bearing rivers; to the east are vast, hot, dense rain forests. On the high, cold plateaus (parts of which are called the sierra and the altiplano) between the majestic Cordilleras, the inhabitants shiver through the nights waiting for the warmth of day. Here the sunworshipping Incas had their cultural center of gravity in pre-Spanish days; here they created a highland empire unique in the world.

Historical Highlights

The imperial system of the Incas was highly efficient. Recently conquered tribes were thoroughly indoctrinated with the culture of their conquerors by being divided into small groups and dispersed among more trustworthy subjects. A system of roads and bridges, a messenger service, and guest houses scattered throughout the country enabled the rulers in Cuzco to maintain communication with the provinces.

Society was divided into the hereditary ruling class, the priestly hierarchy,

* Parts of this chapter were adapted from a 1967 issue of *focus*.

and the people. Each year families were assigned plots of land sufficient to support their members. Most of the products of the soil and the wool of llamas and alpacas went into government storehouses, to be apportioned according to need. Individuals also paid tribute to the state in the form of products of their various skills and crafts or by labor on public roads, buildings, irrigation systems, and agricultural terraces. The ruling and priestly classes lived extremely well, and among the people there was neither extreme affluence nor grinding poverty.

Although the Incas mined the rich deposits of gold and silver, they were not interested in the commercial value of the metals. They associated gold with the sun, their principal deity, and lavishly decorated their temples and palaces with it. It is reported that when the Indians en-

The ruins of Machu Picchu, an old Inca fortress town. The Inca Empire, established in the late eleventh or the twelfth century, controlled a large part of what is now Peru, Bolivia, Ecuador, and Chile. The rigid social, religious, and political hierarchy imposed by the Inca emperors on their subjects functioned efficiently until the arrival of the Spanish *conquistadores*.

Courtesy United Nations

countered the Spanish horses for the first time and saw the horses champing at their bits, they assumed that metal was the horses' customary food and filled up troughs of gold and silver for them.

In 1532, when Pizarro arrived, there was insurrection within the empire, which enabled him to pit the two factions one against the other and thus topple the most sophisticated culture in the New World. Pizarro's inability to control his men in the mad quest for gold left a legacy of violence and lawlessness, and during the following two and a half centuries the condition of the Indians became deplorable. Laws promulgated to protect them were not enforced, and they were constantly being kidnapped to work in the silver mines and on plantations. In 1780, unable to endure more abuses, some 60,000 Indians, led by Tupac Amarú II, revolted against Spanish rule. This rebellion, though unsuccessful, was one of the first of a series sparked by Indians and later by aristocratic creoles (Spaniards born in Peru), who resented being excluded from the highest offices, which were reserved for Spaniards born in Spain.

Even after independence had been achieved in 1821, the struggles of various military chieftains for the office of president kept the country in a turmoil. Then Peru suffered a disastrous defeat in the War of the Pacific at the hands of Chile. Subsequently, efforts were made to reconstruct the country. But from 1908 to 1912 and from 1919 to 1930, under Augusto Leguía, social turmoil and unrest were once again the order of the day. Leguía throttled the press and greatly increased the public debt with very little tangible benefit to the country and none at all to the Indian. Indeed, the Peoples Universities, established to bring education to the masses, were closed down.

Awareness of injustices to the Indians grew steadily in the next decades, even if little was done about it. In 1963 Fernando Belaúnde Terry came to office. He had gained an extensive knowledge of the Indians by traveling widely through the country. Belaúnde had an ambitious program for national development, parts of which will be outlined later in this chapter. His downfall came about chiefly because of the precarious economic state of the country and because of Belaúnde's own increasing political weakness. Since October, 1968, a group of military men headed by Juan Velasco Alvarado has pursued the goals of the Belaúnde government, with the political strength to carry them out. Peru now has what might seem to be a contradiction in terms in South America—a left-wing military government.

The Isolated Indian

The fact that at the time of the Spanish Conquest the Inca Empire was the most sophisticated civilization in South America had a profound effect on the future relationship between Indians and Spaniards. Anthropologist Elman Service has classified the societies of South America into three groups: Euro-American, Mestizo American, and Indo-American. The Indians of Euro-America (exemplified by Uruguay) were hunters insufficient in wealth and numbers to form an organized labor force. They fled from areas of Spanish settlement and were progressively wiped out. The Indians of Mestizo America (for example, Paraguay) were slash-and-burn agriculturalists and occasional hunters or fishers, living in small villages of low population density. Their primitive production techniques and the ease with which they could escape from captivity into more hospitable country saved them from large-scale Spanish exploitation. The mixing of the two societies occurred gradually and on a small scale. Thus the Indian was drawn into the mainstream of society. Paraguay is today the only country in South America where an Indian language—Guaraní—is an official language.

Indo-America is typified by Peru and Bolivia, the heartland of the old Inca Empire. The elaborate organization of that empire at the time of the Spanish Conquest, its stable, surplus-producing agricultural economy, its hierarchical form of organization, highly developed town life, and high population density, brought the Indian into direct confrontation with the Spanish, which led ultimately to his absorption. It must also be remembered that these Indians were accustomed to absolute obedience to a figure of authority.

So the stage was set for the long period of oppression and isolation of the Indian. Furthermore, whereas in Mexico, Ecuador, and Colombia the Spaniards founded their capital cities in the temperate mountains, in the midst of the Indian population, in Peru they founded the capital at sea level, far from the great centers of native life. They faced the sea, engaged in commerce, and kept their backs to the densely populated mountain hinterland. Thus the gulf—racial, social, economic, and political— between the white and the Indian populations has steadily widened, and the process of national integration has thereby been immeasurably lengthened.

It is generally believed that the most urgent problem facing Peru today is incorporation of the Indian into national life. In its attempts to con-

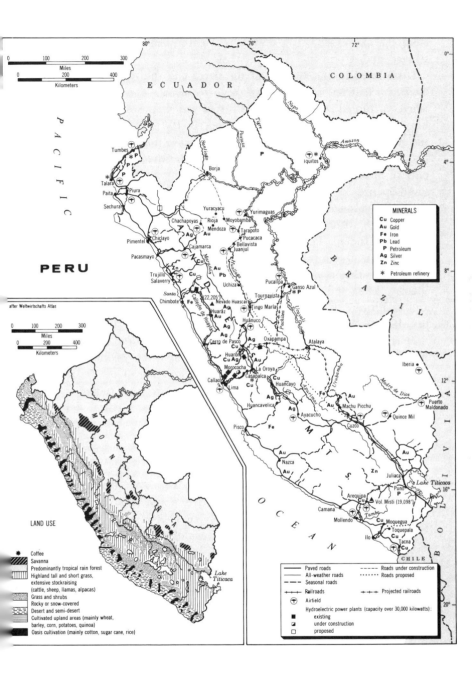

front the difficulties of the Indian, the government has recently passed a stricter land-reform bill (see pages below).

Until recently, the Indians of the sierra and the *selva* (eastern tropical lowlands) had few opportunities to go to school. The owner of the land where an Indian community was situated was supposed to provide schools, but very few owners did so. It was not in the landowner's interest that the Indians become educated and perhaps move into urban areas. Another major barrier to education was that the few schools that existed taught only in Spanish, and some 40 per cent of the population does not understand Spanish or has only a rudimentary knowledge of it. Illiteracy under these circumstances is widespread.

In March, 1972, the government ordered a sweeping reform in education. The Indians henceforth were to be taught in their own languages —principally Quechua and Aymara—as well as in Spanish. Girls will have equal education opportunities. And the educational process will start in infancy, when the child's parents will be instructed in proper nutrition and health care. Radio and television—government-controlled since November, 1971—will be used extensively in remoter parts of the country.

It is estimated that about half of Peru's population of 14 million is Indian. The estimate may not be accurate, however, because few people voluntarily admit to being Indian. Yet, the isolation of the Indian is not, strictly speaking, based on race. A person born into Indian society is not obliged to remain in it because of his birth or physical appearance. He may move into another social group if he is financially able to do so. Andrew Pearse puts it this way:

> The real significance of the Indians lies not in their race or culture, but in their status and social function. The word "Indian" denotes members of social groups to which society apportions special treatment implying a restriction of rights, a limited field of cultural expectations and contractual inferiority to the citizens of the national societies.*

The future of the Indian will depend a great deal on the success of the agrarian reform law instituted in 1969.

Land Reform

It has long been recognized that land reform is necessary in Peru. Until

* Andrew Pearse, "The Indians of the Andes," in Claudio Véliz, ed., *Latin America and the Caribbean*. New York: Praeger, 1968, p. 690.

a few years ago, there was a grotesque inequality in land distribution. On the coast, 10 per cent of the landowners held 89 per cent of the land. In the sierra and the *selva* the situation was even worse: 3 per cent of the landowners owned 83 per cent of the land in the sierra and 93 per cent of the available land in the *selva*.

On the coast, owners of large sugar plantations sometimes forced smaller landowners to sell their land by illegally appropriating their irrigation water. One plantation—the Casagrande—owned some 1,930 square miles, an area only slightly smaller than the state of Delaware. In the sierra the U.S.-owned Cerro de Pasco copper corporation, which controlled a large amount of land, sited its smelter in such a way that the highly toxic fumes it emitted damaged the livestock and crops of the neighboring landowners. The corporation then bought up the land at prices greatly below their true values, cleaned up the smelter, and expanded into the cattle-raising business. Thus the country was divided up into *latifundios* and *minifundios*. The average holding for each farmer was about five acres, and some 290,000 families owned only about two acres each.

In 1964 the Belaúnde government passed an agrarian reform law which provided that land worked by all farmers on the coast and in the sierra would eventually be owned by them. But land reform itself was only a part of the national development plan envisaged by Belaúnde. Expansion of the existing area under cultivation—only 2 per cent of the land in 1964—was a major goal of this plan; over 1.5 million acres of new land were to be irrigated, and the irrigation system in other areas was to be improved. Rich tropical valleys in the *selva* were to be opened by roads and the land was to be developed by landless Indians from the sierra. By the late 1960's, 100,000 peasants had taken possession of land, and 7,000 property titles had been given to settlers in the *selva*.

But there were weaknesses in the 1964 law. For one thing, the rich sugar plantations on the coast were exempt from the law. For another, the government paid market values for expropriated land, which made the costs for large-scale land acquisition prohibitive. And the 1964 law did not regulate private control of irrigation water.

In June, 1969, the military government issued a new decree abolishing many of the provisions of the 1964 law. The sugar plantations were no longer exempt from expropriation. (Indeed, two days after the issuance of the decree the government took control of all the nation's sugar mills and plantations; they are now operated as cooperatives, which are controlled by freely elected workers' councils, but these are closely supervised by government agents.) Under the new law, any area on the coast of over

150 acres of irrigated land is subject to expropriation. Now holdings or parts of holdings that are not directly worked by their owners and that exceed by three times the permissible family agricultural unit may be expropriated. (The amount of land varies from coast to sierra to *selva;* it varies also according to the condition of the land and what it is to be used for.) The price to be paid for expropriated land under the new law is to be based on the valuation made by the taxation office for a property census being carried out by the government. Private water rights have been abolished. Water will be allocated by volume in accordance with the needs of various crops.

But not every Peruvian farmer will be able to own land, no matter how effective the government's program is. There is simply not enough land for all the landless families, who now number about 1.3 million. Even with the most rigorous program of land cultivation and expropriation, it will not be possible to give adequate family units to more than about 25 per cent of the landless small farmers. Other economic activities must therefore be developed.

Economic Troubles and the Move to the City

The Belaúnde government was overthrown in October, 1968, chiefly because of Peru's difficult financial situation. There had been a downturn in export earnings coupled with excessive government spending. The new military government also accused the Belaúnde government of corruption and of signing a new contract too favorable to the United States-owned International Petroleum Corporation (IPC).

Indeed, Peru was in economic trouble. Money in Peru was distributed as unequally as land: 24,000 Peruvians received 44 per cent of the nation's income. In 1969, the average wage in the highly developed coastal region was 35 soles per day (at the time, 38.70 soles equaled U.S. $1.00). In the highlands the landowners often paid the peasants who worked their land only with a little food or coca (dried leaves containing cocaine, which are chewed by the Indians). Many rich Peruvians invested their money outside Peru because they had little faith in Peru's shaky economy. The sol was devalued in 1967. The annual growth rate, which in the early 1960's had been about 6 per cent—one of the highest in South America—had dropped by 1969 to about 1 per cent.

Many Peruvians felt that foreign-owned companies played too large a part in national affairs. Several of the largest concerns were foreign-owned—for instance, Cerro de Pasco Corporation (copper), International Petroleum Company, a subsidiary of Standard Oil of New Jersey, and W. R. Grace Company (sugar refining).

On the other hand, Peru has a much greater diversity of exports than most less-developed nations. It is, for instance, the world's largest exporter of fish meal. The deserts and mountains are rich in minerals. In the bleak mountains of the sierra some of the richest mineral deposits in the world have been found. Silver mines made Peru world-famous during the colonial era. With the coming of the age of electricity, the demand for copper sky-rocketed, and in the early years of the twentieth century copper mining became enormously profitable, with gold, silver, and lead as byproducts. Today copper ranks first in value among the highland minerals. The chief mining centers are at and around Cerro de Pasco, Morococha, Casapalca, and Huarón, and more recently Toquepala.

Many crops can be grown because of the country's wide variety of altitudes, climates, and soils, but only 2 per cent of the land is under cultivation. With a rate of population increase of 3.1 per cent per year, and the massive migration of farmers to the cities, Peru is no longer able to feed its people. Food imports tripled during the 1960's—an expenditure that seriously damaged the balance of trade. About 51 per cent of the population is engaged in agriculture; yet agriculture contributes less than 20 per cent of the gross national product.

Another difficulty is that industry is unhealthily concentrated in the capital. About two thirds of the total value of industrial output comes from some 3,000 factories circling Lima. Uprooted small farmers are migrating to Lima at a rate greater than industry's power to absorb them. The industrial output of the nation is limited because of the smallness of the market (about one third of Peru's population lives outside the market economy). And finally, prices have been rising at inflationary rates.

The new military government faced all these problems and at first seemed to be creating a few of its own. Shortly after it came to power, the government seized the International Petroleum Corporation and refused to pay compensation, claiming instead that the company owed it some $690 million in back taxes. United States-Peruvian relations were also strained by Peru's claim to fishing rights up to 200 miles off its coast. The United States threatened to suspend aid to Peru, and it seemed likely that other U.S. companies would be reluctant to invest in Peru. Loss of U.S. aid and investment would have been disastrous for Peru: In 1968 Peru received $15 million from the United States; at the same time U.S. commercial investment amounted to some $460 million.

But, fortunately for Peru, its government's assertion that the IPC expropriation was a special case seems to have been taken at face value. A U.S. firm, the Southern Peru Copper Corporation, has invested $335 million in Peru, and petroleum companies are continuing to invest.

The military government has moved to control the foreign-owned banking industry, stepped up tax collection, cut nonessential imports, and in May, 1970, declared it illegal for Peruvians to hold cash in foreign currencies or have funds invested in overseas savings accounts or stocks and bonds. Foreign investment will be strictly regulated. Foreign ownership will eventually be limited to 33 per cent in businesses financed by foreign capital and 49 per cent in businesses financed by mixed public and private capital. In most businesses, workers will start to receive a share of the profits and will gradually become majority stockholders.

The government still faces serious economic difficulties. To alleviate them it is trying to make agriculture relatively more productive and to finance ambitious reform programs without causing inflation, and it seems to be making some progress. The government is also trying to set up industries in other parts of the country besides the area around Lima. Membership in the Andean Common Market should also provide greater opportunities for economic development (see pp. 47–60).

Peru is no exception in South America with respect to the migration from rural to urban areas. It has been estimated that since the end of World War II, 1 million people have moved from rural areas to Lima. Looked at in another way, in 1936, 65 per cent of the city's population was native-born; by 1965, this figure had dropped to 35 per cent, and it is probably lower now.

A large number of Lima's migrants (about 750,000 people) live in squatter settlements, known as *barriadas,* that form a belt around the city. To the uninformed or casual observer these settlements may look like slums, with their houses built of slats and roofed with straw matting. In many cases, there is no plumbing or electricity. But closer examination of the *barriada* phenomenon suggests that the designation "slum" is incorrect. A slum is a community that is locked into poverty, one in which the people can look for little improvement in the quality of their lives. Also, a slum may exist partly because of racial or other intolerance on the part of the larger community. As we have seen, racial intolerance per se is not the cause of the Indian's isolation in Peru.

There is a typical pattern to the migration from rural settlement to *barriada*. Most often a small farmer receives assurance of support in the city from a friend or relative; he then moves into Lima's inner city, into a settlement more nearly like a slum. It has been suggested that this period of residence in the center city is necessary because most readily available jobs are there, and because it permits the migrant to become accustomed to an urban life style and a money economy. Also, he will have to learn Spanish, or at least improve his knowledge of it. The migrant and his sponsor will become in time the nucleus of an extended family as other relatives move into the city to join them. This family may embrace two or three generations. When a few members of the family have established themselves in decently paying jobs, it is time for the move to the *barriada*.

The family will move to one of these communities, erect a house of stakes and straw matting (after all, it's not such a hardship to live under a straw roof in a city with an average annual rainfall of 1.6 inches!), and start planning for a more permanent establishment. Living rent-free, the family will be able to devote a fair share of its earnings to building a sturdier home. The government will gradually supply the community with roads, sewage systems, electricity, and perhaps a school. Thus a *barriada* is transformed over the years from a ramshackle squatters' settlement to a respectable lower-middle economic community.

Improvements supplied by the government are granted to those communities that help themselves; they are, in effect, a reward for choosing and following a plan of action. One political scientist sees this as the major difference between rural and urban life:

> Even though the simple and harsh life in the sierra offers, in a sense, a type of security, it is a security based on the absence of choice. To live in the sierra on the level of a subsistence farmer demands certain existence patterns which are so firmly set by tradition and necessity that fundamental and widespread change has simply not been able to occur as yet. On the other hand, the city is heterogeneous and composed of many groups with diverse backgrounds and interests. Such diversity creates opportunities for freedom of personal behavior which do not and cannot exist in a rural context.*

Of course, not all migrants succeed in establishing themselves in a

* Henry Dietz, "Urban Squatter Settlements in Peru; A Case History and Analysis." *Journal of Inter-American Studies*, XI, no. 3 (July, 1969), p. 361.

barriada. Some are lost in the center-city slums of Lima; some return to the country. Good jobs are hard to come by: an estimated 70 per cent of the urban people are engaged in marginal economic activities, for instance, as street vendors, gardeners, and house servants. But the *barriadas* (now sometimes called *pueblos jóvenes,* young towns) have shown the impoverished Peruvian that it is possible for him to change the course of his life.

The Coastal Desert

In the part of Peru lying between the Andes and the coast, the dominant winds, associated with the anticyclonic belt over the South Pacific ocean, are from the south or southwest. Since they blow across the remarkably cool northward-flowing Humboldt Current, they bring no rain. However, during the winter months (from May to October) in the south, their moisture often condenses to form a low cloud cover called the *garua,* which brings a slight drizzle stopping just short of actual rain, like a Scotch mist, that humidifies the gardens along the coast and the pastures in the foothills of the sierra. During the summer the sun is strong enough to prevent the formation of the *garua,* and the whole of coastal Peru then enjoys glorious weather.

This narrow strip, twenty to eighty miles wide, houses about 33 per cent of Peru's people and is the nation's most productive agricultural area. There are some forty fertile oases, to which ingenious irrigation works bring sufficient water to produce abundant crops of sugar cane, cotton, rice, vegetables, grapes and other fruits, and some wheat. However, still more water should be made available for irrigation. The capital for new irrigation works could come from the royalties paid to the government on the petroleum being extracted from the rich fields at Talara.

Offshore, the cool Humboldt Current is rich in fish. The catch, one of the world's largest, is predominantly of surface-swimming anchovies, which are not only a source of income but also food for the birds that live by the thousands on the offshore islands, whose droppings annually provide several hundred thousand tons of guano (used for fertilizer in the oases). Coastal factories convert the anchovies into fishmeal for fertilizer and cattle feed. The fishmeal goes primarily to Germany, the Netherlands, the United Kingdom, and the United States. Although profits remain enormous, overfishing, competition from Chile, and periodic warmings of the coastal waters (sending the cold-water anchovies farther to sea or down to greater depths) are decreasing the catch per boat.

Courtesy United Nations

Until recently, Peru was the world's largest exporter of fishmeal. In 1972, the warm current called El Niño, which every five or six years displaces the cold Humboldt current for a few months, persisted much longer than usual. The warm waters drove the anchovies away, creating havoc in the Peruvian fishing industry. Here anchovies are shown traveling on conveyor belts, ultimately to be converted into fishmeal.

Other principal industries in the coastal strip include the production and refining of petroleum, mainly at Tumbes and Talara (Peru's total output currently is about 4 million tons per year); the making of steel at Chimbote, using local iron and hydroelectric power from the picturesque Santa River; the extraction of copper from mines near Moquegua; the refining of sugar; and the spinning and weaving of cotton, wool, silk, and rayon in Lima and several other cities.

Industrial production has increased rapidly in the last few years, especially petroleum refining, the generation of electric power, and the making of fishmeal, cotton textiles, artificial fibers, plastics, chemicals, fertilizers, and rubber tires. Most of this industrial growth is taking place in Lima, Arequipa, and Callao. Through the enlarged port of Callao pass 75 per cent of the nation's imports and 25 per cent of its exports. The main imports are machinery, vehicles, iron and steel manufactures, chemicals, pharmaceuticals, foodstuffs (chiefly cereals), beverages, tobacco, textiles, and clothing; exports consist primarily of fish and fish preparations, agricultural products such as cotton and sugar cane, and lead, copper, and iron ore.

The Sierra

The great majority of Peru's 3 million Quechua-speaking Indians live on the inhospitable high plateaus, which comprise roughly 25 per cent of the country—or, rather, they live on the floors of the deep intermontane valleys and cultivate carefully terraced plots of ground perched on the seemingly unscalable mountain slopes. With admirable patience and industry, they climb the mountains to till these tiny patches that yield little, yet require enormous outlays of labor to produce at all. The labor involved in building the retaining walls and keeping them in repair is stupendous, to be undertaken only by those to whom the possession of land is almost sacred and whose sense of reward differs markedly from our own. One of the most productive of these mountain-girdled valleys is that of Huancayo (elevation, 10,000 feet), where maize, barley, and 40 per cent of the nation's wheat crop are produced. Coffee and tea are raised in several of the eastern Andean valleys (4,000- to 6,000-foot levels). Coffee is Peru's third most-important agricultural export, after cotton and sugar, and tea production is sufficient for local needs.

In the semiarid altiplano, from 12,000 to 15,000 feet in elevation, Indians graze their cattle, sheep, llamas, and alpacas on the coarse grasses and thorny shrubs native to such heights. The higher and more exposed parts are so cold, rocky, and windswept as to be almost uninhabitable.

Perhaps half of the Andean Indians live in Indian agricultural communities, some of which are completely independent; the others work on *haciendas* (estates) owned by whites or *mestizos*, who have economic, political, and judicial power over their peons. By custom, one adult member of each family is obligated to work a certain number of days a week (usually three) for the *hacienda* in return for the right to occupy a small plot of land supposedly sufficient to support his family. In addition, the peons must supply the *hacienda* with free services as cooks, grooms, watchmen, shepherds, servants, and the like.

The small independent farmer who grows potatoes, barley, wheat, corn, or some other grain can count on an average income equivalent to from U.S. $50 to $110 a year per family of five. This sum must cover production costs as well as living expenses.

To raise living levels to acceptable standards, the first requisites are higher productivity and greater returns for work performed; yet these cannot be envisaged before a comprehensive progam of land reform is carried out and there is a large increase in capital resources, managerial capacity, and trained workers at every level. Even if production doubled, living levels still would not rise to acceptable standards, for farming units are greatly overstaffed. However, the actual manpower and the huge potential hydroelectric power in the Andes, if properly utilized for industrialization, could provide an outlet for labor from the ranks of the underemployed in the rural areas. Among the industries suitable for location in the Andes are the making of shoes, clothing, furniture, soap, and ceramic wares.

The large-scale shifting of rural population from agricultural activities to industrial ones in the Andes and migration to the tropical lands to the east would go a long way toward alleviating the poverty of the Andean Indian.

The Selva

The vast area east of the Andes, variously known as the *montaña* and the *selva,* which encompasses the foothills and some parts of the Amazon Basin, is potentially rich in natural resources, but the settlement of tropical forest areas requires experience and skills that the Andean Indian does not have. Further, the illiterate Indian, almost invariably without capital, rarely has a chance to buy suitably located land at official prices, because of the activities of speculators. However, long-range national—or better still, international—planning undoubtedly could solve most of the problems of opening up the tropical areas suitable for cultivation, such problems as disease, illiteracy, language barriers, and lack of capital, roads, and markets.

The tropical forested lowlands lying east of the Andes comprise about 62 per cent of the national territory (they are larger than the state of Texas); yet only about 14 per cent of the people live there. Exploitation of forest products, such as hardwoods, tannin, and oil nuts, remains the principal economic activity, though the skins of wild animals and some tropical fruits are exported in small quantities.

In 1966 petroleum was discovered near the Marañón River. For some years there has been a feverish search for oil, and additional huge deposits may indeed be found, but at present production is limited to the wells in Ganso Azul, on the Pachitea River, which produce some 101,000 tons of crude oil a year. This is processed at a small refinery in Iquitos into various grades of diesel fuel, low-octane gasoline, and kerosene for the local market.

The new roads into the *selva,* now linked with Brazil's Trans-Amazon

Highway and with the demanding markets of the coast and the sierra, are rejuvenating and opening settlements and surrounding areas previously isolated. The area's potential is enormous, not only for timber but for a variety of crops. Rubber and coffee could be grown. Sugar, tea, cacao, coconuts, and tobacco are now being raised. Pucallpa, for example, once a few thatched huts along the Ucayali River, has become a bustling frontier city of 30,000 inhabitants. Cattle are introduced as rapidly as pasture lands are prepared for them. Rice is being successfully grown; jute production is increasing; dwarf African oil palms are providing much-needed raw materials. Peru's "Wild East" is gradually being tamed.

The Search for Creative Leadership

Much has been done in the last two decades to weld the various regions together by roads and railroads. But much more remains to be done if the eastern forest lands are to be developed and incorporated into the national economy—developed particularly for their potential food resources, which would cut down on the amount spent for imports. And much also remains to be done to incorporate the Indian into the body politic of the nation and into its social and economic life.

The current military government says it intends to initiate a variety of new programs to do just this and has created the National System to Support Social Mobilization (SINAMOS) to implement them. *Sin amos* means "without masters"; the goal is to tackle economic and social problems on the basis of understanding and respecting the local culture, enlisting the active help of members of a community, and organizing and training groups within a community to assume creative leadership. An integrated approach to problems of economic and social development and the encouragement of greater local initiative and responsibility may indeed break the hold of centuries of passivity among the Peruvian Indians and release long-submerged energies and hopes.

Suggested Readings

Brodsky, Jacobo, and Jacob Oser. "Land Tenure in Peru: A CIDA Study." *The American Journal of Economics and Sociology,* XXVII, no. 4 (October, 1968), pp. 405–21. A translation of parts of a controversial land-tenure study published in 1966 by the CIDA (Comite Inter-Americano de Desarrollo Agrícola).

DIETZ, HENRY. "Urban Squatter Settlements in Peru: A Case History and Analysis." *Journal of Inter-American Studies,* XI, no. 3 (July, 1969), pp. 353–70. A study of an individual living in a *barriada,* and the implications of such settlements for the nation as a whole.

FARON, L. C. "Ethnicity and Social Mobility in Chancay Valley, Peru." In W. Goldschmidt and H. Hoijer, eds., *The Social Anthropology of Latin America; Essays in Honor of Ralph Leon Beals,* Los Angeles: Latin American Center, University of California, 1970, pp. 224–55. A description of prominent local organizations (haciendas, villages, and homestead colonies) that appear to characterize rural life in the area.

GRAYSON, GEORGE W., JR. "Peru's Military Populism." *Current History,* LX, no. 354 (February, 1971), pp. 71–77, 116. A clearly written and objective account of recent political events in Peru.

MARETT, ROBERT. *Peru. Nations of the Modern World.* New York: Praeger, 1969; London: Ernest Benn, 1969. A study of Peru's history, and of its present political, social, and economic conditions.

MARIÁTEGUI, JOSÉ CARLOS. *Seven Interpretive Essays on Peruvian Reality.* Translated by M. Urquidi. Austin: University of Texas Press, 1971. These essays, by one of the leading social philosophers of the early twentieth century, discuss economic evolution, the problem of the Indian, public education, and regionalism and centralism. Mariátegui's ideas have profoundly influenced other South American sociologists.

PAULSTON, ROLLAND G. *Society, Schools and Progress in Peru.* New York: Pergamon Press, 1971. An analysis of educational development, with particular reference to socio-cultural change during the 1960's. The author has also attempted to identify major influences on educational change in Peru during that period.

PENDLE, GEORGE. *The Land and People of Peru.* New York: Macmillan, 1966; London: A. and C. Black, 1966. A short history and general survey of the nation.

SACO, A. "In Peru Land is Restored to the Indians." *Land Reform, Land Settlement and Cooperatives,* No. 1 (1970), Rome: Food and Agricultural Organization of the United Nations, pp. 26–39. A study of progress in agrarian reform between 1961 and 1970.

See also Suggested Readings for Part I, pp. 61–63.

13 BRAZIL*

Kempton E. Webb

*Environment and People · Economic Booms and Busts ·
Northeastern Brazil · Eastern Brazil · The Shaping of Southern
Brazil · Centro Oeste · The Changing Face of the Amazon
North · Cities, Backlands, and the Future*

By 1973 Brazil will have surpassed the 100 million population mark. Its economy is booming at a growth rate of 9 per cent per year. The value of exports has doubled every two years since 1966. Intensive efforts to eliminate illiteracy, malnutrition, and food-supply bottlenecks are under way. It is perhaps ironic that these giant economic and social changes have occurred since a military-dominated government took control of the nation in 1964.

The overriding question is not whether or not Brazil is going ahead with changes but what they are intended to do and how they are being carried out. In order to appreciate and understand how Brazil has arrived at its present "take-off" point we must examine what environmental assets it had to begin with and how they are being used, keeping in mind the unique characteristics of the Brazilian people, their history, and their "big-country psychology."

Environment and People

Brazil occupies about half of South America and has half of its population.

* Based in part on Kempton E. Webb, *Geography of Latin America*. Englewood Cliffs, N.J.: Prentice-Hall, 1972, chapter 10.

In an area slightly larger than the continental United States, it has 95.7 million people compared to 203.2 million in the U.S. The country is so vast and encompasses such a wide variety of human experiences that it seems a microcosm of the physical and historical world and a laboratory of racial assimilation. It is distinguished for having had fewer and less bloody political revolutions than most other South American nations.

The physical environment of Brazil is diversified, but generally speaking the land can be divided into two categories: the lowlands, consisting largely of Tertiary deposits in the greater Amazon Basin, and the highlands, which in no way compare to the Andes in elevation but have distinctive characteristics that profoundly affect life and livelihood in those areas.

Underlying the land surfaces of the country and outcropping in some significant places in the east are crystalline basement rocks, which weather to fairly fertile agricultural soils, where the sedimentary cover has been removed by geological weathering.

Brazil has many climates. Most famous, of course, are the humid-tropical conditions in the Amazon Basin. Few people realize that it snows regularly at higher elevations in southern Brazil during the winter, and that there is an enormous area of true desert in the inland sections of the northeast. The highest temperatures, surprisingly, are not found in the Amazon north, where at Santarém the absolute maximum and minimum temperatures are 93°F. and 65°F., respectively; much higher temperatures are found at low elevations in the northeast. Here temperatures as high as 106° have been observed in places of low humidity where the insolation (or sun's radiant energy) at the earth's surface has great intensity and where night temperatures fall sharply from rapid radiation of heat back to space.

The latitudinal fluctuation of the intertropical convergence zone (a zone of warm tropical air moving toward low latitudes from the subtropics, causing uplift and heavy precipitation) is the mechanism that brings the summer season of rains to most of northern and central Brazil. The south, on the other hand, enjoys a moderate rainfall, which is distributed fairly evenly throughout the year. The peculiarities of the rainfall distribution in the northeast mean that in certain years, depending upon the size and strength of a monsoon-like indraft of maritime tropical air off the Atlantic Ocean, the interior areas may not receive rain. These periodic droughts are part of the physical and historical fabric in northeastern Brazil.

The basic vegetation types in Brazil are forest, savanna, grasslands, tropical thorn forest (*caatinga*), and softwood (*araucaria*) forests. The equatorial forests (*mata equatorial*) of the Amazon Basin cover less than half the nation's total area. This is an area of low soil fertility. The shallow-rooted crops, like maize and manioc, that have been planted where the forest has been cleared by slash-and-burn methods, give decreasing yields as that small layer of partially decomposed forest litter is exhausted.

A second variety of *mata,* the semideciduous evergreen forests of eastern Brazil, comprise areas of fertile land and are eagerly sought out by farmers. The very word *mata* is synonymous with fertile farmland. These areas of *mata* are sharply distinguished from those of the savanna (*campo cerrado*), the grasslands covered by scattered trees and soils that are famous for their sterility. The savannas are used mainly as grazing lands for extensive cattle raising or as sources of firewood.

The thorn scrub forest (or *caatinga*) of northeast Brazil is a truly xerophytic vegetation. The plants there are drought-resistant in part because of the dry climate, but also because of the "desertification" of land by repeated clearing, burning, and cropping cycles, which provide an increasingly infertile setting for plants.

In the south, in the state of Paraná, grow the softwood forests of the *araucaria* tree, popularly "Paraná pine," which form the basis for a fairly large lumber industry. The high rate at which the trees are being felled in Santa Catarina and Paraná means that the *araucaria* trees will disappear by A.D. 2000 unless extensive reforestation is carried out.

The people of Brazil cover a broad spectrum, beginning with the indigenous peoples who spoke languages of the Tupi-Guaraní family and who numbered possibly as many as 1 million when the Portuguese landed in 1500. The pre-Conquest Indians were essentially hunters and gatherers and subsistence farmers. None of these tribes had developed the social, political, or technological attainments of the Aztecs, Mayas, or Incas.

The Portuguese arrived in 1500, when Pedro Alvarez Cabral landed in southern Bahia. They were themselves a mixture of Celtic and Nordic peoples with strains of Mediterranean, Moorish, and Semitic origins. Northern Portugal was inhabited by peoples whose original Swabian roots went back to central Europe, so that to view the Portuguese settlers as a single type is clearly a mistake.

The third major population element is African. Negro slaves were brought over in the 1530's to work on the sugar-cane plantations, and this influx continued until slavery was abolished in Brazil in 1888.

In addition to these three principal groups there are the immigrants, mostly Europeans, who came in the nineteenth century. The most recent immigrants are the Japanese, settled in São Paulo and a few areas of the Amazon north.

ADMINISTRATIVE DIVISIONS

The most remarkable thing about Brazil is the fact that so vast an area of the earth's surface has held together culturally and as a single sovereign state for 150 years. Despite its physical contrasts and a population including groups as different as stone-age Indians and recent Israeli immigrants, there is but one overriding national Brazilian culture. In contrast to the ethnic or social loyalties prevalent in so many South American societies, the different kinds of people and groups in Brazil think of themselves first of all as Brazilians and only secondly as particular ethnic or social entities.

The people in different regions of Brazil and at different periods in history have, however, defined and used their resources in different ways. What is the minimally acceptable standard of living to a farmer in Rio Grande do Sul is quite distinct from the standard for a farmer in the backlands of the northeast. As we shall see, this theme of the variations in the cultural definitions of resources from one region of Brazil to another touches on a number of more topical problems, such as the rural-urban migration pattern, underemployment and the impact of modern technology on job opportunities, political and economic inequalities, and the discontinuities and continuities of political institutions and goals.

Economic Booms and Busts

Much of Brazil's history and the geography of settlement can be viewed in terms of the quest for forested (i.e., relatively fertile) lands. However, the initial discovery and exploration derived from quite different motives. In the early colonial period, Brazil was inhabited by adventurers who came in search, not of land, but rather of gold and Indian slaves who could be put to work mining gold. These early explorers often assumed that the whole country was covered with lush, tropical forest—actually only a narrow border along the streams they traveled—or that the dissected edge of plateaus in the distance was the foot of a *serra,* or mountain range. Their disillusionment, added to the fact that Pedro Alvarez Cabral discovered Brazil inadvertently, at a time when Portugal was engaged in a thriving and demanding commercial trade with the East Indies, diminished Portugal's interest in the New World. Brazil offered few commodities and trade items that Portugal could use.

Some attempts to exploit Brazil's resources were made, but few were successful. Nevertheless, some key cities were established in a short time: Salvador (Bahia) in 1502, São Vicente (in the state of São Paulo) in 1532, Olinda (Recife) in 1537, São Paulo in 1554, and Rio de Janeiro in 1567. Still, it must be stressed that Portugal's interest in colonies was essentially economic, and Brazil, which appeared to offer little in the way of wealth, was not considered to be of first importance.

Perhaps for this reason, Brazil's economic history is distinctly cyclical: a series of economic booms followed by equally spectacular declines. Many observers feel that throughout history the Brazilians have been too much interested in fast speculative gain, too impatient for the slow, steady nurturing of the nation's resources and productive capacities that would produce long-term yields to entrepreneurs and their descendants, and to the country in general. Many, in fact, feel that this cyclical history is a major defect in Brazil's development.

The first economic cycle, which lasted only from 1500 to 1550, was based on brazilwood (a source of dye) and involved the establishment of factories where it was collected, processed, and then shipped out to Europe. This activity took place in the tropical forests of the north and northeast and never gave rise to any significant permanent settlement. For that time, the great commercial significance of dyes such as brazilwood (red), indigo (blue), and cochineal (red) cannot be overestimated. Such dyes were the main sources for coloring fabrics, cosmetic products, and paints and inks in the sixteenth century.

The second cycle began around 1532 with the introduction of sugar cane from the Portuguese Madeira Islands off the coast of northwest Africa. African slaves brought in shortly afterwards provided the manpower for rapid development of cultivation to fill the growing European demand. A steady rise in production in the humid coastal northeast from Salvador to Natal reached its peak between 1650 and 1700. Thereafter there was a relative decline. Sugar cane is still produced in northeast Brazil today, although on a marginal economic basis.

In the 1690's, gold and diamonds were discovered for the first time in the interior of Minas Gerais, about 200 miles north of Rio de Janeiro. The *bandeirantes* (literally, flag-bearers), who had scoured Brazil and tramped over much of South America for almost 150 years in search of the precious metal, finally succeeded. The gold deposits were first found in the gravels of the Velhas River, northeast of present-day Belo Horizonte.

This discovery was important for at least two reasons. First, in the Spanish-Portuguese competition for colonies in the New World, Portugal had always lagged behind. The gold and diamond deposits obviously made Brazil more attractive to explorers, colonists, prospectors, and speculators— just about anyone, in fact. Second, the fact that the gold and diamonds of Brazil were located far from the coast (near Ouro Prêto and Diamantina, respectively) led to the first significant settlements in the interior. From that time onward, the currents of settlement have been away from the coast and into the center.

The next outstanding economic boom was based on coffee, for which the world market demands grew after 1850. The search for new lands in which to plant coffee attracted settlement southward and westward into the states of São Paulo, northern Paraná, and eventually Mato Grosso. Great fortunes were made in coffee, and much of the money gravitated toward the financial, banking, and credit center of São Paulo, where it was reinvested to build the industrial complex that has since evolved.

A rubber boom flourished in the Amazon Basin of northern Brazil between 1880 and 1912, when the world market price of natural rubber rose because of the growing demand for rubber tires for automobiles, trucks, buses, and bicycles. As the price of rubber soared, speculators rushed to the Amazon. Competition from plantation-grown rubber of the Malay Peninsula burst this speculative bubble, however, and the market price collapsed by 1913.

A contemporary boom since 1945 has focused upon the urban building industries. Apartments have been constructed at a spectacular rate with the increasing influx of people to the cities. Part of the urban building cycle has been stimulated by Brazil's inflation and the postwar devaluation of the cruzeiro. People sought to protect the purchasing power of their cruzeiros by investing in real estate or hard goods, like automobiles and refrigerators. Finally, in the 1960's, the raising of beef cattle expanded so rapidly that the result might almost be called an economic boom.

While these cyclical economic booms and busts were taking place, a large segment of the Brazilian population continued to exist on subsistence agriculture. The characteristic method of farming is a system of land rotation, or slash-and-burn farming. The farmer clears his plot of land by cutting down the trees and bushes and allowing them to dry throughout the dry season. He burns over the land just before the summer rains and plants his maize, beans, manioc, and sometimes rice and some fruits and other vegetables. The average subsistence farmer does not apply fertilizer, engage in any modern methods of contour plowing, or even use machinery.

The post-1955 period, then, has been one of general inflation in which the industrial sector has developed while the agricultural and rural sectors have languished. And it is the devaluation of the cruzeiro that has stimulated and paid for much of the new industrial development and even for the building of the new capital, Brasília. It remains to be seen whether Brazil will continue this tradition of economic cycles or whether different patterns of sustained growth will emerge.

Northeastern Brazil: The Culture Hearth of the Nation

Some writers have compared the role of Brazil's northeast to that of New England in the United States. Many of the influences that have shaped Brazil first appeared in the northeast. It was here that Brazilian society was forged and that many of the social institutions that have become an integral

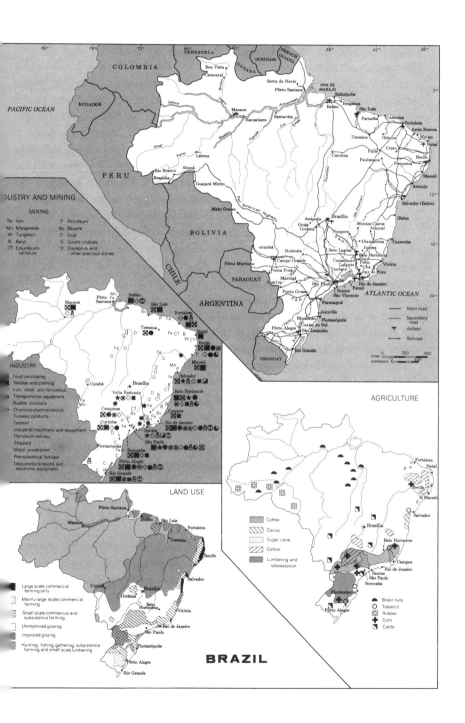

BRAZIL

part of present-day life originated. It was in the northeast that the first permanent settlements were established by the Portuguese in the early sixteenth century. The basic lineaments of the strongly patriarchal "sugar society," based upon slavery, were established here; the dominant modes and systems of land use were also outlined at that time and have changed little in the subsequent centuries. Like New England, Brazil's northeast is composed of small states that have had a disproportionately strong influence on the nation's history in terms of their contribution of statesmen and distinguished men of arts and letters. Unlike New England, however, the northeast of Brazil comprises a huge underdeveloped area—the largest in the entire Western Hemisphere—and it has the only desert in the country.

The brief dyewood boom in the northeast (1500–50) was followed by almost 200 years of prosperity derived from sugar-cane plantations, cultivated mostly by slaves brought from Africa (beginning in 1538). Because land was usually obtained in the form of royal grants, the planters' capital was tied up in slaves. Gilberto Freyre's primary work in social history, *The Masters and the Slaves*, documents the daily life and social significance of the sugar-cane plantation and the close interdependence of the African slaves and their Portuguese masters.

Sugar-cane plantations dominated the colonial period along the coast of northeastern Brazil; beef cattle dominated the interior. The *sertão* (or dry grassland) is not fertile enough for agriculture, but cattle can survive on it, and the vast wilderness of *caatinga* provided ample space to raise cattle. Between the humid coast and the dry *sertão* there has evolved a kind of symbiotic balance: sugar cane and other fruits and vegetables grown in the western *zona da mata* are exchanged for leather products, beef, and manioc from the *sertão*. Many of these items have been exchanged traditionally at intermediate cities in the transitional zone of the *agreste*. Each of the three zones has its own distinct ecology, its own economy, and, in many ways, its own society.

The interior of the northeast has suffered many severe droughts throughout its history. Even old Indian legends tell of them. These droughts occur when the expected fall rainy season does not arrive. Whether or not a particular place receives rain depends upon its orientation toward and exposure to three different air masses of precipitation: there are dependable winter rains brought by polar air masses moving northward in winter along the coast; there are dependable summer and fall rains to the west; and there are autumn rains to the northeast. These are tied to the strong low-pressure cell that moves into South America and spreads eastward to northeastern Brazil.

For many years it was believed that the great poverty of the northeast was due to the droughts. Government assistance was directed toward providing more water. In fact, the federal government set up the Federal Inspectorate of Works Against the Droughts (IFOCS) as early as 1909. Although this organization constructed dams and reservoirs, these efforts did not produce a true irrigation works on the vast scale needed. A lot of agriculture was practiced on the wet lands of the reservoirs as the water slowly evaporated. Before the water level rose, at the beginning of the next year's rainy season, the farmers would have time to harvest their subsistence crops. The successor to IFOCS, the National Department of Works Against the Droughts (DNOCS), continued to improve the water supply but also branched out into other related activities.

It was not until the 1950's, with the Bank of the Northeast and its successor, SUDENE, that attention was drawn to man-made causes of poverty, such as lack of forage due to overgrazing, lack of financing by banks, and lack of marketing systems. Most of the land in the northeast, of course, is owned by a small percentage of the population. The history of land use in the area is one of destructive exploitation of the soil and vegetation

Northeast Brazil is the least developed part of the nation. ANCAR (Associacão Nordestina de Crédito e Assistencia Rural) was formed to provide incentives and technical and financial assistance to small farmers in the area, many of whom live in conditions of extreme poverty. The farmer at the right is receiving advice from an agronomist on how to improve his yield of cactus (used for cattle feed).

Courtesy United Nations

resources with the result that some degree of desertification has occurred in all areas. In an area of sparse and unreliable rainfall, the vegetation and soil cover are highly susceptible to abuse by man through overcropping and overgrazing without the application of land conservation techniques. The droughts of the northeast, in effect, are as much man-made as they are natural.

A comparison of Philip von Luetzelburg's study of vegetation density in 1910–20 and recent air photography and field work by the present writer * reveals that in most areas vegetation is much less dense today than it was early in the century. The rate of deforestation has accelerated because of the cities' increasing demands for charcoal. The extension of paved highways has meant that charcoal buyers are able to reach new charcoal sources deep in the interior of the *caatinga*. Virtually no conservation techniques are practiced in the northeast; most farmers plant and cultivate the same way their grandfathers did. The only instance I know of contour plowing and strip farming on slopes is the Pesqueira tomato-paste factory farm. Although the legacy of the land is a poor one, man has chosen not to make the most efficient and productive use of the resources at his disposal. The farmers' habit of treating the dry areas as though they were humid, planting maize and beans year after year, frequently experiencing failure because of drought, must give way to a new approach to agriculture in this area.

In the 1960's SUDENE invested large amounts of money to bolster and stimulate the economy of the *sertão*. The attack was mainly on the institutional level, through existing government agencies, banks, and educational institutions, and not on the "hydraulic solutions" (i.e., dam building, water storage), which former government organizations such as IFOCS and DNOCS had emphasized. It is too early to evaluate the effectiveness of these efforts.

Land taxes in the interior of the northeast are extremely low: There are large areas where the average land tax is less than a dollar per square mile per year! This means that a farmer is not penalized for inefficiency. He can *afford* to use the land ineffectively or to leave it fallow. A discriminatory tax would tend to bring unused land into production, or at least promote its sale by placing a tax burden on unused land. In many instances, such legislation has been passed, but as yet there is no evidence of results.

* Kempton, E. Webb. *The Changing Face of Northeast Brazil.* To be published by Columbia University Press.

Eastern Brazil: Gold, Agriculture, and Industry

The tumultuous rush of people into the wild backlands of interior Minas Gerais in the 1690's can be explained in two words: gold fever. For over 150 years the *bandeirantes* from São Paulo had been seeking gold similar to that which the Spaniards had found in Mexico, Peru, Guatemala, and practically all the territories of Spanish America. The Brazilian version of El Dorado was finally achieved, at least in the gold-bearing gravels of the Velhas River, northeast of present-day Belo Horizonte.

The eastern half of what is now the state of Minas Gerais was composed of relatively infertile metamorphic schists and gneisses, with some fertile limestone enclaves to the west (Sete Lagoas) and north (Montes Claros). In the immediate area of the mines were some especially sterile soils, known as the "hunger schists." As is common in all gold rushes, the early years saw enthusiastic miners who had gold dust in their pockets but nothing to eat; astronomical prices were charged for basic food commodities, and many people went hungry. The high prices offered for food at the mining camps had the effect of diverting the food commodities northward from São Paulo and southward from Salvador. All supply currents became deflected toward the gold mining area.

In the early days, the pack trains from the south had to come to the gold fields by way of São Paulo; from Rio de Janeiro, a boat trip was necessary before the trail could be used from Parati or Taubaté, two major junctions along the gold route. Because so much gold was escaping the royal *quinto* (the one fifth gold tax) and because of contraband to and from the mines, the Portuguese colonial government decided to build a New Road (the *Caminho Novo*) linking the Minas Gerais mines directly with the sea. Rio de Janeiro, the port that served the Minas Gerais hinterland, began to thrive. Its location at the end of the gold trail assured its success as a viable urban center in the eighteenth century.

The discovery of diamonds in 1630 went almost unnoticed in the midst of all the gold fever, but the yield of diamonds and of gold continues, although at a reduced rate, even today. The more recent exploitation of iron ore at Itabira and the manganese mines at Conselheiro Lafaiete have further diversified the mining industry of this part of Brazil.

Although eastern Brazil attained an early reputation for its mineral resources and has continued to benefit from them, it is agriculture that has furnished the livelihood for the great majority of people there.

Some of the people who flocked to the mines were miners from other areas, but there were also some sugar planters from northeast Brazil who made their way southward with their slaves, who were subsequently put to work in the placer gold diggings. Because of the high price of food, some of the sugar planters had their older and less robust slaves cultivate food crops. Any surplus could easily be sold at a handsome price. As the mines petered out, more and more people turned to commercial and subsistence farming; by the nineteenth century, southern Minas Gerais had become a food supplier to the growing metropolis of Rio de Janeiro and other nearby cities. As the decades passed, the denser populations tended to cluster in areas of forested lands, with extensive cattle raising taking place mostly in northern Minas Gerais, in the areas with savanna and grasslands.

The two most dynamic cities in eastern Brazil are Rio de Janeiro and Belo Horizonte. Rio has for many years enjoyed a position as the primate city of the nation. Only as recently as 1962 was Rio surpassed by São Paulo in population. Belo Horizonte is interesting because it is the regional capital of a mining area and yet its hinterland, Minas Gerais, is extremely diversified. Minas Gerais is a state of vast mineral wealth and also of increasing agricultural production. Its western *triangulo* area and south-eastern *zona da mata* are among the breadbaskets of the country.

Belo Horizonte was a planned capital that was designed and inaugurated in 1897 to provide a central place from which a fast-developing area could expand and flourish. Ouro Prêto, the former capital, was too remote to serve as a state capital. In the brief period since Belo Horizonte's inauguration, it has grown from a small village of 14,000 inhabitants to a metropolis of over 1 million people. As recently as 1956, Belo's population was only half a million. Belo Horizonte is the center of the metallurgical industries and has also attracted other kinds of industry.

Much of eastern Brazil falls within the area called the "Great Region of Rio de Janeiro." Brazilian geographers have undertaken to delimit the hinterland of several Brazilian cities, and the prototype study was done for Rio. The distribution of patients coming to Rio's hospital, of newspapers published in Rio, and of branch offices of banks with headquarters in Rio have all been plotted and mapped.

The western boundary of the Great Region lies halfway between Rio and São Paulo and trends northward, cutting Minas Gerais in two and leaving the "triangle" within the economic orbit of São Paulo. The contestant to the north is the city of Salvador, in Bahia. Just as Rio has its "Great Region," the interior, smaller cities have their local hinterlands and trading areas. Because of this interdependence between the hinterland and the area of central influence in eastern Brazil, the growth of cities has progressed at a very rapid rate (5–6 per cent per year) since World War II Eastern Brazil is one of the most prosperous areas of the country, and it shares with the south the distinction of evolving highly productive and dynamic metropolises.

São Paulo is the cultural and economic heartland of Brazil today. The city of São Paulo, like Buenos Aires, experienced most of its incredible growth during the last hundred years. It remained a small provincial town until 1850, when the coffee boom caused it to prosper. Coffee was first grown in the Paraíba Valley, north of Rio de Janeiro. Cultivation spread westward and southward, eventually across the states of São Paulo and Paraná into new areas of virgin forests. A growing world market guaranteed the success of this pioneer area of southern Brazil.

A number of factors account for São Paulo's emergence as the leading and most powerful center of industry and manufacturing within all South America. First, São Paulo had a source of investment capital in the fortunes earned from coffee production since 1850. Secondly, although it was peripheral to "settled Brazil" in the colonial period, São Paulo is the center of Brazil's population in the twentieth century. By 1969 São Paulo state had grown to approximately 16 million inhabitants, of which over one third, or 6 million, lived in metropolitan São Paulo. Thirdly, São Paulo has always had an adequate, if not abundant, supply of hydroelectric power thanks to the far-sighted construction of the hydropower facilities, using the precipitous Serra do Mar escarpment. Fourthly, although the city is located on a plateau about 2,700 feet high, overlooking the Santos lowland, a cable railway and a modern superhighway have erased any barrier to transportation to its port city of Santos. The degree of concentration of industrial activity in São Paulo is suggested by the fact that 30 per cent of all Brazilian industry and 40 per cent of the industrial workers are located in São Paulo state. Most of the markets for São Paulo's industrial production are in eastern and southern Brazil, especially in and around the metropolises of São Paulo and Rio de Janeiro. São Paulo city has the highest per capita income and is the richest aggregate market in the entire country.

The Shaping of Southern Brazil: European Colonization

The dominant theme in southern Brazil for any geographer, historian, or social scientist is colonization. Southern Brazil resembles Argentina and

Uruguay in that it has become essentially European, although less so than these nations because of the strong indigenous Brazilian culture.

The area is distinguished by its solidly expanding frontier. Agriculture in southern Brazil is the most advanced in the country and follows the most modern practices in other parts of the world. Farmers use fertilizers and soil conditioners; they plow along the contour and use selected breeds of animals for higher yields. The south is an area of generally high elevations and therefore cool temperatures; it is also an area of fairly fertile soils, such as the weathered diabase lavas in the states of São Paulo, Paraná, and Santa Catarina.

Two main currents of penetration opened up the south. The *bandeirantes* pushed southward from São Paulo on the plateau. Another current of explorers pushed southward along the coast from São Vicente (near Santos). The first towns of Curitiba and Paranaguá started out as gold-mining centers. The early roads in the south were no more than cattle and pack trails over which not only beef cattle but also horses and mules were driven northward, especially during the colonial period, from their breeding grounds in the Rio Grande do Sul and Uruguay.

Rio Grande do Sul was the earliest nineteenth-century center of recent European colonization. The first group of colonists comprised some 20,000 Germans, who came to São Leopoldo in Rio Grande do Sul between 1824 and 1859. They grew rye and potatoes as they had done in Germany because the land in the south was similar in many ways to that of their homeland. The key to the economic success of São Leopoldo was its accessibility to the markets in Pôrto Alegre, the state capital.

To the north, Santa Catarina became a largely German community. In 1848 Dr. Herman Blumenau arranged to bring 6,000 Germans to the area between 1850 and 1870, and subsequently the Itajaí Valley has remained a strong center of German culture. The traveler in this area today hears much German spoken and is able to buy locally printed German language newspapers. The German tradition of frugally managed, highly productive small farms operates to supply food for the growing markets in the cities. Towns like Blumenau and Joinville are centers of manufacturing. The state of Paraná also received large numbers of Poles, Russians, and Ukrainians in the years from 1876 to 1879.

Large-scale immigration of Italians occurred between 1870 and 1890. These newcomers established themselves higher up on the plateau, around Caxias do Sul, where they set up small farms and vineyards. On the lowermost areas of the Jacuí Valley and its well-watered banks are rice-growing areas settled by Portuguese people. The *gaucho* tends his livestock in the extreme southern grasslands of Rio Grande do Sul. These four main areas are distinct not only in their physical characteristics but also in the culture that has evolved.

In the twentieth century, the spread of coffee has attracted pioneers from other areas of Brazil to the northern and western parts of Paraná, areas whose diabase soils are free from coffee-killing frosts. The latest chapter in the story of colonization is the opening up of western Paraná. This is the area to which surplus populations from Rio Grande do Sul have been moving, applying their advanced agricultural techniques to a new area. People from the north are also relocating there. It will be interesting to observe just how these two different outlooks and attitudes toward land and farming are resolved in the same area of western Paraná.

The Rôdovía do Café (the Coffee Highway), constructed in the mid-1960's in Paraná, represents Paraná's attempt to compete with São Paulo for economic dominance. The new highway makes it possible for northern Paraná coffee to pass through Curitiba and on to the coffee port of Paranaguá, cutting travel time from the northwestern parts of Paraná to Curitiba and Paranaguá by 40 to 50 per cent.

Centro Oeste: *The Awakened Hinterland*

This vast interior area of Brazil comprises one third of the area and houses only 3 per cent of the nation's population. Probably more than any other part of the country, this area is considered Brazil's *sertão*. The word *sertão*, meaning the dry interior of northeast Brazil, also has a generic connotation, meaning the mysterious backlands or unknown areas of the country. The basic problem is whether this area will remain a remote hinterland or become a dynamic new center of innovation for Brazil. In many ways, the *centro oeste* of Brazil is in the vanguard of developments, largely because of the new capital of Brasília, which was inauguarated in April, 1960. Formerly on the periphery of the zone of concentrated settlement, west central Brazil now lies directly in the path of the nation's future.

The early history of the west central zone is a story of small gold rushes which quickly lost momentum, leaving abandoned mining towns in their wake. The fertile soils eventually found in Minas Gerais, whose cultivation provided an alternative economic development when the gold mines became exhausted, had no equivalent in west central Brazil. This area has remained the domain of gold and diamond prospectors, as well as that of extensive cattle raisers who supply beef to the growing markets of São Paulo and southern Brazil.

In the late 1940's, a small but important area of fertile forest, the Mato Grosso de Goiás, was made accessible by a new road. The rich potential farmland attracted thousands of new settlers, and southern Goiás has since become a breadbasket, not only for Goiás and São Paulo, but for Minas Gerais and Rio de Janeiro as well.

The state of Goiás followed the example of Minas Gerais and moved its capital city from the sleepy colonial mining town of Goiás to Goiânia in 1934; this, of course, was followed by the move of the national capital from Rio to Brasília in 1960. The main purpose of the new city was to locate the national capital in the center of the country, to stimulate the interior development of Brazil, and to remove the capital from the local interests and domination of the coastal states.

This most unusual act of deliberately establishing a national capital entirely outside the zone of concentrated settlement has already brought rewards to Brazil. Brasília provides a market destination for the highways penetrating inland from the coastal state capitals. Already, roads are extending northward from Brasília to Belém and Fortaleza. Some food commodities are coming into Brasília from the areas to the west of the capital over a road that will soon link Brazil with Pucallpa, Peru.

There are still many problems to be resolved with Brasília. Some are political, some geographical, and some personal-psychological, for it is difficult to attract people to live in a remote area. Brazilians and most South Americans are city lovers if they are not city dwellers: They like the bustle of the city life. Brasília, with its broad avenues and great open spaces, lacks congestion and the sense of *movimento*. Brasília is not like traditional Brazilian cities where one gets jostled on the streets by noisy, good-natured crowds. The absence of human contact is one reason many people dislike the new capital as a place to live, despite its architectural beauty and careful planning. Nevertheless, the city remains a source of national pride for Brazilians.

The agricultural picture of the west central region holds little promise if traditional Brazilian farming techniques are continued. The future of the area depends to a large extent on the discovery and application of effective techniques of making the acid soil of the savanna suitable for agriculture.

The Changing Face of the Amazon North

The north of Brazil contains 4 per cent of the nation's population on almost 42 per cent of the land. It comprises the two states of Amazonas and Pará and the four territories of Roraima, Guaporé, Amapá, and Rio Branco.

There are many myths about the Amazon's supposedly unbearable climate and boundless resources, but they are mostly inaccurate. The Amazon north is neither so rich nor so poor as legend implies. Most of the land is flat and is never flooded. Although it is an area of sustained high temperatures, Manaus having a range between 69° F. and 98° F., it is the sustained high relative humidities of around 78 per cent that make life uncomfortable. Rainfall averages 80 inches per year over much of the area, but occurs mainly from November to June. Although most of the area is covered by tropical forest or *selva*, there are considerable areas of savanna and grasslands. These open spaces, observable from airplanes, appear to be the result of soil rather than climate differences.

Belém was founded as early as 1616, and its easy access to the Amazon River allowed the early Portuguese explorers to probe the interior reaches of the Amazon Basin. Portugal set up a few dyewood-gathering stations and forts in order to secure the territory from other competing powers, but for the most part, the Amazon north was ignored in favor of Portugal's East Indies ventures. It has always been a low-priority area in Brazil, although within the last decade efforts have been made through the Superintendency for the Economic Valorization of the Amazon (SPVEA) to subsidize development of the area.

The north had a short-lived rubber boom, from 1890 to 1913, which left such reminders of the precariousness of the area's economy as the run-down palatial residences of former rubber barons. Charles Goodyear's discovery of the vulcanization process in 1839 made rubber much more useful and valuable. In 1827 Belém exported some 70,000 pounds of crude rubber; in 1853, it shipped out 5.2 million pounds. The market suddenly dropped when more efficiently produced rubber from the Malay Peninsula successfully competed with Brazilian rubber. It was believed that if Brazil could grow rubber on plantations, as in Malaya, it would regain a large share of the world's rubber markets. The Ford plantation attempts in Fordlandia and Belterra, near Santarém, failed for a number of reasons, ranging from remoteness to plant diseases to unavailability of labor.

In the 1960's the Amazon regained some economic strength and a new basis of economic development with the infusion of government and private-investment capital through tax incentives. The Amazon north became an area of priority within the national goals of regional development. The Belém-Brasília Highway, opened in 1962, provided the first overland link between that area and the core area of southeastern Brazil. Another road is planned to extend northward from Cuiabá to Santarém. These roads, which have a north–south trajectory, are significant not only because they provide overland communication with the Amazon north but also because the contact comes from a new direction. The general highway plan for Brazil aims to incorporate the Amazon north and other remote areas into the effective national territory. The Amazon River is also part of the highway network through a series of ferries and other transfers.

The modern Amazon includes the manganese mines at the Serra do Navio in Amapá, where a part of the profits are channeled to the Regional Institute for the Development of Amapá (IRDA), which is trying to diversify the economy of that area. A plywood factory has already been established, and research is going on to discover what kinds of commercial crops can be successfully produced in Amapá. The conversion of Manaus to a free port has had a striking impact, although it is too soon to analyze the long-term results of such an action.

Cities, Backlands, and the Future

As one looks over the enormous area of Brazil and considers its long history, the sharp discontinuities in both are noticeable. There is a basic cleavage today between traditional and modern Brazil, and between urban and rural Brazil.

Traditional Brazil is characterized by low productivity, extensive cattle raising, and subsistence agriculture—the growing of crops such as manioc, which has little nutrient value and which requires large expenditures of energy to produce. Modern Brazil is reflected in the efficiently grown rice of São Paulo or Rio Grande do Sul and in the modern manganese mines of Amapá. The traditional is reflected in the low-productivity city worker, whether he is a public functionary in a nonessential government branch in Rio or a street vendor in Fortaleza. The new Brazil is distinguished by the increasing number of consumer products available as well as by the application of rational analysis to ordinary problems. The modern approach is to increase productivity: of land, labor, and industry. Traditional

A supermarket in Campinas, not far from São Paulo. Various types of rice are being offered for sale. Supermarkets are still a rarity in South America, but their numbers will probably increase as more factories are established with the success of the drive to industrialize and produce more consumer goods locally.

Brazil is isolated and feudal, its social, economic, and political life dominated by a small élite group. Masses of poorer people are without resources or the means for rising above their positions. The new Brazil is undergoing a profound revolution; improving education and valorizing land by applications of modern technology will result in a wider distribution and greater democratization of economic gain and, it is hoped, greater political democratization as well.

The question persists whether the conditions of living for the average Brazilian or for the poorest 25 per cent of the people are really improving. It is ironic that during 1962–64, under the João Goulart government, which loudly preached agrarian reform, there were unprecedented inflation, food shortages, unemployment, and economic decline. What the strong military governments have done since 1964 is provide institutional, economic, and political stability, but without political participation by the public. Inflation dropped from over 80 per cent in 1963 to around 20 per cent per year in 1971. The economy is receiving investments from abroad and from local capital owing to tax incentives. It is probably true that there are more jobs in Brazil today, but the demand is for skilled labor, not for unskilled labor, of which the northeast has a surplus. The poorest 25 per cent of the population is probably not much better off, but some of the benefits of the general growth process may eventually reach this socio-economic group.

The emphasis has been on raising productivity in agriculture through mechanization, the spread of electricity and transportation networks, education, and the like, rather than by the division and redistribution of large estates to workers. In general, the laws that have been passed have been designed to placate the poorest people, but without really changing the authoritarian system or limiting the power of the élite in decision-making. Also, the passage of a law does not necessarily mean that it will be fully executed. Given the present attitudes of the politically powerful groups, it seems unlikely that there will be significant changes in agrarian policies, even if there is a change in government leadership. Income and land taxes, however, are being collected much more thoroughly than ever before, and these tax revenues can enable the state and national governments to undertake vast programs to improve the nation's infrastructure. Important programs that will help to shape the future include (1) the physical integration of the entire country by a network of all-weather roads, such as the Belém-Brasília and the new Trans-Amazon Highways; (2) the building of a large merchant marine fleet to ship Brazil's burgeoning industrial production to foreign markets; (3) the exploration and development of large new mineral deposits (iron in Pará state, manganese in Amapá) and oil exploration in the interior; (4) the belated but massive increase of investment for the rationalization of agriculture, including dissemination of hybrid seeds; (5) the rationalization and expansion of Brazil's beef industry, traditionally an inefficient and low-quality industry; and (6) campaigns to raise literacy and extend education to more people. All these developments reflect a strong confidence in the nation's future—a confidence rare in this troubled continent.

Suggested Readings

ADAMS, DALE W. "What Can Under-Developed Countries Expect from Foreign Aid to Agriculture? Case Study: Brazil, 1950–1970." *Inter-American Economic Affairs*, XXV, no. 1 (summer, 1971), pp. 47–63. Argues that foreign assistance to Brazilian agriculture will decrease over the next ten years, and that viable programs to alleviate rural poverty in the northeast should be developed by the Brazilian government before it seeks foreign aid.

American University. *Area Handbook for Brazil.* Washington, D.C.: U.S. Government Printing Office, 1971. A comprehensive analysis of social, economic, and political aspects of the nation.

FREYRE, GILBERTO. *The Masters and the Slaves: A Study in the Development of Brazilian Civilization.* Translated by S. Putnam. New York: Knopf, 1946; abridged edition, 1964. A pioneering study of the development of a dual society in Brazil. As valuable today as when it was first published.

GARCIA-ZAMOR, JEAN-CLAUDE. "Social Mobility of Negroes in Brazil." *Journal of Inter-American Studies and World Affairs,* XII, no. 2 (April, 1970), pp. 242–54. The number of Negroes in Brazil has diminished tremendously since the 1870's. White Brazilians claim that this is due to miscegenation; the author feels that the gradual mixing of the races is not true miscegenation, but rather, from the point of view of the Negro, a means of moving upward, socially.

HUMMERSTONE, ROBERT G. "Putting a Road through Brazil's 'Green Hell.' " *The New York Times Magazine* (March 5, 1972). An account of the building of the Trans-Amazon Highway, which eventually will connect the Atlantic ports of Recife and João Pessoa in the east with the Pacific coast in Peru. The highway will bring profound changes to the huge Amazon Basin.

NICHOLLS, WILLIAM H. "The Brazilian Food Supply: Problems and Prospects." *Economic Development and Cultural Change,* XIX no. 3 (April, 1971), pp. 378–90. Analyzes factors that have contributed to the lag in agricultural productivity, including the long neglect of the rural infrastructure.

POPPINO, ROLLIE E. "Brazil's Third Government of the Revolution." *Current History,* LX, no. 354 (February, 1971), pp. 102–7, 115. An analysis of Brazil's recent political history; suggests that the nation's achievement of status as a world power depends on a nonviolent transition to constitutional government, and the development of hoped-for national capability in science and technology.

ROSENBAUM, H. JON. "Brazil's Military Regime." *Current History,* LVIII, no. 342 (February, 1970), pp. 73–78, 115–16. A study of Brazil's recent political history, focusing on the possibility of the military government's continuing to hold power, even if it does not achieve popular support.

———, and WILLIAM G. TYLER, eds. *Contemporary Brazil: Issues in Eco-*

nomic and Political Development. New York: Praeger, 1972. A collection
of articles by experts on Brazil, discussing tax reform, foreign trade policy, agrarian reform, urbanization, and the changing political role of the
Catholic Church.

See also Suggested Readings for Part I, pp. 61–63.

14 BOLIVIA

Robert J. Tata

*Social and Population Factors • A Difficult Environment •
The Economy • Transportation and Trade • focus on the Bolivian
Revolution and Its Aftermath*

A social revolution is under way in Bolivia, but it is being sorely tested
by difficult cultural and environmental problems. In 1952, when the revolution began, Bolivia was the second poorest country in South America
and had almost all the basic disadvantages of less-developed nations.
The major features of the Spanish feudal agrarian and mineral-exploitation
system, established in Bolivia in 1532, persisted until 1952. The Spaniards
found dense concentrations of Indians practicing a productive sedentary
agricultural economy around Lake Titicaca and a few favored valleys in
the Cordillera Oriental of the Andes. They divided up the lands and
Indians into large *encomiendas* (a royal grant to an individual settler),
thus giving the Spanish officers the right to Indian labor and the obligation
to oversee the Indians' welfare, but reserving land ownership to the crown.
Silver was discovered in the fabulous Potosí lode in 1545. It was exploited
by use of the *mita* (a system of forced Indian labor) and exported to
Europe.

Independence in 1825, due chiefly to the armies of Antonio José de
Sucre and Simon Bolívar, freed the Bolivian élite from Spanish control
and formalized their economic, political, and social dominance. But
the only perceivable effect on the lives of the Indians, who comprised
70 per cent of the population, was to eliminate what little protection the
Crown had offered them. By 1950, 92 per cent of the farm land was

in holdings averaging 2,470 acres each, and this was owned by 6 per cent of the landowners. Material poverty, social and political disenfranchisement, and hopelessness were the sad facts of life for the great majority of Bolivians. Compounding these social problems was an ambivalent physical environment, on the one hand offering enormous potential sources of wealth, and on the other posing obstacles that hindered the realization of this wealth. In 1952 the social system made a revolutionary turnabout; the cultural and physical factors, however, remained about the same as before. Bolivia's current problems stem from its attempt to reconcile the aspirations of the former with the realities of the latter.

Social and Population Factors

Human settlement in the Bolivian highlands is believed to be ancient. A basic subsistence food, the potato, was first domesticated here more than 2,000 years ago. The elaborate ruins of Tiahuanacu on Lake Titicaca's south shore indicate that an advanced, organized, and populous society existed around the lake from about A.D. 600 to 900. In about A.D. 1440, the Incas conquered the highland Indians from their Peruvian bases and established their autocratic, paternalistic, welfare-state type of social organization. One Inca policy was to set up colonies of loyal supporters on the margins of the empire while keeping recently conquered peoples near the administrative centers, where they could be watched. This policy probably explains the present distribution of Aymara Indians (descendants of the Tiahuanacu culture) around lakes Titicaca and Poopó and the Quechuas farther south in the Cochabamba area and other Valles basins. Agriculture and communal landholding were the important components of the economic system that the Spaniards took over about 1532.

The Spaniards effected significant changes in Bolivian society. One major change was the reorientation of the national economy to a mineral-exploitation and export-based system. In order to permit this system to function, transportation routes were built to the Pacific coast and cities. All of today's large cities, Sucre, Potosí, La Paz, Santa Cruz, Cochabamba, Tarija, and Oruro, had been founded in that order by 1610. New crops and animals produced significant changes in agriculture. Barley, wheat, rice, sugar cane, coffee, citrus and other fruits, cattle, sheep, horses, hogs, and poultry were all introduced by the Spaniards, but the native potato, *quinoa* (a grain), maize, and llamas remained most important in the predominant Indian subsistence agricultural system.

Under the leadership of the International Labor Organization (ILO), U.N. agencies have joined with the governments of Bolivia, Peru, and Ecuador in the so-called Andean Indian Project. Some 6 million Indians will eventually benefit from efforts to integrate them into the life of their nations. Here altiplano Indians are being taught how to rid their sheep of internal parasites.

Another drastic change was the great reduction in total Indian population. No one knows for certain how many people existed in pre-Columbian Bolivia, but estimates go as high as 10 million. This figure was probably reduced by 80 per cent in the early years of the Spanish era. Roman Catholicism blended easily with the native religions, but the Spanish language was adopted by only a small portion of the Indians, and Indian cultural systems persisted as Indian society became introverted in reaction to the force and intensity of Spanish domination. Thus, a dual society was born. The dominant whites enjoyed political, economic, and social mastery from their urban centers, while the Indian majority lacked education, economic security, a political voice, and virtually any stake in the national system. People of mixed blood, called *cholos* in Bolivia, occupied a middle position in the society, usually living in the cities and fulfilling the roles of artisan, small-scale businessman, or laborer. The *cholo* had some possibility for upward social mobility, but he was generally looked down upon by both white and Indian. These basic societal patterns persisted up to the revolution of 1952.

Bolivia's present population approaches 5 million. While ethnic lines are not distinct, it is estimated that at least 50 per cent is Indian, 35 per cent *cholo*, and 15 per cent white. Even within these groups there are differences. The Indian element is composed of one million Quechua, somewhat fewer Aymara, and a scattering of primitive groups in the eastern sections of the country. The Quechua seem more amenable to assimilation in the modern nation, whereas the Aymara have been described as taciturn, hostile, morose, and withdrawn. One expert states that, until recently, the Indians never considered themselves part of the national state. In addition to the Spanish-speaking whites, there are small numbers of Brazilians, Mennonites, Semites, Japanese, and Okinawans, most of whom live in colonies in the Oriente.

About 65 per cent of the population is considered rural. Relatively reliable estimates indicate that 67 per cent of the people are illiterate, and that only one child in ten attends school. Only 3.5 per cent of the gross national product is spent on education. The age structure of the population is also typical of a less-developed economy. Some 49 per cent of the population is nineteen years old or younger, 38 per cent is between twenty and forty-nine years old, and only 13 per cent is fifty years old or older. The population is growing at a high rate, about 2.4 per cent annually. Life expectancy is only fifty years, and considerably less for miners. With only one physician per 2,680 people, infant mortality is about 108 per 1,000 live births, and general health standards are low.

Like most South American countries, Bolivia is not densely populated, at least by Asian standards. The national average is eleven people per square mile; the most densely populated rural areas are around Lake Titicaca–La Paz, where there are sixty per square mile, and around Cochabamba, where the figure reaches eighty-four per square mile. (The average for the United States is about fifty-seven). The largest cities and their populations are: La Paz (679,000), Cochabamba (149,900), Santa Cruz (124,900), Oruro (119,700), Potosí (96,800), Sucre (84,900), Tarija (35,700), and Trinidad (22,800). The size of Trinidad and Santa Cruz is indicative of recent movement toward the Oriente.

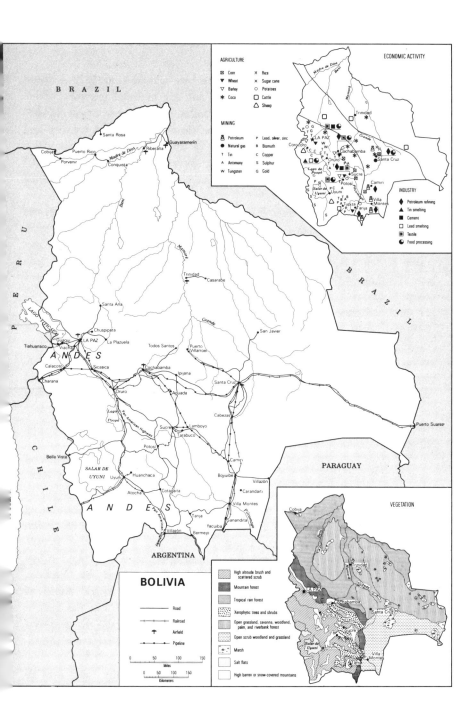

A Difficult Environment

Unfortunately for Bolivia, independence was achieved in 1825 without clearly defined international boundaries, and the national territory, which once encompassed some 850,000 square miles, is now only about 424,000 square miles. Much of this land was lost through ill-advised treaties and wars with neighbors, especially the War of the Pacific, 1879–82, in which Bolivia lost its Pacific littoral to Chile, thereby becoming a landlocked nation. Considering an outlet to the sea to be a national necessity, Bolivia still claims this territory.

The landscape varies from high, rugged mountains that exceed 21,000 feet to almost flat plains that lie only about 400 feet above sea level. Some 250 miles north of the Bolivian border, the Andes split into two more or less parallel chains of high peaks, which eventually merge into one chain again toward the southwest, where Chile, Bolivia, and Argentina come together. In the west the high, arid, barren, and steep crests of the Cordillera Occidental form the Chilean boundary south of 20° S. Volcanic peaks, rough lava flows, and salt flats are typical of this generally inhospitable area. East of the Cordillera Occidental lie the 38,000 square miles of Bolivian altiplano. The altiplano is a high intermontane plain, formed by water- and ice-laid sediments and volcanic ash, which filled an ancient chasm between the two main Andean chains. It has an elevation of about 12,500 feet just south of Lake Titicaca and tilts down slightly to Lake Poopó at 12,119 feet, then rises again south of Poopó, reaching 15,000 feet at the latitude of Tarija.

The Cordillera Oriental, east of the altiplano, is again very high, and it is deeply dissected on its eastern flanks. Known as the Cordillera Real, from the Peruvian border to the latitude of Oruro, this chain contains many snow-clad peaks that tower over 20,000 feet. The northeast-facing slopes of the Cordillera Real are known as the Yungas. Within fifty miles of the 21,000-foot crests of the Cordillera Real, the Yungas drop steeply in narrow, V-shaped valleys and sharp, elongated, heavily forested ridges to elevations of only 2,000 feet. Numerous tributaries of the Amazon, which rise in the area, have produced this dramatic relief. South of the Yungas, the crests of the Andes reach only 16,000 feet, but the broken terrain and the sharp local relief represent a severe obstacle to west–east transportation. The valleys of Cochabamba, Sucre, and Tarija are prominent places in this zone.

The eastern plains, comprising about two thirds of the land area of

Bolivia, range from tropical rain forests *(selva)* in the extreme north to tropical savanna in the extreme south. In contrast to the very difficult terrain elsewhere, the land drops only 400 feet in elevation in the 250 miles from the foot of the mountains in the north to the Brazilian border.

With this diversity of terrain all within tropical latitudes, a variety of climates is to be expected. The major climatic controls are latitude, altitude, surface configuration, and air-mass sources. Virtually all the precipitation is derived from the Atlantic. The altiplano is arid and windswept, with great temperature changes from day to night. Aridity increases from north to southwest. Annual precipitation is about 22 inches at La Paz and about 5 inches at Uyuni; no altiplano station receives as much as 28 inches. Heavy showers are experienced from November to February, while the rest of the year is relatively dry. Thunder storms and hail are common during the rainy period. The annual mean daily maximum temperature at La Paz is 64°F., and the minimum is 39°; Tarija records a high of 82° and a low of 54°. Nights are cold even in summer, and temperatures may fall to 12° in winter. (A classic story of cultural misunderstanding relates to the high Andean climates. In proselytizing the Catholic faith, Spanish missionaries told the Indians that the damned on earth are punished for eternity in a place of perpetual fires. Used to the numbing cold of their habitat, the Indians thought that such a place must obviously be paradise.) In the lowlands, temperatures range from an annual average maximum of 88° to a minimum of 68° to 61°; temperature ranges increase from about 7° in the north to 20° in the south. But rainfall differences are the main determinators of the lowland climates. Rainfall varies from about 62 inches in the north to 38 in the south, while one station near the northeast Brazilian border records more than 200. All lowland stations also record a distinct dry season from May through September (winter). The stations in the southern Oriente not only record less total rainfall, but their dry season also lasts two months longer. This factor influences soil types, vegetative cover, and drainage characteristics.

Bolivia's three basic drainage systems include the interior drainage of the western altiplano, the vast Amazon system, which drains the north-eastern two thirds of the country, and the La Plata system, which drains a portion of the southeast highlands and the far eastern lowlands. The western altiplano is the largest area of interior drainage in South America. Ichú grass and low woody shrubs *(yareta* and *tola)* are the dominant vegetative cover in this barren landscape, except for the immediate locales of salt flats, which are altogether devoid of vegetation. This terrain has often been compared to a moonscape. Furthermore, soils in the western altiplano are mostly thin and stony, with the exception of some deeper and more fertile soils around the margins of Lake Titicaca and east of Lake Poopó. Altiplano soils on level land have a great water-absorption capacity, whereas those on slopes are susceptible to erosion and landslides.

Other environmental hazards in the east stem from the many broad, deep, and swift tributaries of the Amazon, which overflow during the rainy season, flooding many square miles with up to six feet of water. The extreme northeast plains are covered by true *selva,* while the middle plains have a semideciduous forest. Large areas of grassland are interspersed among the forested zones, the most extensive grassland being located between the Beni and Mamoré rivers. The Yungas are covered by a lush tropical *montane* forest. *Galeria* forests along the water courses are another vegetation feature of the region. Local residents have a rule of thumb that soils under forests are generally good for cultivation while those under grasslands are not. This probably has some validity because the major difference between forest or grass cover seems to be the length of the dry season.

Tributaries of the Pilcomayo River drain a small portion of the southeast altiplano and the Bolivian Chaco, and tributaries of the Paraguay River drain the easternmost section of the Oriente. Many streams in these areas are nearly dry in the six months when little rain falls, and they too overflow in the rainy periods. In the vicinity of Sucre, the La Plata drainage system comes within fifty miles of the Amazon drainage system. Scrub forests, extensive swampy areas, and savanna grasslands are found in this region. The only soils effectively utilized are those in the highland valleys.

The Economy

Agriculture employs some 60 per cent of the 1.9 million members of the labor force, and most of these are subsistence farmers, isolated physically and economically from modern national life. Agriculture on the high altiplano is an unrewarding occupation: potatoes, *quinoa,* barley, and *habas* (broad beans) are the major crops, and yields are limited by poor soils, aridity, hail, frost, disease, lack of scientific techniques, and until recently a feudal economic organization. *Chuño,* a preparation of mashed or dehydrated potatoes, is the most common peasant food.

The margins of Lake Titicaca are more favorable for agriculture, and their proximity to La Paz encourages the production of wheat, alfalfa, vegetables, and meat for the urban market. The Yungas and Valles are lower and warmer, and the former gets more rainfall than the altiplano. Maize, wheat, cows, truck crops, and temperate and subtropical fruits are raised in the Valles, whereas the terraced slopes in the Yungas are planted in coffee, cacao, coca, citrus, bananas, rice, sugar cane, and cassava. Soil erosion and high transportation costs limit commercial development here. Most crops grown in Bolivia can be grown in the Oriente, subject to the serious physical limitations mentioned above, and cattle are raised there. The principal economic deterrents to commercial operations in the Oriente are a lack of refrigeration for perishable tropical products and prohibitive transportation costs to highland markets.

Historically, Bolivia's soil, water, and forest resources have been neglected because mineral resources are so rich and abundant. Copper, tin, gold, and silver were mined long before the Spaniards arrived. Most of the mineral wealth is found in and around the margins of the altiplano. Some 300 minerals are known to exist in Bolivia, but only a few are intensively used. Copper, sulphur, and salts abound in the Cordillera Occidental and on the altiplano proper. Tin, silver, lead, zinc, bismuth, and antimony are often found together in the Cordillera Real and in the southern extension of the Cordillera Oriental. Gold occurs in placer deposits in the Yungas north of La Paz. More than 40 billion tons of 50 per cent iron ore are located in the Oriente southwest of Corumbá, Brazil.

The most important mineral of the Oriente is petroleum. The potential petroleum zone forms a wide arc at the eastern base of the Cordillera Oriental from the Peruvian border all the way to the Argentine and Paraguay borders. The present zones of exploitation lie northwest of Santa Cruz at Caranda, south of Santa Cruz at Camiri (the largest field), and south of Camiri to the Argentine border at Sanandita, Yacuiba, and Bermejo.

Mining, including petroleum, contributes only about 13 per cent of the gross domestic product but about 95 per cent of the value of all exports. Tin is still the leading income earner after several years of drastically reduced production in the early 1960's. Tin produced nearly 50 per cent of export earnings in 1969 while petroleum earnings rose sharply to second place with 14 per cent of the total. Other minerals, in order of export importance, are silver, tungsten, copper, antimony, and zinc and lead, together accounting for 24 per cent of exports. Petroleum production increased by 250 per cent from 1966 to 1967 but has remained static since then. Bolivia hopes that exports of petroleum and natural gas to Argentina will more than make up for the decreasing trend in metallic minerals.

Manufacturing is oriented toward local markets. Most of the 1,689 firms are small, with fewer than ten employees. Outstanding industries are oil refining, food processing, beverages, tobacco, textiles and clothing, leather, wood and furniture, paper, rubber, chemicals, cement and related products, and metallurgy. Most of the industry is located in the La Paz area, and almost all manufacturing types are represented there. Cochabamba, which has about 16 per cent of the nation's industry, specializes in leather, wood

Bolivian tin miners, earning less than $1 per day, live in constant fear of rockslides, landslides caused by dynamiting, and gas emissions. To counteract these fears, they have formed a sort of cult, seeking to enlist the devil as an ally. The miners, who have given the devil the nickname *Tio* (uncle), believe that he controls the rich veins of ore, revealing them only to those who make ceremonial offerings of cocoa, alcohol, and cigarettes. Shown here at a mine in Oruro, a 13,800-foot-high mining center in the Cordillera Real, is the president of the Oruro Devil Fraternity in the traditional mask. In the background is the miners' monument. Tin is Bolivia's most important mineral; in most years it accounts for over 50 per cent of export earnings.

Courtesy United Nations

and furniture, and brewing, and this is the location of the largest petroleum refinery. Oruro and Santa Cruz each have about 10 per cent of the industrial plant. There is almost no heavy industry. A small domestic market, a shortage of capital, excessive transportation costs, and extensive smuggling of foreign goods into Bolivia all limit the prospects for further expansion of manufacturing.

A shortage of energy is another serious hindrance. Bolivia has the lowest per capita energy consumption on the continent, with only 250,600 kilowatts of installed capacity; electric light and heat are rare in the rural areas, although there are an estimated 2.7 million kilowatts of electrical potential in the rivers which flow from the highlands to the Oriente. Some 83 per cent of installed electrical capacity is derived from hydro-electric works and the remainder from thermal installations. There are no workable coal deposits, but new discoveries of natural gas and petroleum could increase the generation of thermal electric power.

Transportation and Trade

Of the many problems Bolivia faces, the lack of adequate transportation is perhaps the most serious. Harold Osborne, writing in the early 1950's, described the roads as "uniformly bad, usually incredibly bad, and most often dangerous." * Some progress has been made since then, but even now less than 450 miles of roads are paved; the best road in the country, a two-lane asphalted road, runs 311 miles from Cochabamba to Santa Cruz. Of the 12,000 miles of roads reported by the government, most are unsurfaced, poorly constructed, and subject to washouts and landslides during the rainy season. Roads were originally constructed to link the altiplano mining centers and to provide egress from Bolivia to the Pacific ports, and most internal routes are still concentrated on these highlands. The northern half of the Oriente plains has virtually no overland transportation system. There are important plans for roads, aimed at further penetration of the Yungas from La Paz and Cochabamba and extension of the colonization area northeast and northwest of Santa Cruz. The difficult road from La Paz to Caranavi in the Yungas has spawned considerable spontaneous colonization to exploit the agricultural potential of the area, which had not been done previously because of the lack of people

* Harold Osborne. *Bolivia: A Land Divided*. London: Royal Institute of International Affairs, 1954, p. 49.

and transportation. The only international connections by road are provided by the Pan American Highway, which joins the altiplano roads to Puno in Peru and San Salvador de Jujuy in Argentina.

The railroad network is likewise inadequate, consisting of two unconnected systems, one in the east and one on the altiplano. Centered on Santa Cruz, the eastern system has a line that stretches eastward to Corumbá in Brazil and thence to the Atlantic port of Santos, also in Brazil. A southern branch goes from Santa Cruz to Yacuiba and then extends to San Salvador de Jujuy in Argentina, with connections to Buenos Aires. The altiplano system connects all the important cities in the highlands except Tarija and offers four external connections. The southern prong leaves Bolivia at Villazón and again connects with Jujuy and Buenos Aires. A southwestern line goes from Uyuni through Oyahue (Ollagüe) to the port of Antofagasta in Chile. The third foreign connector goes from La Paz through Charaña to Arica, Chile. The Arica line, which has twenty miles of rack rail because of steep terrain, is the principal route of foreign commerce. The fourth line connects La Paz to the Lake Titicaca port of Guaqui. Goods are unloaded at Guaqui, shipped by lake steamer to Puno, Peru and then loaded on Peruvian trains for the final haul to the Pacific ports of Mollendo and Matarani. These two ports, plus Arica, Antofagasta, and Santos, are all free ports for Bolivian goods. Locomotives are steam-powered, and the condition of the rolling stock ranges from adequate to inferior. Fifteen new diesel locomotives and new rolling stock have, however, been ordered from Japan, and this will improve the operations of both rail systems. Petroleum pipelines connect all the eastern fields with the highland centers of Sucre, Cochabamba, Oruro, La Paz, and, by connector, from Sicasica to Arica.

The transportation map is somewhat deceptive because the connections among the major population centers suggest that the transportation system is adequate. The meager cost data available, however, suggest otherwise. Argentine meat is often cheaper in La Paz than meat from nearby Beni in the lowlands. Meat and even timber are flown to the highlands from Beni because good surface travel does not exist. The price of a bottle of beer produced in La Paz increases sixfold by the time it arrives in the hands of the Beni consumer. And at one time, the transportation costs from Santa Cruz to La Paz were ten times greater than the transportation costs from Arica to La Paz. It has been estimated that 28 per cent of the price of Bolivian tin on the world market can be attributed to transportation costs. Economic modernization requires good, cheap, and dependable surface transportation.

Bolivia's foreign trade has been dominated by the United States and Great Britain. Both of these together have taken about 80 per cent of all of Bolivia's exports over the past decade. Britain now purchases 45 per cent of the exports, principally minerals, and refines them in its technologically advanced industrial plants. Recent trends indicate growing exports to Japan and the Netherlands and a large increase in exports to the Latin American Free Trade Association countries. The United States supplies Bolivia with about 42 per cent of its imports. West Germany, the LAFTA nations, and Japan contribute a major portion of the imports, which include machinery, vehicles, iron and steel, and wheat flour. Bolivia's trade pattern is typical of a less developed economy. Membership in the Andean Common Market may, however, bring some changes, since both Bolivia and Ecuador, the two poorest nations in ANCOM, will receive special trade and tariff considerations (see pages 47–60).

focus *on the Bolivian Revolution and Its Aftermath*

Chaotic is the only accurate adjective to describe Bolivia's political history. Since independence in 1825, it has averaged more than one government per year. Bolivia is officially a constitutional republic, with a popularly elected president who serves for four years, a two-house legislature, and a separate judicial system. But most elected governments have not served a full term, and military intervention has been the rule rather than the exception.

Before 1952, literacy and property-ownership requirements for full rights of citizenship effectively excluded the great majority of the population from political participation. Minority rule and the traditional Spanish allegiance to a strong man *(personalismo)* rather than to a legal system produced extreme political instability. A strong personality readily found armed support and thus the path to the presidency. Ineffectiveness in foreign relations and the consequent loss of much of Bolivia's national territory resulted from political weakness. The many military coups, however, should not be called "revolutions," for they most often meant virtually no change in the élitist system, but merely in the top personnel.

Mexico, Cuba, and Bolivia are the only Latin American countries to have experienced something like a true revolution. Some say that the seeds of the Bolivian revolution were formed in the disillusionment with the government aroused by the humiliating defeat in the Chaco War of 1932–35. Whatever the cause, agitation for change began in earnest on

August 25, 1941, when the National Revolutionary Movement (MNR) was formed. The new political party claimed to be a patriotic movement with a socialist orientation aimed at affirming and defending the Bolivian nation. While the party tried for a power base among the poor majority, organizationally it depended upon an élitist cadre to effect "changes from above." Also in the 1940's, radical students formed the Party of the Left Revolutionaries (PIR), which sought power and "change from below." The miners became a potent political force at this time. Having grown in numbers from 30,000 to 50,000 during World War II, they began to flex some muscle in a union movement under the leadership of Juan Lechín. The three large mining corporations tried violent union busting but accomplished nothing more than to unite the miners into a disciplined and determined organization.

Much unrest in the country preceded the presidential election of 1951. With less than 7 per cent of the population eligible to vote (less than 4 per cent actually voted), the MNR candidate, Víctor Paz Estenssoro, won the most votes. He failed to achieve the required majority, however, and the power structure would not allow his government to take office. When a general uprising took place in 1952, it was Juan Lechín and the armed miners who turned the tide, defeating the regular military and placing Paz in power.

Paz's program, aimed at restructuring Bolivian society, consisted of the following five principal points: (1) universal suffrage, accomplished by removing the literacy and property-ownership restrictions for voting; (2) nationalization of the three large mining companies, carried out October 31, 1952; (3) dissolution of the army and establishment of a popular militia, accomplished by arming the miners and small farmers; (4) agrarian reform by confiscation of *latifundios*, accomplished by law on August 2, 1953; and (5) establishment of the principle of worker participation in the management of national enterprises, enforced by the formation of twenty-eight to thirty unions, ranging from teachers' to small farmers' organizations.

Paz's program succeeded in shaking the Bolivian system to its foundations. The traditional power structure, comprising landowners and the military, was effectively eliminated in favor of labor, small farmers, and a small group of middle-level intellectuals. Osborne, having observed much of the program from close quarters, believes that the MNR program was carried on with a mixture of genuine idealism, political opportunism, and hard-headed realism.

The immediate social success of the revolution can hardly be denied, but political and economic evolution remained uncertain. The MNR ruled Bolivia for twelve consecutive years, something of a record in the political affairs of the nation. But factionalism, lack of discipline, lack of capable administrators, failure to institutionalize the revolution as Mexico did, and too many urgent causes to support at the same time all weakened the MNR and led to its overthrow by the re-established army in 1964. And this occurred despite massive financial support from the United States, whose State Department, in a most unusual and enlightened fashion, proclaimed the Bolivian revolution to be "Marxist, but not communist."

When the civilian political institutions of an underdeveloped nation are not capable of mobilizing its physical and human resources to get on with the nation-building job, the military establishment can, and often does, assume leadership. Because Bolivia's modernization problems are so great, even the military is not united in its views of the proper course to solve them. Rightists, leftists, nationalists, internationalists, hard-liners, moderates, populists, and élitists are some of the labels that might be pinned on the leading figures of the seven or eight military governments that have run the nation between 1964 and 1972. The saddest part of this story is the confusion and profusion of disparate policies which the various governments have tried to follow, some seeming to make headway, only to be replaced with others which seem to head in the opposite direction. Piecemeal plans rarely work.

Experiencing a near-catastrophic decline in the first decade after the revolution, the economy has made slow but steady progress in the last five years. The mining and industrial sectors suffered from an irresponsible power orgy by the newly formed unions. Between 1952 and 1958, an average of 350 strikes per year were called, probably setting a world record for lost man hours of work per worker. Inflation, low productivity, the poor tin market, food shortages, inept management of new government enterprises, corruption, and a brain drain complicated the problems of a nearly paralyzed system.

Many small farmers were given title to the land they had worked for years on the large *haciendas*. *Sindicatos* (farmers' leagues) were formed to provide a corporate institution through which the land reform could function and a communications channel to the central government, at the same time affording some local controls. One author comments that the *sindicatos* readily became a functional equivalent of the displaced feudal *patrón*. Initially, while consumption by the small farmers increased, agricultural production declined because some land was taken out of production, there was a spell of bad weather, and the new owners lacked agricultural credit, knowledge of new techniques, and transportation to urban markets. Output in agriculture, manufacturing, and mining has now risen at least to prerevolutionary levels and petroleum production, sugar refining, and smelting have increased markedly.

As far back as the early 1940's Bolivia made a firm commitment to public participation in the economic sector with the founding of the Bolivian Development Corporation to stimulate economic growth. In 1952 COMIBOL (Mining Corporation of Bolivia) took control of the three largest mining operations, Patiño, Aramayo, and Hochschild, along with eleven smaller companies. This action was something of a national crusade because the large mining corporations had wielded such overwhelming power in national affairs that they were considered a state within a state. Government control over the smaller mines came about indirectly, mostly by the Mining Bank of Bolivia's control of the purchase and sale of output, including exports. The YPFB is the government petroleum agency, which became a virtual monopoly in 1969 when Bolivian Gulf Oil Corporation was expropriated. Railroads and the airline likewise were nationalized, and the government operates various manufacturing plants, including a sugar mill, a cement plant, and a powdered-milk plant. The limited managerial group that was left after the revolution was thus greatly strained in attempting to meet these new responsibilities. Many government enterprises have been run at a loss in recent years and this perhaps is the price that must be paid for such a far-reaching revolution. One unfortunate consequence of this situation is that an average of about 50 per cent of the government's annual budget has had to go to administration and only about 15 per cent has been allocated to economic development projects.

The revolution has not lacked detractors. The middle economic and social group has been particularly hard hit (it is said that inflation has reduced its standard of living to that of the laborers), and they are fond of saying that the revolution has done little more than socialize poverty. The small farmers seem to have gained the most, even if the short-term benefits are nothing more than psychological. Liberated from feudalism, they are beginning the slow process of attaining full citizenship: The word *indio* (Indian) is now taboo, and the designation *campesino* (small farmer or peasant) has been substituted in a first attempt to assimilate the Indian majority of the population. This will undoubtedly be a long process because the small farmers will not only have to learn the traditional three R's (in Spanish), but they also will have to learn how to produce and consume in a commercial economy. Encouraging the small farmer's desire for the benefits of the revolution will require a major readjustment of his traditional culture patterns: He has successfully resisted this for more than five centuries.

Even though Bolivia has accomplished the first part of its revolution, the nation's difficult physical and cultural environments pose immense problems which must be solved if political, social, and economic evolution is to be realized. Stability in the political sphere is a prerequisite to growth. The military coup in 1964 billed itself "The Revolution of Restoration," trying to convince everyone that reaction was not about to set in, but rather a return to ideals of the 1952 revolution, which had been corrupted by the MNR. The one-year Torres government in 1971 formed a "Popular Assembly" of labor and students headed by Lechín. The Assembly was supposed to be an advisory group without any legislative powers. This action, and the call of the press for a "people's war," were apparently too leftist for at least one faction of the military, and Colonel Hugo Banzer took control of the government on August 22, 1971. The new government is a coalition of the military right-wing Bolivian Socialist Falange and the MNR.

One obvious project for the new government is to establish order. A longer-term but equally obvious goal is to build an institutional political structure that will represent the aspirations of the majority. Such a structure might create the political stability needed to ensure continuity in development policies. The current government has passed a law to stimulate foreign private investment, but under strict Bolivian controls.

The social aspects of the revolution have not been entirely successful either. The gross pattern of large landholdings, absentee ownership, and serfdom have largely been broken, but vital problems remain. Education and the dissemination of knowledge and technical skills are especially important to create the means and the desire among the small farmers to modernize. Other requirements include technological improvements in agriculture and ensuring that all farm families have enough land to raise themselves above the subsistence level. This probably means more extensive colonization of the Oriente. Colonization started back in 1920, but recent growth of the program has just kept up with population growth rather than relieving population pressures on the unproductive altiplano. An

International Labour Organization consortium in 1958 proved that colonization of the Oriente by highland Indians can be successful. Potential
colonists were carefully selected: They were disease-free and immunized
against endemic lowland diseases, and work hours were regulated to
avoid exhaustion. They were fed proper diets, obliged to wear shoes
to protect them from hookworms, drink filtered water, and use sanitary
latrines. Insect repellents and antibiotics were provided to prevent skin
ulcers and infections. The results were that the Indians bathed every
day, most of the colony enjoyed good health, clothing was gradually changed
to suit the climate, food habits were improved, coca-chewing ceased,
alcoholism became insignificant, and the people were no longer shy and
taciturn but laughed and talked unreservedly. A case, perhaps, for environmental determinism? Such a program on a large scale would probably
not be within Bolivia's financial capabilities. Some recent spontaneous
colonization has occurred in the Yungas as transportation routes have
opened up some areas. Back in the cities, miners and manufacturing
workers are beginning to become more productive and take more responsibility for national welfare, along with their newly acquired power and
freedom.

Economic solutions, of course, are related to political and social accomplishments. It has been noted that no goverment since the 1930's has
been strong enough to enforce the needed economic reforms. The most
fundamental requirements are for capital accumulation and infrastructure
development. A vicious circle prevails: domestic savings are not sufficient
for capital accumulation because the economy is not efficient; and the
economy is not efficient because capital for improved infrastructure is
lacking.

The single greatest infrastructure lack is adequate transportation. Costs
to both Pacific and Atlantic coasts are high, and it is unlikely that they
can be lowered much for Bolivia's cheap, bulky, and heavy mineral exports,
given the topographical constraints. Petroleum and natural-gas exports by
pipeline should help, if reserves prove to be large enough. Another means
of lowering the transportation costs on exports is to increase the value per
bulk and weight of the product shipped, but Bolivian mineral ores are
reputed to be very complex and difficult to smelt: Increasing smelting
capacity within the country will require more technology and more power.

Effective exploitation of the Oriente would provide additional meat,
timber, and other tropical exports (rice is already being shipped from
the Oriente to Peru and Chile). But good roads are needed to do so.

More energy is another requisite for further economic development. Bolivia has a choice of energy sources to develop: hydroelectric, natural gas and petroleum, and uranium deposits have recently been found southeast of La Paz. The list could go on, but Bolivians find it a little depressing because the nation needs more of everything it now has a little of, except anarchy.

Suggested Readings

BURKE, MELVIN. "Does 'Food for Peace' Assistance Damage the Bolivian Economy?" *Inter-American Economic Affairs,* XXV, no. 1 (summer, 1971), pp. 3–19. The author believes that this U.S. aid program should be more sensitive to the needs of the recipient country.

CARTER, WILLIAM. *Bolivia: A Profile.* New York: Praeger, 1972. A study of Bolivia's society from the aboriginal Tiahuanacu cultures through the Spanish conquest and colonization, and the implications of the country's cultural heritage.

CLARK, RONALD JAMES. "Problems and Conflicts over Land Ownership in Bolivia." *Inter-American Economic Affairs,* XXII, no. 4 (spring, 1969), pp. 3–18. The author suggests that land redistribution should have been carried out more efficiently, that lands of all large landholders should have been expropriated, and that strong local and national peasant union organizations are the best security against landlords' repossessing their expropriated land.

COHEN, ALVIN. "Bolivia: Internal Instability and International Dependence." *Current History,* LX, no. 354 (February, 1971), pp. 78–83. An examination of the detrimental effects of Bolivia's unstable political situation, difficult topography, and dependence on foreign investment.

EDELMANN, ALEXANDER T. "Colonization in Bolivia: Progress and Prospects." *Inter-American Economic Affairs,* XX, no. 4 (spring, 1967), pp. 39–54. In the opinion of the author, colonization of Bolivia's sparsely settled areas is imperative to increase the nation's agricultural production, and to provide land to many landless small farmers. He examines the colonization program in Alto Beni.

FIFER, J. VALERIE. "Bolivia's Pioneer Fringe." *Geographical Review,* LVII, no. 1 (January, 1967), pp. 1–23. An examination of the difficulties the country faces in resettling people from overcrowded areas, particularly in view of the nation's poor system of transportation.

_____. *Bolivia: Land, Location, and Politics Since 1825. Cambridge Latin American Studies, No. 13.* Cambridge: The University Press, 1972. A historical and political study of the nation in the light of its land-locked position on the continent and underdeveloped internal transportation system.

HEATH, DWIGHT B., CHARLES J. ERASMUS, and HANS C. BUECHLER. *Land Reform and Social Revolution in Bolivia.* New York: Praeger, 1969. A study of the development and results of land reform since the 1953 law. Includes detailed ethnographic descriptions of important regions that differ ecologically, historically, and culturally.

PRESTON, DAVID A. "New Towns—A Major Change in the Rural Settlement Pattern in Highland Bolivia." *Journal of Latin American Studies,* II, no. 1 (May, 1970), pp. 1–27. A study of a development unique to Bolivia: the spontaneous formation of new nucleated small-farmer settlements in certain parts of the highlands.

SMITH, PETER SEABORN. "Bolivian Oil and Brazilian Economic Nationalism." *Journal of Inter-American Studies and World Affairs,* XIII, no. 2 (April, 1971), pp. 166–81. Analyzes an incident typical of the difficulties facing South American economic cooperation.

See also Suggested Readings for Part I, pp. 61–63.

15 PARAGUAY*

Raymond E. Crist and Edward P. Leahy

Historical Highlights • The Social Environment • Transportation and Industrial Problems • Rural Poverty and Land Reform • focus *on Political Power*

A fertile soil, a generally pleasant climate, and an industrious people do not add up to a prosperous nation in the case of Paraguay, where centuries of isolation, war, and revolution have spelled economic stagnation. During the Spanish colonial period, in the 1600's and 1700's, the inhabitants, neglected by their far-off rulers, were almost continuously besieged by Indians from southern Brazil. The "mother country" was too busy with its mines in Mexico and Peru to develop agriculture in this tiny territory. Since 1811, under a republican regime, local demagogues have tended to follow the state-of-siege pattern in the face of political, military, and economic pressure from powerful neighbors.

The eastern third of the country, ranging in altitude from 1,000 to 2,000 feet, is an extension of the plateau of old basement-complex rocks of southern Brazil. These underlying crystalline rocks are covered almost everywhere with thick beds of red sandstone, into which lava, diabases, and basalts of volcanic origin have been intruded. Westward the ancient massif plunges beneath more recently deposited alluvium. The whole eastern region is a gently rolling, well-watered land of luxuriant grasslands and forests, sloping slightly westward as far as the Paraguay River. Beyond this lies the Chaco, a vast piedmont plain made up of unconsolidated sands, silts, and clays brought down from the slopes of the Andes.

The Chaco is a gray wilderness of scrub thorn trees, dwarf shrubs,

* Parts of this chapter were adapted from a 1967 issue of *focus.*

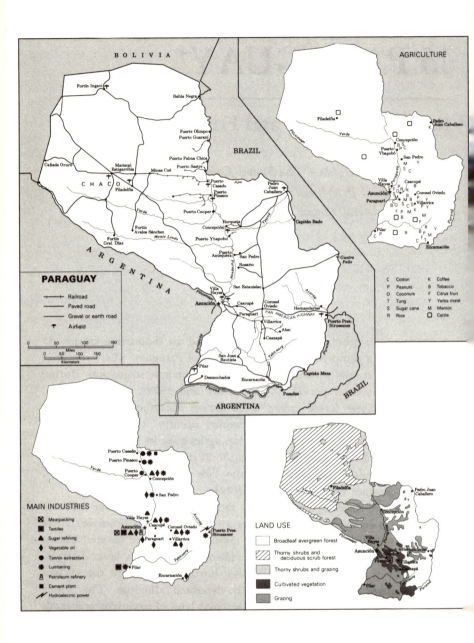

AGRICULTURE

Filadelfia

Concepción
Puerto Ybapobó
San Pedro
Caacupé
Villa Hayes
Asunción
Paraguarí
Coronel Oviedo
Villarrica
Pilar
Encarnación

Pedro Juan Caballero

C	Cotton	K	Coffee
P	Peanuts	B	Tobacco
O	Coconuts	Y	Citrus fruit
T	Tung	Y	Yerba maté
S	Sugar cane	M	Manioc
R	Rice	▢	Cattle

PARAGUAY

+—+— Railroad
——— Paved road
——— Gravel or earth road
+ Airfield

Miles
0   50   100   150
Kilometers
0 50 100 150

BOLIVIA

Fortín Ingavi
Bahía Negra
Puerto Olimpo
Puerto Guaraní
BRAZIL
Puerto Palma Chica
Cañada Oruro
Mariscal Estigarribia
Minas Cué
Puerto Sastre
CHACO
Filadelfia
Puerto Casado
Puerto Pinasco
Pedro Juan Caballero
Puerto Cooper
Horqueta
Capitán Bado
Fortín Avalos Sánchez
Concepción
Fortín Gral. Díaz
Puerto Ybapobó
Puerto Antequera
San Pedro
Rosario
Guairá Falls
Villa Hayes
San Estanislao
Asunción
Caacupé
Coronel Oviedo
Hernandarias
Paraguarí
PAN AMERICAN HIGHWAY
Puerto Pres. Stroessner
Villarrica
Abaí
Caazapá
San Juan Bautista
Pilar
Desmochados
Encarnación
Capitán Meza
Posadas
ARGENTINA
BRAZIL

ARGENTINA

MAIN INDUSTRIES

Puerto Casado
Puerto Pinasco
Puerto Cooper
Concepción
San Pedro
Villa Hayes
Caacupé
Asunción
Coronel Oviedo
Paraguarí
Villarrica
Puerto Pres. Stroessner
Pilar
Encarnación

⊠ Meatpacking
▪ Textiles
▲ Sugar refining
◆ Vegetable oil
✳ Tannin extraction
✱ Lumbering
⌂ Petroleum refinery
▣ Cement plant
⟋ Hydroelectric power

LAND USE

Filadelfia
Pedro Juan Caballero
Concepción
Villa Hayes
Asunción
Hernandarias
Villarrica
Caazapá
Pilar

☐ Broadleaf evergreen forest
▨ Thorny shrubs and deciduous scrub forest
░ Thorny shrubs and grazing
■ Cultivated vegetation
▓ Grazing

and giant cacti. Scattered, gnarled hardwoods, casting little shade because scantily leaved, stand like sentinels above the dense growth of bush. In the east, the quebracho tree perdominates The *campos,* the natural grass areas, are covered with coarse, stubby grasses *(espartillo)* up to three feet high. These are burned in the spring. Cattle like the young green shoots but find the mature grass unpalatable.

Except in some parts of the Chaco, the climate of Paraguay is fairly good for man and crops. From October to March, temperatures range from the high seventies to the nineties, but the heat is often broken by strong winds that may bring a drop of thirty degrees in a half hour; during the winter months, April to September, the range is from the sixties to the seventies. Extremes of heat and cold increase from the Paraná Plateau westward across the Chaco.

The eastern part of the country gets about fifty inches of rainfall, fairly evenly distributed throughout the year. Toward the west the amount gradually decreases, and in the Chaco the higher rate of evaporation and the permeability of the alluvial soil mean periodic droughts, often succeeded by floods.

Historical Highlights

From the first the Paraná-Paraguay river system offered the Spanish conquerors an easy route into the heart of the great green continent, on the western edge of which was the fabulous Inca Kingdom of the Sun. Asunción, an inland port that could be reached by small cargo boats, was established as a base of operations. Through Asunción passed the first transcontinental shipments of silver from the world-famous mine at Potosí (Bolivia) on their long, hazardous voyage to Europe.

The present citizens of Paraguay, some 2.5 million, are descendants of the small group of Spaniards who settled here and native women and men of Guaraní stock. Guaraní was the language spoken by the original inhabitants, and even today the country is bilingual. In fact, it is the only country in South America where an Indian language is an official one (along with Spanish). Periodicals, plays, and poems are published in both Guaraní and Spanish.

The Spaniards found the local people around Asunción enjoying an abundance of maize, beans, pumpkins, manioc, sweet potatoes, chickens, ducks, game, fish, and a wide variety of tropical fruits, such as melons and bananas. By the end of the 1500's sugar cane, wheat, barley, rice, and grapes had been introduced, and good-quality wines were beginning to be made. But these agricultural riches did not interest the Spanish Crown, which was eager for gold and silver. The country was treated like a poor relation. The farmers received no encouragement; on the contrary, they fell afoul of customs regulations and tax officials.

With the establishment of Jesuit missions in the early 1600's, things began to pick up. The Jesuits converted and baptized large numbers of Indians and gathered them into mission towns, called "reductions." Besides taking care of the people's spiritual welfare, the Jesuits taught them how to build magnificent churches and how to maintain settled farms. Within a few decades the "reductions" had become thriving agricultural centers from which yerba maté (used to make tea), cotton, tobacco, dried meats, hides, and hardwoods were exported.

Such success could not but excite the envy of Spanish landholders in Paraguay, who wanted cheap Indian labor for their own yerba maté forests, cotton plantations, and cattle *estancias* (estates). The result was that in 1767 a royal decree banished all Jesuits from Spanish dominions and confiscated their property. Within a few years much of their work had been destroyed, the orchards and fields had reverted to forest, and the herds were scattered.

Throughout the latter half of the seventeenth century and the whole of the eighteenth, the country was torn by periodic revolts of the Guaranís against Spanish authority. Even after Paraguay finally obtained independence in 1811, upheavals were the rule. A succession of powerful dictators one by one took the governmental reins, often by force. Disasters and wars took their toll, and the recent history of Paraguay has been essentially a slow struggle to reconstruct and repopulate the country.

The Social Environment

In addition to problems related to historical events, Paraguay is struggling with a 3.4 per cent annual rate of growth in population, one of the highest in South America and the world. This annual increment, plus the fact that a very large percentage of the total population is young, places a heavy burden on the adult population with respect to education, health, housing, and employment.

Although primary education is compulsory and free, financial support for the schools is inadequate. As a consequence, nearly 40 per cent of the people are illiterate, and many of those included as literate can barely manage to write their own names. In the late 1960's, 25 per cent of the instructors apparently did not have teaching certificates. Fewer than one quarter of the students complete four years of schooling. Of those who complete primary education, only approximately one in eight goes on to secondary school.

Paraguay has two institutions at the college level, the National University at Asunción, with an enrollment of 5,500 students, and the Catholic University, with about 2,000 students. The emphasis in both universities is on law and the social sciences. In 1965, however, the Inter-American Development Bank made a substantial loan to the National University to upgrade its programs in physics, mathematics, chemistry, pharmacy, agronomy, veterinary medicine and economics—all much needed in Paraguay. The university is also expanding its medical school to meet the needs of the nation. At the same time, the Ministry of Education and Worship is working with a grant from UNESCO to carry out a teacher-improvement program and to establish regional educational centers that will provide basic training in the humanities and some branches of technology.

With respect to health, Paraguay occupies an intermediate position in South America. According to the Ministry of Public Health, life expectancy is fifty-eight years for men and sixty-one years for women. A marked difference, however, can be seen between Asunción and the country districts: in the late 1960's the death rate was 7.8 per 1,000 in the capital but 12.1 per 1,000 in the outer areas. The leading causes of death are listed as gastroenteritis, pneumonia, tuberculosis, emphysema, and cardio-vascular failure. Per capita food intake is estimated at 2,560 calories per day, above the average in South America. A critical situation exists, however, with regard to the availability of medical services. In 1969 there were only 4,300 hospital beds to serve the national population of 2.5 million, and more than half the hospital beds and three fourths of the physicians were located in Asunción. Obviously, many *campesinos* (small farmers, or peasants) live and die without ever seeing a doctor.

The government has, however, inaugurated programs to improve health conditions. The Ministry of Public Health has established six clinics to serve as centers for maternity and infant-care programs. They have also set up nutrition programs for children. Another federal agency, the National Sanitary Works Corporation, has been established with over-all responsibility for design and construction of water-supply and sewage systems. About half of Asunción is now served by piped water, but service beyond the city limits is minimal.

Although there is some migration from the farms to the city, the strong tide of urbanization so characteristic of most South American nations is hardly beginning in Paraguay. Perhaps this is because of its isolation and general tendency to lag a few decades behind its neighbors in socio-economic development. In any event, the crowded shantytowns so typical of Rio de Janeiro and Santiago are not seen in Asunción. Only 36 per cent of the national population is classified as urban. Of these, 437,000 lived in Asunción (1970). The next largest towns are Encarnación, with 23,500, and Concepción, with 21,000.

In spite of the relative immobility of the population, a critical shortage of housing exists. In 1970 it was estimated that 60 per cent of all dwellings were inadequate. Some 160,000 new units are needed, of which 120,000 should be built in rural areas.

The Paraguayan Housing and Urban Institute (IPVU) was established in 1964 with over-all responsibility for making studies of housing needs, formulating plans for urban development, and supervising construction programs aimed at improving this aspect of the social environment. Meanwhile, the Inter-American Development Bank made $6 million available to IPVU for construction of 2,600 housing units. The loan was payable in thirty years at $1\frac{1}{4}$ per cent interest. Progress was slow at first, but in 1967, 126 units were completed; in 1968, another 126; and the following year, 750. At the end of 1970, 1,100 additional units were under construction. Present plans call for a total of 6,200 units by the end of 1973.

It is anticipated that the pace of construction will pick up substantially by the mid-1970's as the basic infrastructure expands in response to projects now under way. Also, a new cement plant completed in 1970 will increase annual production capacity by 120,000 tons, and the creation of a trained cadre of construction personnel and a trend toward mechanization should increase productivity. It is not realistic, however, to foresee any significant decrease in the housing shortage much before 1980.

The employment structure inevitably reflects the underdeveloped nature of Paraguay's economy. About 54 per cent of the labor force makes a living from agriculture. Most of these people are engaged in subsistence agriculture, which is characterized by low productivity. Some of them work as temporary help on the commercial farms during the harvest season. The result is that there is considerable waste of human resources in the rural areas. The *campesinos* suffer from unemployment and underemployment and the deprivation that goes with them.

The industrial sector is small. Only 3 per cent of the manufacturing establishments employ more than twenty workers. More than half employ fewer than five workers. The labor code recognizes the rights of both workers and employers to unionize. The one central union, the Paraguayan Confederation of Workers, has 163 locals with a combined membership of just over 16,000. This is a very small proportion of the total labor force. The social security laws as currently written could provide protection for 300,000 workers, but as yet only about 70,000 actually enjoy coverage.

The armed forces are relatively large for so small a country. They consume about one third of the federal revenues, and they really represent a form of disguised unemployment, since their contribution to national productivity is minimal.

Transportation and Industrial Problems

Like California two or three generations ago, Paraguay has enormous potential, but its rich resources of grassland and forest cannot be realized until the transportation problem, common to so much of South America, is solved.

Landlocked Paraguay, the size of California, has fewer than 3,000 miles of surfaced roads. A plan for increasing the highway network has been initiated, under the auspices of the Central Bank of Paraguay in cooperation with the U.S. Agency for International Development. A major project is completion of Paraguay's part of the Pan American Highway, which runs from Cañada Oruro, on the Bolivian border, to Filadelfia (in the Chaco), to Asunción, and then eastward through Coronel Oviedo to the Paraná River. This river is spanned by an international bridge at Puerto Stroessner. The road then continues through Brazil to Paranagua, where Paraguay enjoys free port facilities on the Atlantic coast.

Another project recently undertaken was the building of a road linking Coronel Oviedo with the new route between Concepción and Pedro Juan Caballero. Plans also call for a road northeastward from Asunción to Capitán Bado; one from Encarnación northward up the valley of the Paraná; and one to link the central road system and the Guaira Falls in the northeast, which are a spectacular attraction for tourists and a potential source of enormous hydroelectric power.

The one main railroad, running from Asunción through Villarrica to Encarnación, has suffered from highway competition in recent years, for the principal roads duplicate its services rather than act as feeders. The roadbed is poorly maintained, and the rolling stock is antiquated. National air transport is a monopoly of the Líneas Aéreas Paraguayas. Various foreign lines link Paraguay with other parts of the world. From Asunción, Buenos Aires can be reached in only one and a half hours and Rio de Janeiro in two. Centrally located on the South American continent, Asunción is almost certain to become an increasingly important international airport.

Paraguay has none of the fuels and minerals needed for industrialization. The rivers are potentially rich sources of hydroelectric power, but so far little has been done to harness it. Most of the 100,000 people engaged in industry process agricultural, pastoral, and forestry products, mainly for export, or manufacture consumer goods on a small scale for the domestic market. Cotton, lumber, quebracho extract, hides, and canned and frozen meats are the principal earners of foreign exchange, along with some yerba maté, tobacco, and vegetable oils. The textile industry is one of the most important for the home market, and there is room for expansion: Large quantities of raw cotton are exported, and yet cotton cloth is imported. Local manufacture of more cotton goods would create additional jobs and cut import expenses. Small factories and shops provide lumber and furniture, matches, soap, cigars, bricks and tiles, and shoes, and an oil refinery near Asunción is producing 248,5000 tons per year.

Each year some 400,000 hides become available for tanning, and, by great good fortune, enormous stands of the quebracho tree (Schinopsis lorentzii), rich in tannin, lie on both sides of the Paraguay River. This could be the basis for a thriving leather industry if the quality of the hides were improved. The logs were formerly sent to Argentina for processing, but transportation costs were too high. Five tannin factories have now been established at Puerto Cooper, Puerto Pinasco, and Puerto Casado. Of these, one is controlled by North Americans, the others by Argentines, who have forced Paraguay to sign an agreement not to produce more than 20 per cent of world production.

German and Japanese interests are playing an increasing role in the industrialization of Paraguay. In 1967, the Federal Republic of Germany and Paraguay signed an agreement which continues a supply of credit for the development of small and medium industry; a Japanese firm is currently interested in building a plant for the extraction of tung and soybean oil in the Alto Paraná area.

Rural Poverty and Land Reform

In the cattle country most farmers own at least a few acres of land. But in the real heart of the country, the agricultural zone around Asunción, which occupies only 5 per cent of the total area of the republic but contains more than half its people, a large proportion of the farmers do not own the land they work. In fact they are simply squatters, paying no rent or taxes. Many are slash-and-burn farmers who clear their small plots of brush with machete and fire, cultivate them for two or three 'years, and then move on to other plots when the soil begins to lose its fertility.

If Paraguayan agriculture is to be improved, one of the first steps should be to provide the farmers with security of tenure to land of their own. In 1936, a law was passed authorizing the government to expropriate 5 million acres, pay for them with bonds, and sell them to farmers in plots of 25 to 250 acres. Lands subject to expropriation were public lands not required for other purposes, private land in the vicinity of communities needing it for expansion, and any private land suitable for farming that was not being "rationally exploited" by its owner. In the eastern part of the country, "rational exploitation" meant that at least half of an estate must be under cultivation. Since then other measures have been introduced to increase agricultural production. Special credit terms have been granted to farmers who undertake to plant a specified area, and price floors have been established for basic crops such as maize and manioc.

Despite all this, large estates are still the rule, and agricultural production is still low. Total production of foodstuffs has not kept pace with the increase in population since 1950. Rural areas are characterized by high rates of unemployment. Crops have suffered from drought and rain damage. This situation is causing some flight to the cities and also an exodus from the nation. It is estimated that about a half million Paraguayans are currently residing in Argentina and Uruguay, most of them because of adverse economic and political conditions in their homeland.

Realizing that these migrations away from the farms have hindered the development of agriculture, the government has encouraged the immigration of agricultural settlers. For example, it gave a group of Mennonites 2,100 square miles of land in the nearly empty Chaco, assured them freedom to practice their religion in peace, and granted them virtual self-rule, perpetual exemption from military service, and generous concessions as to taxes and tariffs. These people have opened up the Chaco to uses other than the traditional grazing and extraction of tannic acid.

focus *on Political Power*

Paraguay has been called the "Sparta of South America," and there is some justification for the cliché. Proud, austere, warlike, despising the soft pursuits of a liberal bourgeois philosophy, it has traditionally been governed by militarists, including some extreme examples of ,the genus. Francisco Solano López, for instance, had a career in keeping with the most robust requirements of *machismo.* Sent to Paris by his father in 1853, he acquired a beautiful Irish mistress, Eliza Lynch. Eventually he returned to Asunción to take over the reins of power from his father. Under his leadership, the army was trained by Germans and supplied with European equipment. It became so formidable a force that Paraguay was viewed as a menace by its neighbors.

The upshot of all this was the War of the Triple Alliance (1865–70) against Brazil, Argentina, and Uruguay, which left Paraguay in ruins, its fields barren, its herds of cattle decimated, its people starving. Even the generals were barefoot. The population had been reduced to less than half what it had been in 1864, and virtually no males over fifteen years of age were left. López was finally cornered by the enemy and killed, and Mme. Lynch buried him with her own hands.

Times have changed in Paraguay; the present incumbent, General Alfredo Stroessner, is less flamboyant in his life style. He qualifies as the longest-reigning military dictator in South America, having assumed office in 1954 by a bloodless coup. It is maintained, in fact, that his regime exemplifies a one-party rule rather than personal dictatorship. Stroessner himself is mild-mannered and diffident, a professorial type rather than a demagogue. His power is based on control of the military establishment and a demonstrated willingness to deal firmly with opponents. Civil liberties are marginal. The officer corps is a favored class, and Stroessner has established working relations with other elements of the oligarchy in finance and industry. Thus, effective political power is in the hands of a relatively small clique. The rest of the people are privileged to choose between two alternatives: they can remain politically inert, or they can leave.

There has been growing protest against the government on the part of the Roman Catholic Church, however. A crisis long in the making was brought to a head in May, 1972, when the goverment expelled a Spanish-born Jesuit who had been working in one of the small farmers' agrarian-reform leagues. These are sponsored by the Jesuits to improve the lot of the country's impoverished farmers. The government objects to the leagues, on the ground that they are infiltrated by Communists. The Interior Minister has said that all Jesuits will be expelled if they continue their "nonpriestly" activities. The church charges that it is living in a "climate of systematic persecution."

Apparently Stroessner does not believe that Paraguay is ready for democratic institutions, but this has not prevented him from proceeding with a program of economic development. He has improved the highway network, encouraged the settlement of unexploited lands, and encouraged enlargement of the industrial infrastructure. Also, he has brought order to the financial sector of Paraguay by inaugurating a series of reforms, starting in 1957 whereby taxes were raised, credit was restricted, and wages were made subject to control. The result was that the disastrous inflation was brought under control, and the guaraní became one of the strongest currencies in South America.

Suggested Readings

ARNOLD, ADLAI F. *Foundations of an Agricultural Policy in Paraguay.* New York and London: Praeger, 1971. An assessment of the country's agricultural potential, and problems related to it. Makes recommendations regarding land-tenure problems, research in the *minifundio* and colonization areas, and programs to help the organization of agricultural cooperatives and credit unions.

Inter-American Development Bank. *Socio-Economic Progress in Latin America; Tenth Annual Report.* Washington, D.C., 1970. Discusses Latin American progress toward achieving institutional development and social progress. The section on Paraguay describes the economy, housing, urban development, education, health and sanitation, rural development, and labor and social security problems.

Kolinski, Charles J. *Independence or Death: The Story of the Paraguayan War*. Gainesville: The University of Florida Press, 1965. The Paraguayan, or Triple Alliance, War was, in many ways, a counterpart of the U.S. Civil War. The author relates the events leading to the war, gives an interesting account of the major battles, and summarizes the effects of fighting on the belligerents.

Pendle, George. *Paraguay: A Riverside Nation*. London and New York: Oxford University Press, 1967 (third ed.). A somewhat dated, but valuable, summary of political events, and an analysis of the people and their occupations.

Pincus, Joseph. *The Economy of Paraguay*. New York: Praeger, 1968 (third ed.). This outstanding volume explores many economic, social, and political factors essential to an understanding of Paraguay. There are special appendixes on the physical geography, historical development of land-use patterns, and characteristics of immigrant groups.

Service, Elman R., and Helen S. Service. *Tobatí: Paraguayan Town*. Chicago: University of Chicago Press, 1954. A pioneering study of community life in rural Paraguay, focusing on the relationship between Hispanic and Indian societies.

Stewart, Norman R. *Japanese Colonization in Eastern Paraguay. Foreign Field Research Program; Report No. 30*. Washington, D.C.: National Academy of Sciences–National Research Council, 1967. An informative, pertinent report on Japanese acculturation; discusses elements of the colonizers' culture that survived the thirty-six years of settlement in eastern Paraguay. Today, the Japanese are a dominant minority, with an agriculture adjusted to Paraguayan conditions, and a successful commerce.

See also Suggested Readings for Part I, pp. 61–63.

16 URUGUAY

Raymond E. Crist and Edward P. Leahy

Political Instability, Early Reforms, and Immigrants • *Farm Products and Practices* • *Transportation and the Growth of the Primate City* • focus *on the Welfare State*

With an area of only 72,172 square miles, Uruguay is the smallest sovereign nation in South America, and it is squeezed between two giants —Brazil to the north and Argentina to the west and south; yet it has been able to maintain a sturdy hold on its rolling pasturelands, the traditional basis for the nation's economy and large-scale international trade.

In 1603 an attempt to establish a colony from Buenos Aires failed, but a population of 300 horses and 300 head of cattle left by the Spaniards foreshadowed future developments. At present, livestock outnumber people by about ten to one. The most recent estimates are 21.8 million sheep and 8.7 million cattle; the number of inhabitants is estimated at 2.9 million. Naturally, the consumption of meat is high, averaging a little over a half pound per person per day. The average Uruguayan's diet is one of the world's best as far as calories and proteins are concerned.

Political Instability, Early Reforms, and Immigrants

Uruguay's position between Portuguese settlements in Brazil and Spanish settlements in Argentina resulted in conflicts over control of the territory during the seventeenth and eighteenth centuries. The history of Colonia del Sacramento, a city on the northern bank of the Plate River (Río de la

Plata) thirty miles from Buenos Aires, illustrates these struggles. The Portuguese founded the city in 1680 and were immediately pushed out by forces from Buenos Aires. The following year the town was given back to its founders. Later it was attacked by the Spaniards because of flourishing contraband activities. In 1713 it was ceded back to Portugal. During the next few decades it again changed hands several times and finally was secured by Spain.

After Uruguay and neighboring areas won independence, Uruguay became a buffer state between Argentina and Brazil. A treaty was signed in 1828, largely in response to the mediative efforts of the British minister at Buenos Aires. For most of the next century, South America was the scene of uprisings, revolts, revolutions, and foreign wars. Uruguay was no exception. Finally, after decades of instability, a man appeared who defined some of the nation's basic political, economic, and social ills and attempted to lay the foundations of an orderly, progressive, viable community.

During his first term as president (1903–7) José Battle y Ordóñez was engaged mainly in attempting to achieve civil stability in a liberal atmosphere. At the expiration of his term he rigidly adhered to the constitution, which prohibited a president from immediately succeeding himself, and sailed for Europe to study methods of government. Returning to Uruguay in 1911 to become president for the second time, he recommended that the state have a monopoly on insurance and electric light and power, and he urged legislation for the protection of labor, for the establishment of research institutes and experiment stations, for universal free education, and for the construction of state railroads and highways. "There is great injustice in the enormous gap between the rich and the poor," he declared. "The gap must be narrowed—and it is the duty of the state to attempt that task." He believed that most of Uruguay's ills had been caused by corrupt elections and the abuse of presidential power, and he saw to it that elections were reasonably honest and that the personal power of the president was severely curtailed. Although abuses of presidential power did occur after 1920, especially during the depression of the 1930's, Uruguayan democracy eventually reached a high level of performance.

Among the social reforms that were accepted early are old-age assistance, pension systems, an eight-hour workday, compulsory liability insurance, vacations with pay, free medical services, legalized divorce, women's suffrage and right to own property, and work codes for children. In the eyes of many South Americans, these reforms make Uruguay a virtual Utopia.

Nor does Uruguay suffer from the high rates of population increase so common in South America, and a source of many of the area's basic problems. Uruguay's population growth rate is the lowest on the continent; indeed, it is the lowest in the Western Hemisphere. Because of the declining birth rate (about 24 per thousand), the population increased an average of only 1.2 per cent per year during the 1960's.

The people of Uruguay are almost all of European descent. Although traces of Indian ancestry are still apparent among some rural families in outlying districts (the Spaniards and Portuguese killed off most of the Indians), the *mestizo* group is estimated to be no more than 10 per cent of the total population. Most of the immigrants have come from Spain and Italy; some 650,000 of them arrived between 1836 and 1926. Since World War II the only immigrants permitted have been farmers and skilled workmen who had employment contracts. Unfavorable economic conditions have also discouraged immigration into Uruguay in recent years, and there has perhaps been a small net outflow of people. In consequence, the number of foreign-born living in Uruguay has dropped from 450,000 in 1957 to about 250,000 in 1970. Some 48 per cent of the nation's inhabitants live in Montevideo, the capital city; only about 25 per cent live in communities having fewer than 2,500 inhabitants.

Farm Products and Practices

Uruguay's gently rolling hills receive a moderate rainfall averaging about 40 inches a year, well distributed through the seasons. A subtropical and essentially maritime location provides mild average temperatures, which range from 50°F. to 72°F. Of the land area of nearly 42 million acres, fewer than 1 million are classified as wasteland—rocky land, swamps, sand dunes, and alkaline flats. But only 3 million acres are cultivated, and another half million lie fallow each year. Only about 1 million acres are in planted pastures; the vast expanse of over 36 million acres is in range grassland. The largest part of the country (about 70 per cent) is devoted to livestock raising. Moreover, the intensity of use is high: the average density of livestock is almost one per acre, and very little supplementary feeding is done.

During colonial days Uruguay consisted chiefly of huge *estancias,* or estates. Cattle, considerably more numerous than sheep, were valued primarily for their hides; salted meat, although important, was distinctly secondary. When a meat-extract plant opened at Fray Bentos in 1865,

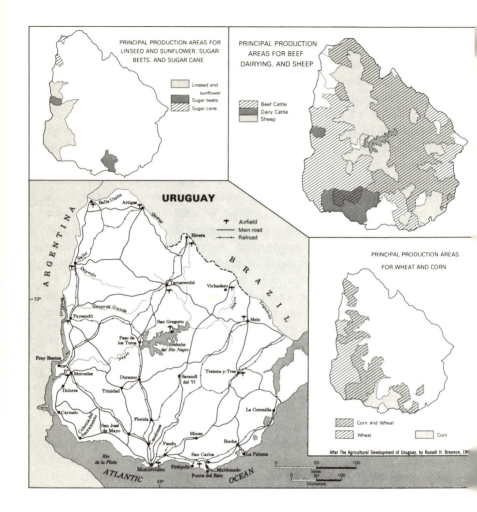

PRINCIPAL PRODUCTION AREAS FOR
LINSEED AND SUNFLOWER, SUGAR
BEETS, AND SUGAR CANE

Linseed and
sunflower
Sugar beets
Sugar cane

PRINCIPAL PRODUCTION
AREAS FOR BEEF
DAIRYING, AND SHEEP

Beef Cattle
Dairy Cattle
Sheep

URUGUAY

Airfield
Main road
Railroad

ARGENTINA

BRAZIL

ATLANTIC OCEAN

PRINCIPAL PRODUCTION AREAS
FOR WHEAT AND CORN

Corn and Wheat
Wheat
Corn

After The Agricultural Development of Uruguay, by Russell H. Brannon, 19

sheep numbered 2 million and cattle more than 3.5 million. By 1900, however, the picture had been reversed, with 18.5 million sheep and not quite 7 million cattle, and the numbers have not greatly altered since then.

The livestock industry, however, radically changed during the latter part of the nineteenth century because of the introduction of barbed wire to fence in the ranges, the development of refrigerated ships to carry chilled and frozen meats to European markets, and the improvement of livestock quality, due to the importation of European breeding stock.

The shift from salted meat to chilled, frozen, and canned meats increased the demand for better grades of beef. Herefords and shorthorns now constitute a large proportion of the stock.

Cattle and sheep raising are closely associated; in fact, the herds and flocks commonly graze together. In general, the northern part of the country is the area of the largest *estancias* and of stockbreeding: the topography here is more rolling than in the south. The better grazing lands for fattening cattle and most of the cultivated croplands are south of the Negro River.

Landholdings are large: only 1 per cent of the farms occupy one third of the total farm area. In the late 1960's, 4.9 per cent of the estates had 2,500 acres or more each, comprising 62.4 per cent of the land. On the other hand, 30 per cent of the farms with less than twenty-five acres accounted for 0.7 per cent of the total farm area. Reflecting a national trend to accumulate property, two thirds of the agricultural land was controlled by 3,000 enterprises. Government efforts to increase the number of small farms are hampered by lack of money. Between 1948 and 1967 fewer than one and a half million acres of land had been redistributed, and, given Uruguay's deteriorating economy, it is unlikely that much more land has since been made available to settlers. The great estates readily lend themselves to mechanization, and the mechanized area has been conservatively estimated at well over a million acres. Ownership and tenancy are about equally divided.

The chaotic political situation during the nineteenth century delayed the growth of farm communities and put a premium on cattle and sheep raising. Only with the encouragement of the government's guaranteed price-support program for crops has agricultural production notably increased. The country now grows enough rice for its own needs with even a surplus for export. The wheat crop has more than doubled since World War II and in a good year gives Uruguay a sizable export of wheat for the world market. Nearly as much wheat is shipped out in the form of flour as in grain, proof of the growth of the flour-milling industry.

During the 1960's a strong demand in world markets stimulated production of wool, which became the main Uruguayan export, eventually accounting for an average of almost half the national export income. The proportion is slightly less than that now, but Uruguay is still among the six leading wool exporters in the world. The United Kingdom is the best customer, followed by the United States and the Netherlands. Uruguay also ranks among the top half dozen exporters of beef, mutton,

Because the government has concentrated most of its investments in the cities, many rural areas lack adequate educational and health facilities. In this small community it has undertaken a health program to improve nutrition, sanitation, and maternal and child care.

and hides—in spite of the fact that the livestock industry has been handicapped by weak prices and unfavorable tax policies.

Yields of grains and the output in livestock have been disappointing in recent years and remain below the average for South America. It is estimated that improved methods could raise productivity by as much as 40 per cent for both grains and animal products without increasing either the herds or the area under cultivation. Major agricultural problems include animal diseases, especially hoof-and-mouth disease (aftosa) and undulant fever; poor health standards in slaughterhouses; inadequately managed grazing and arable lands; and inefficient grading, transporting, storing, and marketing of crops and livestock. In addition to these problems, periodic droughts and soil erosion create some difficulties.

Although the effects of animal diseases are serious, the principal diseases—aftosa, undulant fever, and tick fever—can now be controlled. The problems of land management hinge upon the relationship of pasturage to crops Undoubtedly, more attention should be given to high-yielding legumes. Legumes for pasturage would improve permanent pastures and, planted in temporary plots, would provide feed reserves to meet the shortages that occur during periods of drought. The use of legumes in rotation with cash crops would not only improve yields but also help to retard soil erosion. Moreover, increasing the yield from a given amount of cropland would release land for the production of feed crops for fattening cattle and for emergency use. More diversified farming would provide a more stable income through crop and livestock combinations.

In order to compete in world markets, Uruguay should handle its crops and livestock products with greater care and efficiency. This means more concern with rural Uruguay on the part of those who control investment capital, as well as local incentives such as better marketing procedures and prices.

Transportation and the Growth of the Primate City

Gradual extension of the railroad system, begun in the late 1860's, facilitated the nation's economic development. Since then the government has carried out an extensive program of highway construction and has encouraged road transport by granting truckers partial relief from import duties and certain taxes and by providing relatively cheap gasoline and diesel oil. Increasing traffic is overtaxing the roads, however, and a nationwide program for the construction of paved roads is about to get under way, with financial help from the Inter-American Development Bank.

New life was pumped into Montevideo by the building of railroads and roads, into the interior and the installation of modern public utilities and port facilities. Products such as wool and meat are processed there for export. Most of the internally oriented consumer-goods industries —textiles, shoes, soap, wines, and dairy products—are also located in the capital, as are petroleum refineries and cement works, railway shops, and the electric power system. The textile industry has grown rapidly and now ranks second to meat processing. The wool used is domestic; the cotton comes from either Paraguay or the United States. There is also some manufacture of synthetic materials. And, as in most welfare states, much of the economy of the primate city is devoted to providing services for its large number of public employees. Another thriving industry is tourism: both foreign and local visitors flock to the internationally famous beach resorts along the Atlantic coast.

As the amenities of the capital have become ever more attractive, one new suburb after the other has developed. From a population of 300,000 in 1908, Montevideo has more than quintupled in size to about 1.5 million (1971). A bright, modern city, with fine schools, museums, libraries, and hospitals, it has acted as a magnet to the people of the hinterland. As a result, the rural provinces have lost many of those who might have created vigorous regional centers. Outside the capital city, household industries such as cigar wrapping, rice hulling, weaving, and the manufacture of tools and leather goods are carried on, but there are few modern industries and few cultural activities. Incomes and job opportunities have increased somewhat in the city, but there has been no comparable increase in the countryside. Effective political and commercial power are likewise concentrated in the capital city. Thus a dual society has evolved, and, unless conditions in the rural areas are improved, the gap is likely to widen, causing mounting political unrest.

focus *on the Welfare State*

A guiding principle in the operation of the public agencies that play such a large role in the economy has been to control the role of foreign capital in the industrial and financial life of the nation, but the primary motive has been to render service to the public in the form of low-cost insurance, low interest rates, low utility rates, and low prices for meat, gasoline, and other commodities. Some state enterprises compete with private business, others enjoy a monopoly. Some state enterprises are profitable; others are subsidized. Examples of deficit ones are fisheries and the Montevideo meat monopoly. The fisheries agency operates fishing boats, warehouses, and ice plants and distributes fish at low prices through wholesale and retail outlets. Montevideo's fresh-meat monopoly suffers from the attempt to lower the prices charged to customers and simultaneously raise the prices paid to producers. Difficulties in delivering cattle to the stockyards, delays in payments, and high operating costs have plagued the agency. The railroad system, also government-owned, is another deficit enterprise.

There are state agencies in the fields of banking and insurance. The government also has a monopoly on the distilling of alcohol and the refining of crude oil. It manufactures cement in competition with private companies and controls the sale of cement for public works. It also controls the import and sale of coal, mainly used for the manufacture of gas, and all electricity and telephone services.

There are those who assert that the welfare state has contributed to complacency in Uruguay, and they point to the widespread custom of taking summer afternoons off to enjoy the beautiful beaches that stretch from Montevideo past Punta del Este. But widespread and repeated strikes and political disorders in recent years would seem to indicate a quite different mood. There have been several general strikes, mainly in opposition to restrictions on wage increases, which virtually paralyzed the nation, as well as strikes by various groups, such as government employees, meat packers, and teachers. Farmers have withheld milk from urban markets to protest low prices. Unemployed farm workers have marched on Montevideo to demand jobs. Kidnappings, armed robberies, and other terrorist activities of dissatisfied political groups, including students, have endangered the democratic form of government and it is also being threatened by the increasing role of the military.

The basic problem stems from the fact that the government instituted ambitious social and welfare programs but failed to stimulate sufficient economic growth to pay for these programs. Not enough capital has been used to increase productivity in the two basic elements of the economy: agriculture and livestock. The grasslands are not intensively managed, the croplands are not sufficiently fertilized, the soils of sloping fields continue to erode: yields in crops and meat have in fact declined, and the yearly per capita income has fallen by 10 per cent over the past decade.

Because of the lack of investment in rural areas, the rural population is also underprivileged in terms of per capita income, education, health services, diet, and social welfare. This has helped to stimulate migration from the countryside to the capital city. The influx of these migrants has in turn strained Montevideo's facilities.

Industry grew rapidly in the years after World War II, but the boom leveled off in the mid-1950's, and since then expansion has been slow. The domestic market for manufactured goods is small; accordingly, industry is organized in small production units, which tend to be high-cost producers characterized by inefficient methods, inefficient equipment, and high labor costs. Consequently, Uruguay's manufactured goods cannot meet foreign competition unless protected by a high wall of tariffs.

In order to increase the efficiency of industry, a basic reorganization is needed. This would require large-scale investment. But high taxes, high interest rates, inflation, and government red tape have combined to undermine confidence in capital markets so that Uruguay has one of the lowest investment coefficients in South America. The current rate of investment barely replaces worn-out equipment, and there is little or no provision for improvement or for expansion of existing facilities.

Another factor contributing to Uruguay's economic difficulties is the disproportionately large number of people on the government payroll (almost 40 per cent of the total labor force). Many of these people are not only unproductive but in fact counterproductive, since the many agencies of the overblown bureaucracy tend to reduce production in other activities. Also, the population of Uruguay has the highest average age in South America—about thirty-two years. The fact that the nation now has more people over fifty years of age than under, plus early retirement for many people, means that the nation has a relatively large unproductive group that has to be supported by the national economy. In addition, the labor-force unemployment rate exceeded 10 per cent during most of the 1960's and early 1970's. Almost all of the unemployed are eligible for benefits. As a consequence, there is a top-heavy economic structure, with a large group of unproductive consumers and a small group actively engaged in economic production. Sad to relate, the situation is worsening; the unproductive groups, which already represent more than one third of the active population, are expanding at the expense of the productive ones.

Since the social-welfare programs distribute purchasing power throughout the population, living standards tend to be relatively high. But nothing in this world is without cost. Uruguay's high rate of consumption tends to prevent capital accumulation. It would seem that people are enjoying present comforts at a level they cannot afford. At best, they are failing to build for the future.

This situation creates severe problems for the government. Revenues have fallen while demands on the treasury have remained high. In order to meet expenses the government has turned to deficit financing. Such methods are, of course, strongly inflationary. Bank credit and the money supply have expanded rapidly; wages rose by an average of about 50 per cent per year during the 1960's; inflation rose to a peak of 135 per cent in 1967. A stringent economic-stabilization program affecting wages and prices has now, however, begun to show results. In the 1970's, the cost of living has risen by only about 10 per cent per year. But the social-security funds and the deficit-operated nationalized corporations continue to be a heavy drain on the federal treasury. Who has borne the brunt of this inflation? Most probably the middle-income group, because they tend to have their wealth in savings accounts, insurance policies, pension funds, and other fixed investments. In order to break this pattern a program of austerity is needed, featuring more exports, less imports, a balanced budget, higher tax collections, wage and price controls, tight bank credit, and high interest rates. A program like this is not particularly popular, but it is the usual medicine required to dampen inflation.

Despite its current troubles, Uruguay has advantages not enjoyed by some South American nations. There is slack in the economy; the resource base is underutilized; the population is well fed, healthy, well educated, skillful, resourceful, and of high morale. Also, the Uruguayans are aware of their cultural heritage and values. Those familiar with the Uruguayan spirit are confident that the nation will reorganize and institute the measures needed to reduce social and economic inequalities and restore political stability.

Suggested Readings

ALISKY, MARVIN. *Uruguay: A Contemporary Survey.* New York: Praeger, 1969. Emphasizes modern Uruguay's government, finances, social structure, and education.

American University. *Area Handbook for Uruguay.* Washington, D.C.: U.S. Government Printing Office, 1971. A comprehensive analysis of social, economic, and political aspects of the nation.

FINCH, M. H. J. "Three Perspectives on the Crisis in Uruguay." *Journal of Latin American Studies,* III, no. 2 (November, 1971), pp. 173–90. Suggests that Uruguay's current crisis is rooted in the way in which modernization was imposed on traditional structures in the early decades of this century.

PENDLE, GEORGE. *Uruguay.* New York: Oxford University Press, 1963 (third ed.). A somewhat dated, but well-written, general account of the nation.

REDDING, DAVID C. "The Economic Decline of Uruguay." *Inter-American Economic Affairs,* XX, no. 4 (spring, 1967), pp. 55–72. A study of the long-term deterioration of the nation's economy, caused partly by over-reliance on foreign borrowing, overemphasis on industrialization at the expense of agriculture, and inefficient operation of state enterprises.

WERNER, ELLIOT. "Basic Data on the Economy of Uruguay." U.S. Bureau of International Commerce, *Overseas Business Reports, OBR 68–113* (December, 1968). A brief analysis of the structure of the nation's economy.

See also Suggested Readings for Part I, pp. 61–63.

17 ARGENTINA

Morton D. Winsberg

The Physical Environment · Historical Background · The Agricultural Base · The Growth of Industry

For more than a hundred years, Argentina has been second only to the United States in the dreams of Europe's landless and jobless. In search of a piece of land on the Argentine pampa (flat fertile grassland) or steady work in one of the nation's rapidly growing cities, millions of immigrants have come in, most of them from Italy and Spain, but also from other parts of Europe. Yet despite a physical environment more favorable than most and an enormous investment of money, talent, and energy, Argentina has not quite fulfilled the destiny predicted for it.

In the past few decades, and especially in the 1960's and early 1970's, serious economic and political problems have brought strikes, demonstrations, riots, robberies, urban guerrilla violence, and a growing disillusionment, particularly among the young. The economic problems include inflation (the cost of living went up by 60 per cent from July, 1971, to July, 1972), huge deficits in trade and in state-controlled industries, lagging agricultural production (once the backbone of the nation's wealth), and a lack of sufficient investment money. The most difficult problem in the political realm is the deep division among the various parties which are daily manifesting themselves in demonstrations, riots, kidnappings, and killings; they concern the form of government desired and basic policies and goals. In the opinion of Argentine leaders, no solution to the increasingly pressing economic problems will be found until the political equation is solved.

As a result of this continuing economic and political crisis, many

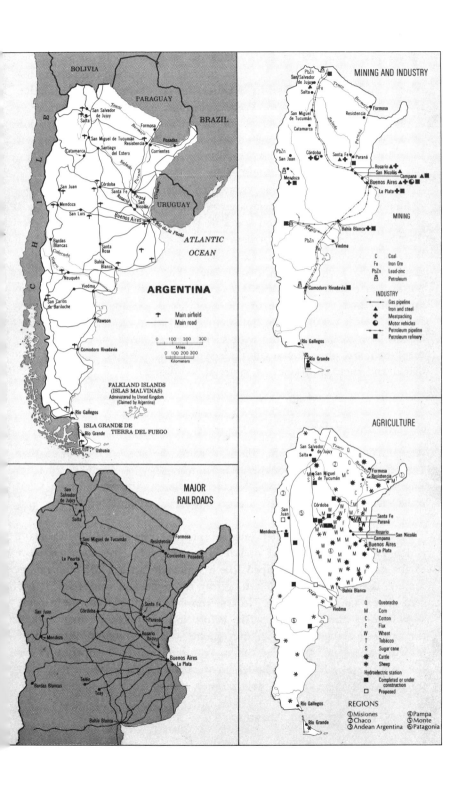

among the young and skilled, unable to find good jobs or to rise in the ranks of the big industrial firms because of nepotism, are leaving the country in the hope of finding a better life elsewhere. Their destination is usually the United States, Western Europe, or Brazil, where there is a shortage of skilled personnel for new industries. This out-migration of skilled workers is becoming so serious that the Argentine government is seeking ways to stem it, so far unsuccessfully; the newly arrived immigrants do not have equivalent skills.

Yet, the average Argentine enjoys the second highest annual income in South America: $820, as compared to $950 in Venezuela. This is a good deal lower than in the United States or Western Europe but much higher than in Colombia ($310). Furthermore, it is far more evenly distributed than in most South American nations. Nor does Argentina suffer from many of the problems that beset some others, such as a high rate of population growth (Argentina's 1.5 per cent per year is one of the lowest anywhere) and a high rate of illiteracy (its 8 per cent compares very favorably with Brazil's 39 or Bolivia's 67). In other ways, too, the Argentinians have created a culture with a "European" flavor, in their architecture, their arts, their literature, their sports, their clothes, their food and drink, and their enjoyment of material well-being.

The Physical Environment

Argentina is a large nation, about a third the size of the continental United States. Shaped roughly like a triangle, the distance from its base in the tropics to its apex deep in the South Atlantic is about 2,300 miles and it has consequently a great variety of climates, vegetation, and land forms.

Argentina may be divided into six physical regions. Most important is the pampa, the grassland underlaid by rich soils that attracted most of the early immigrants. Shaped like a semicircle, with a 375-mile radius around Buenos Aires, this flat to gently rolling region comprises 20 per cent of the national territory. No one knows for certain what the natural vegetation of the pampa was like before it was altered by man. When the Spanish arrived, however, they found a large grassland interrupted only by trees and shrubs in the more humid north. Temperatures on the pampa are mild, and although snow occurs in the southern half, it is infrequent. Average annual precipitation varies from 40 inches in the northeast to 20 inches or less in the southwest. Variability is a constant threat to agriculture, however, especially on the drier margins of the pampa, where droughts are frequent. One of the great assets of the region is its soils. Developed under temperate-climate grasses, these highly organic soils rival in fertility those of the United States Corn Belt. Unfortunately, poor agricultural practices have caused considerable wind erosion in the drier portion of the pampa and water erosion in the more humid parts.

Surrounding the pampa are regions with less temperate environments. In the extreme northeast is an extension of Brazil's volcanic Paraná Plateau. Although it accounts for only 1 per cent of the national territory, this hot, wet, and forested region is the closest approach to a humid tropical climate in Argentina. West of the Paraná River lies the Chaco, a low alluvial plain covered in scrub forest and grass. During the summer this flat plain experiences some of the highest temperatures recorded anywhere in South America. On its western margin the pampa merges with the Monte, a dry basin and range region, with short grass in the more humid east and cacti and other drought-resistant plants in the drier west. Southwest of the pampa is Argentina's largest physical region, the high, dry, barren plateau of Patagonia. Covered with bunch grasses, it is broken by deep canyons etched by rivers whose sources are the high humid areas along the Argentine-Chilean border. Separated from the pampa by the Monte is Andean Argentina, which extends from Bolivia to just south of Mendoza. Argentines divide their Andean region into two subregions, the Northwest and Cuyo. The Northwest, where the cordillera is broadest, is actually an extension of the Bolivian Plateau, experiencing the same aridity and coldness. Farther south, in Cuyo, the cordillera narrows and plateaus and basins disappear. Heavy snowfalls occur on the mountain tops, but the eastern face of the mountains, or rain-shadow side, is desert.

Historical Background

Argentina was neglected by Spain during most of the colonial period; in fact, until 1776, it was actually governed from Peru. Early expeditions sent from Spain to ascertain the wealth of the pampa found nothing to encourage attempts at colonization along the Plate River (Río de la Plata) except the wish to provide buffers against Portuguese expansion.

Northwestern Argentina appeared more promising to the Spanish, and agricultural communities were founded here to provide hides, food, and work animals for the mining centers of Bolivia and Peru. Such towns as Salta, Tucumán, and Córdoba, though small, prospered while Buenos Aires languished, disease-ridden and neglected, sometimes waiting more than a year for the arrival of a ship from Europe; in 1750 its population barely exceeded 12,000.

In time, the descendants of the cattle set free on the pampa shortly after the first Spanish arrived began to have commercial value. During the eighteenth century, increasing numbers of Argentina's famed horsemen, the *gauchos,* set forth from Buenos Aires in search of the wild herds. They returned with hides and tallow, both of which found markets in Europe. Later, cattle were driven to Buenos Aires to be slaughtered; their meat was dried and salted for shipment to Brazil and the Caribbean, where it was used as food for slaves. Only at the close of the colonial period, when the wild cattle had disappeared from areas easily accessible to Buenos Aires, did the large cattle ranches begin to form around the city.

Even at the eve of independence in the early 1800's Argentina had no national unity. Fewer than a half million inhabitants, mostly Indian and *mestizo,* occupied a vast region extending from Buenos Aires to Bolivia. The little port of Buenos Aires and its small hinterland faced Europe; the agricultural settlements of the northwest, by then suffering an economic depression as a result of the exhaustion of the Andean silver mines and the disruption of trade with upper Peru (present-day Bolivia), were virtually self-sufficient. Crude ox cart roads connected the port with the northwest, but travel along them was slow, costly, and subject to constant harassment by the nomadic bands of Indians.

The Argentina that achieved independence from Spain in 1816 was not to have any degree of internal coherence for another seventy years. At the risk of oversimplification, the struggle during this long period was basically between the port of Buenos Aires and the rest of the nation. The port sought to convert the nation's resources into exports to be sent to Europe. To do this most efficiently, and also to serve their own interests, its leaders sought to modernize the Argentine economy and to centralize (under their control) the national government. Spanish colonial traditional society survived much longer in the interior. Its leaders, the *caudillos,* bitterly resisted the growth of the economic power of Buenos Aires and sought a loose confederation of the provinces, permitting great local autonomy.

Until these differences were resolved, economic and social evolution was slow. Civil and international wars constantly sapped the vitality of the nation. For much of the period large sections were beyond the control of national authority: They were the domain of local *gaucho* leaders or Indian tribes. Not until 1880 did Buenos Aires conclusively establish its supremacy.

While the young republic was achieving internal coherence, industrialization in Great Britain led to a de-emphasis on domestic agriculture and a demand for imported wheat and beef in exchange for British manufactured goods. Even before this demand for imported food arose, Britain had sought to incorporate Argentina into its empire: In 1806 and 1807 two unsuccessful military expeditions were launched to seize it from Spain. In the following decades large numbers of British arrived in Argentina and invested in land; by midcentury, British capital was going into the nation's infrastructure, particularly railroads. The event that solidified the close economic union between Argentina and Britain occurred about 1870, however, when the invention of refrigerated ships made it possible to send fresh Argentine beef to Europe.

As a result, the Indians were rapidly driven from the pampa, estates were fenced, and the cattle herds improved by the introduction of British purebreds. Great numbers of laborers were needed by the landowners to increase agricultural production and productivity. The cities required workers to build and staff the food-processing plants, build the workers' houses, and supply services. The railroads employed thousands to lay the tracks to connect the pampa with the port. Of the millions of immigrants who arrived, many eventually returned to Europe, others came annually to work in the Argentine harvest, but millions chose to remain. In the 1930's almost three fourths of the Argentines were born of European parents and one fourth were immigrants.

Today Argentina has 24.7 million people, 97 per cent of them of European ancestry (the other 3 per cent are Indians). A large proportion of the people can be classified in the middle-level socio-economic group, are urban dwellers, and make their living from industry and services: Only 19 per cent of the labor force is engaged in agriculture, compared with 32 per cent in Venezuela and 72 per cent in Bolivia. Buenos Aires, with a population of about 9 million in the metropolitan area, ranks among the world's fifteen largest cities. In addition there are two other cities (Rosario and Córdoba) with populations over 500,000 and five more between 250,000 and 500,000.

The Agricultural Base

Since the 1880's, Argentina has emerged as one of the world's great agricultural export nations, placing on the world market large quantities of meat, wheat, wool, maize, hides, vegetable oils, dairy products, and many other agricultural commodities. It controls 80 per cent of the world market of linseed oil, nearly 50 per cent of the fresh and canned beef, 21 per cent of the oats, and between 20 and 7 per cent of the grain sorghums, wool, and wheat. The nation is also self-sufficient in almost all agricultural commodities, importing only those it cannot produce domestically, such as coffee and rubber.

The main agricultural region is the pampa, which produces the majority of the nation's exports. Farms are large, often absentee-owned, and many are none too efficient. Agricultural productivity on the pampa has stagnated during the past forty years, largely because foreign markets have been lost and the government has controlled agricultural exports. This control, designed to give priority to urban rather than rural investment, has restricted the pampa landowners' investments to increase efficiency, especially in grain production. As elsewhere in South America, agricultural reform is needed in Argentina, but it is doubtful if the typical land reform, involving reduction in the size of the farm units and distribution of land to the landless, would help. The agricultural products the nation can most profitably sell on world markets are produced most efficiently as large, highly capitalized farm units.

Virtually every section of the pampa is deeply committed to cattle ranching, but it is most prevalent in the southeast and in Entre Ríos (between the Uruguay and Paraná rivers). Cattle production has become highly specialized: A breeding zone has developed in the southeastern part of Buenos Aires Province and a fattening zone in the northwestern part of it, where alfalfa is cultivated. Two important dairy regions supply dairy products as well as exports of casein and cheese. The Argentines eat an average of 130 pounds of beef per person annually; other types of meat play a small role in their diet.

In the twentieth century, crops have successfully competed with animal products for primacy among Argentine exports. During the two world wars, animal products predominated, but normally, during periods of relative international stability, the grain trade is most valuable. Wheat, the most important grain, is raised on the drier margin of the pampa, particularly north of Bahía Blanca, where oats, rye, and barley are also grown. Maize is raised in the more humid center of the pampa. Flax and sunflowers are grown for their oil. Flax production is concentrated in an area between the Uruguay and Paraná rivers, and sunflowers are grown farther to the west, in the center of the province of Buenos Aires. Enough citrus fruits to meet domestic demand and about one quarter of the nation's vegetables are raised near Buenos Aires.

Outside the pampa there has been a spectacular rise in agricultural production in the past forty years, mainly because of the rising standards of living and increasing domestic demand for a variety of foods. Large areas of cropland are irrigated. Major zones of oasis agriculture are around Mendoza and San Juan, famed for their wines, but also for fruits, vegetables, and alfalfa. The valleys of the Negro and Colorado rivers in Patagonia also support large irrigation projects growing much the same crops as Mendoza and San Juan. A half-billion-dollar project on a tributary of the Negro River (El Chocón), currently under construction, will greatly increase irrigated acreage as well as electrical power. Older, less efficient irrigated oases are found around the cities of Córdoba, San Miguel de Tucumán, and Salta. The last two produce the majority of the nation's

Virtually all of the Argentine pampa is used for cattle ranching. Cattle production has become highly specialized in Buenos Aires Province. The main breeding zone is in the southeast; the main fattening zone, in the northwest. Many of the cattle later to be butchered for export pass through the huge stockyards of Buenos Aires. Here mounted cattle-buyers, many of them British or Anglo-Argentine, ride among the lots of cattle, choosing those to be sent to packing plants.

Courtesy Moore-McCormack Lines

sugar. Normally enough cotton is raised in the Chaco, usually under irrigation along the Bermejo River, to supply domestic demand.

The Growth of Industry

Argentina is poorly endowed with mineral resources for industry. Mining accounts for less than 1 per cent of the gross domestic product, and its share is declining. There are large reserves of petroleum and natural gas in Patagonia, near Mendoza, and in the northwest, and these are the major exploited minerals. Since 1958 the state oil monopoly has striven for self-sufficiency but, despite a large increase in production, it has to import oil in most years. Newly built pipelines now connect oil and gas fields with refining and consumption centers. Low-grade bituminous coal is available in southern Patagonia but production still meets only half the national need; the rest is imported. Despite newly discovered iron-ore deposits of considerable magnitude in northern Patagonia, only 10 per cent of the iron ore smelted in the national steel industry is mined domestically; the remainder comes from Brazil, Chile, and Peru. A wide variety of other minerals occur in small deposits throughout the county, but Argentina is self-sufficient in only a few.

The industrial base of the country is highly developed and is capable of producing virtually everything needed by the Argentine consumer, one of the most affluent in South America. In addition, the capital-goods industry has developed rapidly in recent years. To achieve this advanced industrial stage, Argentina has practiced a high degree of protection against imports and has taxed agriculture heavily. Because of the proliferation of small, inefficient firms, encouraged under the protective trade laws, some products suffer, however, from low quality and high production costs, making expansion into foreign markets difficult. Industrial expansion has also been restricted by a continuing shortage of energy.

Most of the energy is derived from petroleum and is consumed primarily in the form of electricity. The largest generating capacity is in the Buenos Aires region, but production normally lags behind demand. In 1968 the government contracted with a German firm to build a large nuclear electric plant near Buenos Aires, which will use domestic natural uranium. The El Chocón hydroelectric-irrigation project in Patagonia will double existing electric production when it is completed.

Manufacturing is highly concentrated in an area extending from Rosa-

Courtesy United Nations
Argentina's highly developed industrial base is capable of producing virtually everything needed by the Argentine consumer, one of the most affluent in South America. At this Fiat plant in Córdoba, a worker is inspecting the flywheel of a diesel engine.

rio to La Plata, particularly in Greater Buenos Aires, which has the majority of the nation's population and consequently the largest market. It is also most accessible for the imported raw materials so essential for Argentina's industries.

Although most factories are small, there are several that employ large numbers of workers. The big meat-packing plants, often foreign-owned, are situated along the shore, facilitating loading for export. A steel plant with over a million-ton capacity located on the Paraná River north of Buenos Aires is convenient for the assembly of raw materials from overseas. Large plants also produce, among other things, transportation and farm machinery, electrical equipment, petrochemicals, textiles, and cement. Nevertheless, most items, particularly consumer goods, are made in small workshops.

In the interior only Córdoba, with approximately 10 per cent of the industrially employed, has a large industrial base. This city has attracted a sizable share of the nation's vehicle and farm-machinery industry, largely because of the production of cheap hydroelectricity in the nearby mountains. The rest of the nation's industrial workers live in regional centers, where most are employed in food and beverage industries or in plants that supply local needs.

In recent years there has been an attempt to decentralize industry. The government has built several plants outside the established centers, and private industry is being encouraged, primarily through tax concessions, to build in previously unindustrialized areas. To date this program has not met with great success. Most regional towns are still mainly market and service centers and probably will continue to be such until the nation's transportation network is improved sufficiently so that raw materials can be assembled efficiently there and the finished products marketed economically.

The railroad network is the densest in South America but since it was nationalized by Juan Perón immediately after World War II it has been plagued with recurrent labor problems and starved of public investment. Equipment is old and often out of order, and rails are frequently in a dangerous state of disrepair. Although freight and passenger rates are inexpensive, service is unreliable. In recent years private capital has been invested in trucks and buses in an effort to offer alternate means of transportation, but the government has spent very little money for the improvement of existing highways or the construction of new roads.

Rapid industrialization has brought serious growth pains to all the large cities. Millions of unskilled agricultural laborers, out of work, underemployed, or simply discouraged by stagnation and lack of opportunity in the rural areas, have migrated to the cities in search of work—where they have been joined by millions who had come from Europe. This tremendous influx has strained public services of all kinds and at times has caused temporary breakdowns. Some public housing has been built, but not nearly enough: Vast areas in the suburbs are covered with sprawling slums known as *villas miserias* (misery villages), where most people suffer from the lack of pure water, sewage facilities, schools, health clinics, doctors, and jobs or good transportation to jobs. And although industry has been expanding, it has not expanded fast enough to create enough jobs for the immigrants. Unemployment and underemployment are critical problems in all urban areas.

Argentina must export in order to obtain the foreign exchange needed to purchase raw materials and capital equipment for its complex industry. To buy from abroad it sells, primarily in Europe, a wide variety of agricultural commodities, principally cereals, meat, vegetable oils, and wool. Historically Britain has been its best trade partner, but since World

War II, other member nations of the European Economic Community, the Soviet bloc, and Spain have had the lion's share. Exports have dropped in recent years while imports have risen steadily. If exports continue to drop at the present rate, there will not be enough money available to pay the nation's debts and import the raw materials needed for industry.

Argentine governmental policy throughout most of this century has been to give priority to industrialization. Since World War II it has nationalized or established many industries, most of which are inefficiently operated. Money for industrialization and vast urban programs has, to a great extent, been obtained from taxing agricultural exports. This, in turn, has discouraged agricultural production, especially of grains, which require a higher degree of mechanization than beef production. Other factors that have discouraged production for export include inflation: The cost of living rose by 11.3 per cent in one month in 1972, and the biggest increases were in the prices of such essential items as beef, cotton, wool, and clothing. Furthermore, the nation has had to face increasing competition from other countries that are able to produce the same agricultural products more efficiently and cheaply. Also, the increased use of synthetic fibers has acted as a deterrent to the wool trade, plastics have lowered the price of hides, and an outbreak of hoof-and-mouth disease in Great Britain, attributed to Argentine beef, has caused that nation to place periodic embargoes on Argentine beef since 1967.

It seems unlikely that in the near future Argentina will be able to substitute new and more profitable exports (although in the distant future it might be able to sell industrial products to fellow members of the Latin American Free Trade Association and possibly to Andean Common Market nations). Furthermore, it is doubtful if foreign food purchases by Argentina's trading partners will increase significantly in the coming years since the population in these areas is increasing very slowly and gains in income are likely to be spent on products other than food.

Since 1970 the government has obtained loans of more than $50 million from the Inter-American Development Bank and the World Bank to improve all sectors of agriculture, particularly to expand livestock breeding and develop herds. It is now seeking $1 billion from the United States and Europe in an attempt to make a "fresh start" financially. But the best way for Argentina to achieve a favorable balance of trade is to improve agricultural efficiency on the pampa, thus reducing the price of exports and making them more competitive in world markets. If this can be done, the nation may find markets now closed to it. To reduce imports, efforts might be made to further develop mineral deposits and encourage the capital-equipment industry. A considerable saving could also be achieved by the government by improving the efficiency of the nationally owned enterprises: Most are excessively staffed and notoriously low in worker productivity.

With a well-educated population and a reasonably good resource base, Argentina should look with confidence to the future, but social scientists have predicted a bright future for its economy so many times, only to see their predictions proved false, that prophecies must be made with caution. If the Argentine government can devise a better system of priorities between industry and agriculture, if it can bring greater efficiency to both, and if it can improve the operation of nationalized enterprises, it would be well launched on a program leading to greater prosperity. The big questions are: Can the people of Argentina agree on a form of government, and can the government accomplish economic tasks of this magnitude?

Suggested Readings

ALEXANDER, ROBERT J. *An Introduction to Argentina.* New York: Praeger, 1969; London: Pall Mall Press, 1969. A general survey of the nation, treating its geography, history, economy, politics, and culture.

American University. *Area Handbook for Argentina.* Washington, D.C.: U.S. Government Printing Office, 1969. A comprehensive study of social, political, and economic aspects.

EIDT, ROBERT C. *Pioneer Settlement in Northeast Argentina.* Madison: University of Wisconsin Press, 1971. A study of a colonization zone, characterized by varied topography, unusual settlement evolution, and immigrants of widely differing backgrounds.

FIENUP, DARRELL F., RUSSELL H. BRANNON, and FRANK A. FENDER. *The Agricultural Development of Argentina: A Policy and Development Perspective.* New York: Praeger, 1969. A study of the recent changes in agricultural production and productivity, with recommendations for implementing its growth and development.

GERMANI, GINO. "Mass Immigration and Modernization in Argentina." In William Petersen, ed., *Readings in Population.* New York: Macmillan, 1972, pp. 223–41. A study of the effects on Argentina of the arrival of huge numbers of immigrants between 1856 and 1930.

McGANN, THOMAS F. *Argentina: The Divided Land.* Princeton, N.J.: Van

Nostrand, 1966. An analysis of the nation's domestic and international situation, in terms of the dilemmas posed by its geography and history, and the social psychology of its people.

SCOBIE, JAMES R. *Argentina: A City and a Nation.* New York: Oxford University Press, 1972 (second ed.). The emphasis is on the nation's formative years—the nineteenth century—during which Buenos Aires came to dominate the development of Argentina.

SMITH, JOHN N. *Argentine Agriculture: Trends in Production and World Competition.* Washington, D.C.: U.S. Department of Agriculture, 1968.

See also Suggested Readings for Part I, pp. 61–63.

18 CHILE

Donald D. MacPhail

Varied Uses of the Environment • A Diverse and Dynamic Population • Political and Economic Changes • Land Reform • Fisheries and Forestry • Mineral Wealth and the Rise of Nationalism • Changing Sources of Energy • Future Prospects

Chile's social revolution, which began in earnest during the administration of Pedro Aguirre Cerda (1938–41), is now moving along swiftly. By initiating drastic internal reforms to try to diminish political, economic, and social inequalities, Chile is making a dramatic break with its past. Transformations in the ownership and operation of farms and industries are fundamental. Increasing political awareness is also likely to bring further efforts to reduce the role of foreigners and foreign capital in mining and industries, for the spirit of nationalism is running high.

Varied Uses of the Environment

In describing Chile's physical environment one tends to use superlatives. It is an extremely long land, spanning over thirty-eight degrees of latitude along South America's west coast. It is very narrow: Its broadest areas are only 224 miles wide in the north near Antofagasta and 263 miles wide in the south near Punta Arenas. Its northernmost provinces have some of the bleakest, driest landscapes known on earth. The far south is a land of ice-gouged fiords and huge cordilleran icefields, where precipitation exceeds 120 inches a year.

A large continental plate of the earth's crust, slowly moving westward from Africa during the last 150 million years, has deformed the western fringe of South America. Where the plate encounters another, which underlies the Pacific Ocean, great crustal instability occurs. Along the contact of these plates, a short distance offshore, submarine trenches marking the edge of the continent commonly exceed depths of 16,000 feet and sometimes 23,000 feet. Inland, along the Argentine frontier, many Andean peaks exceed 19,000 feet, and elevations of 13,000 feet are commonplace. In these circumstances, volcanic and seismic activity is to be expected. Chileans are used to earthquakes. Some in recent times have been particularly destructive. Usually seismic disturbances are localized, as in Valparaíso in 1822 and 1906, or Chillán in 1939, but sometimes entire regions are affected. In 1960 the southern half of the populated core of the nation, devastated by two weeks of continuous quakes and tremors, suffered landslides, volcanic eruptions, tsunamis (seawaves produced by seismic activity), and widespread destruction of towns and cities.

Despite the fact that Chile has an area of 286,396 square miles, much of the land is too steep, wet, or dry to sustain great numbers of people. Only the hardy brave the rigors of the austere Atacama Desert in the north. Descendants of the ancient Atacameño ethnic group occupy a string of small interior oases on the flank of the Andes and the altiplano along saline rivers, only one of which (the Loa) manages to reach the sea. Port cities, especially Arica, Iquique, and Antofagasta, are the present foci of development and growth in the Norte Grande (Big North).

South of the Atacama and north of the Central Valley, the Andes reach to the shores of the Pacific. This Norte Chico (Little North) cactus-covered landscape of semidesert has much in common with northern Mexico. Adobe huts of subsistence miners dot the remoter areas. Away from the highways and railroads, burros are used, and herds of goats are everywhere. Favored transverse valleys such as the Copiapó, Huasco, Elqui, and Choapa are noted for irrigated specialty crops such as papayas, figs, raisins, and walnuts.

In the far south, vast areas of glaciated mountains separate isolated communities in this, the least populated part of Chile. Great herds of sheep graze the broad, short-grass plains at the extreme southern end of the mainland and in northern Tierra del Fuego.

The populated core of Chile includes a chain of inland basins and valleys between the Coast Range and the Andes, which coincide with a great longitudinal structural trough. North of the Bío-Bío River is a Mediterranean environment with warm, rainless summers and mild, rainy

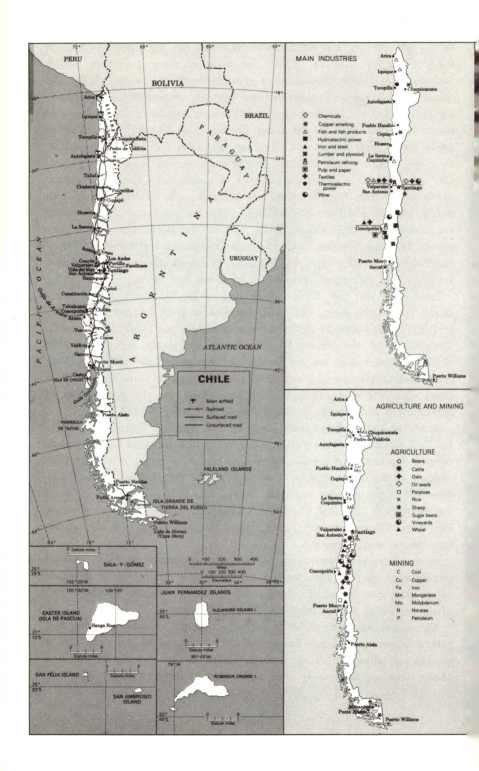

winters. Southward there is a marine, west-coast climate with mild summers and winters that are cool and exceptionally rainy.

The Aconcagua Valley north of Santiago is densely populated. Irrigation agriculture prevails, with an emphasis on specialty crops such as table grapes for export and orchards of oranges, lemons, nectarines, peaches, plums, and avocados. Hemp also grows here. Traditional food crops such as maize, beans, potatoes, squash, and watermelon are of secondary importance except in areas of subsistence farms.

Mountains completely encircle the Santiago Basin. The urban sprawl of the national capital converts more and more prime farm land into residential, commercial, and industrial uses. The shape of the basin helps to trap gases emitted by the burning of fossil fuels in cars, buses, trucks, and domestic and industrial furnaces. Winter temperature inversions create severe air-pollution problems, which the Chilean government is now confronting. On the fringe of the metropolitan area, much land is devoted to the production of truck crops. At greater distances from Santiago the usual pattern of Mediterranean land use occurs—traditional food crops and some industrial crops such as sunflowers, plus wheat, irrigated alfalfa and clover for dairy herds, and vineyards.

The traditional pattern of settlement in the Rancagua Basin and Central Valley combines the large estate, or *fundo,* side by side with clusters of *minifundios.* The landholdings of the *minifundistas* are too small to sustain a family adequately. Thus the residents of these diminutive parcels have been a source of part-time labor in nearby *fundos* or towns. In the past a typical *fundo* covered 1,000 to 7,400 acres, with large fields, a third to a half mile on a side. There were a half dozen to a score of families of farm laborers in adobe row houses along the main roads of the farm, guarded by stately rows of poplars or eucalypts. Some land was dedicated to semillon, cabernet, pinot, or other types of grapes, and the rest of the farmland was used for winter wheat, rapeseed, sunflowers, sugar beets, maize, oats, beans, and rotation pasture of alfalfa and clover. Fruit and nut orchards were also common. Less productive spurs of the Coast Range and the Andes provided wood for charcoal, scrub pasture for peasant-owned livestock, or otherwise unused acacia thickets. All this is changing now (see below).

One of the least studied regions of Chile is a low tableland, the Montaña. It first appears in the north as a narrow belt of upland between the Central Valley and the Andes east of Curicó. It extends southward, ever widening, until it fills the entire structural trough at the Bío-Bío

River. The Montaña is a region of flat, west-sloping strata of volcanic mud and debris flows, volcanic loess, glaciofluvial materials, and alluvial deposits which are deeply incised by the main rivers from 300 to 1,000 feet. The area is noted for dryfarming of wheat combined with livestock on rotation pastures, yet the surface of the tableland is still covered by open groves of broadleaf evergreen *Nothofagus* forest. The southern limit of the Montaña occurs northeast of Valdivia, where transverse sections of the Coast Range join the Andes. The tableland south of the Bío-Bío River is the home of the proud Araucanian Indians, or Mapuche, as they call themselves. In 1969 there were 322,916 Mapuche living on 3,048 reservations (1.4 million acres) between Bío-Bío and Llanquihue provinces.

Spectacular snow-capped volcanoes rise well above the summits of the Andes in the Lake District. Along the eastern flanks of the mountains, huge moraines have impounded a chain of beautiful, elongated lakes in ancient glacial gorges. A large and fertile glacial plain, adjacent to the lakes, focuses on the city of Osorno. Here, and on the smaller Cruces River plain near Valdivia, well-managed farms produce dairy products, small grains, rapeseed, potatoes, sugar beets, and apples. Pioneers from Germany colonized this area in the nineteenth century: House styles, land-management practices, family-run farms, and regional dialects still show the influence of a northern European life style. Blended with this style, however, is the Chilean system of commerce and land tenure. In terms of population, the Chileans of *mestizo* and Spanish origin far outnumber those of German ancestry.

The city of Puerto Montt lies at the southern end of the Chilean coreland. Along the shore near this port, and southward through an extensive zone of islands, channels, and fiords, *minifundios* blanket the landscape. Here men take to the sea to supplement the meager resources of the land and women weave beautiful woolen goods as a form of cottage industry. The nuclei of settlement of these farmer-fishermen are at Calbuco, near the mainland of Llanquihue Province, and the islands off the town of Castro on Chiloé Island.

A Diverse and Dynamic Population

Although most Chileans are *mestizo*, there are significant numbers of Germans, Yugoslavs, Spanish, Basques, French, Italians, English, Atacameños, and, as noted before, Mapuche. The population of Chile was 10 million in 1971, and it is growing at the rate of 2.3 per cent per year. Almost 35 per cent of the entire nation lives in Santiago Province (3.2 million). Of this number, 2.6 million are in the greater Santiago area. Well over one quarter of all Chileans live in the nation's capital or its suburbs.

Most of the people in Chile are urban dwellers. Migration from provincial town and farm to city has been steady in recent years: in 1940, the rural and urban populations were about equal; by 1952, the proportion was 40 per cent rural and 60 per cent urban; in 1960, it was 32 per cent rural and 68 per cent urban. The latest census (1970) indicates a continued shift, with 26 per cent rural and 74 per cent urban.

In numbers the rural population has remained almost static during the last two decades. In 1952, there were 2.4 million rural residents compared to 2.5 million in 1970. Thus, the significant absolute and relative increases in population have been in the cities. The influx of rural migrants has created enormous problems because they come at a rate too rapid to be absorbed in the urban working force or to be provided adequate shelter, even though the government has an active housing program. The present Chilean administration sums up the plight of the rural emigrant in a 1971 report:

The accelerated migratory process from the countryside to the city [and] the low level of qualification of the rural working force [coincide] with a development in the productive industrial and service sectors [which are] insufficient to absorb the increase in population. [This,] together with inadequate urban development, contributes to a high percentage of the emigrants not finding adequate working and living conditions. [They] pass into a contingent of underemployed urban population with extremely low levels of income—which lives in highly unsatisfactory conditions.*

In summary, the rural migrants often face conditions in the city that are worse and more dehumanizing than those in the countryside. The slums of Santiago are an ever-pressing problem. It will be interesting to see if, by placing rural farm wages on a par with the wages of industrial workers, the government is able to substantially diminish the rural–urban

* Oficina de Planificación Nacional, *Plan de la Economía Nacional 1971–76: Antecedentes sobre el Desarollo Chileno 1960–70.* Santiago, 1971, p. 107.

migration. Higher farm wages may slow the urban squeeze in Chile, but they are not likely to hold the farmers unless rural social services, such as educational and health facilities, are greatly improved. Illiteracy in rural areas is about 20 per cent because of the lack of educational facilities at all levels, whereas in the cities the rates are as low as 6 per cent. In the outlying, dominantly rural provinces, such as Bío-Bío and Chiloé, there is an average of one doctor for as many as 8,000 people; in Santiago the ratio is one for 900. Similarly, the highest reported infant mortality rates come from the essentially rural provinces outside the central zone.

Political and Economic Changes

Chile has a long and varied history. The northern half of the country came under Inca domination in the fifteenth century. A century later,

Most Chileans are now urban dwellers, and almost 35 per cent live in Santiago province. Of these, 2.6 million are in the greater Santiago area. The huge influx of rural migrants has created enormous problems because industry is not expanding fast enough to absorb them into the urban work force and adequate housing for them does not exist. The government is taking steps to encourage industries, however, and has an active housing program that may eventually ease some of these problems. This is Lo Valledor Sur, a self-help housing project in Santiago, sponsored by the government with assistance from the United Nations.

Courtesy United Nations

the Spanish arrived and incorporated the area into the Viceroyalty of Peru. The early colonial years were marked by unending struggle between the Spanish and creoles and the formidable Mapuche. Warfare with the Indian population did not cease until 1882.

Turbulence continued all through the nineteenth century. Between 1810 and 1814, there was civil war between patriots and royalists. Three years later, an army led by San Martín and O'Higgins crossed Andean mountain passes from Argentina and successfully concluded the War of Independence in 1818. In 1833, constitutional government was established; this has continued to the present. The late nineteenth century saw the eruption of the War of the Pacific between Chile and its northern neighbors, Peru and Bolivia. Chile, the victor, gained undisputed control of the desert provinces of Tarapacá and Antofagasta and the vast mineral treasures that lay therein. This was followed by the last of the Indian battles and a period of internal conflict in 1890 and 1891.

Chilean society was predominantly agrarian: The landowners were in control of the economy and the government. This led to the tradition of conservative, authoritarian, centralized government by the aristocracy. The conservatives continued to hold most of the power well into the twentieth century.

By contrast, during the twentieth century—a time of great economic, social, and political change—Chile has been free of direct military involvement abroad and at home. Conservative power in the legislature and in the executive branch has been steadily waning. There have been liberal and social administrations for brief periods, especially those of President Arturo Allesandri (1920–25) and President Pedro Aguirre Cerda (1938–41). The political conservatives have been steadily losing ground during the past decade. In 1958, Jorge Allesandri, son of former President Arturo Allesandri, ran as an Independent and was supported by a coalition of the Liberal and United Conservative parties. He won an extremely narrow victory over another coalition candidate, Salvador Allende of the leftist Popular Front. The next administration was dominated by the new left-of-center Christian Democrats, led by President Eduardo Frei. The Frei regime was replaced by the Popular Unity government of Marxist President Salvador Allende in 1971. It was and is composed of a coalition of Socialists, Communists, and Radicals. In November, 1972, Dr. Allende named a new cabinet, which included three top military leaders. Inclusion of the traditionally apolitical military was interpreted as an effort to increase confidence in the socialist-minded government. The key appointment was that of Commander in Chief of the Army, General Carlos Prats, who was given control of internal security. The shift in politics follows the nation's population shift from rural to urban. Under conservative politicians, whose strength was in the provinces, the main thrust of economic development was in the Santiago basin, the two big port cities of Valparaíso and Concepción, and the mines. Conversely, the present administration, whose main support comes from the urban centers and the mines, seeks to create greater economic diversification in the depressed, underdeveloped provinces. The Popular Unity government proposes to develop underused or unemployed manpower and resources in such a way as to give greater strength to separate regions and thus to the entire nation. Even under the reform-minded Frei government, the priorities of economic development were aimed at the central zone and the extreme northern and southern provinces were regarded as "zones of colonization." * The rationale of the new economic policy of President Allende is that the flow of goods in the past has been out of Chile or into Santiago, discouraging local development and creating great disparity between economic groups and regions.

Complicating the development process is what some analysts describe as the existence of two distinct subcultures. Writing in 1963, Pike estimated that about 30 per cent of the total population at that time consisted of a demoralized, fatalistic, immobile mass of workers outside the mainstream of economic life. The other 70 per cent of the Chilean people, he says, do or will actively participate in the vital processes of the nation.† Some of the present internal socio-economic changes and those that come in the immediate future may have their roots in this persistent dual social system, which is, however, disintegrating under present population increases and political evolution.

The implementation of new economic policy in Chile in facilitated by its centralized, republican government. An *intendente*, appointed by the president, governs each province. The provinces are divided into departments headed by governors whom the president also appoints. The National Planning Office (ODEPLAN), which sets the direction of regional programs and national priorities, operates directly from the presidency of the republic. Its principal goals are to initiate regional and

* Oficina de Planificación Nacional, *Politica de Desarollo Nacional.* Santiago, 1968, pp. 44–46.
† Frederick B. Pike. *Chile and the United States, 1880–1962.* South Bend, Indiana: University of Notre Dame Press, 1963, pp. 292–93.

national development plans; to further improve living conditions, employment opportunities, and wages in the depressed rural areas, where vestiges of a feudal socio-economic system persist; and to reduce unemployment and underemployment in manufacturing, construction, and other industries in the cities, especially among the new immigrants.

The role of government in the economy increased with the trend of national politics. The best example is the Chilean Development Corporation (CORFO). Established in 1939, it emerged as one of the most powerful Chilean institutions. It can act with absolute autonomy within the framework of its charter for economic development. CORFO plays the role of development bank within the country. Important and vital affiliates of CORFO include the Pacific Steel Company (CAP), the National Petroleum Enterprise (ENAP), the National Electric Enterprise (ENDESA), the National Enterprise of Telecommunications (ENTEL), the National Sugar Industry (IANSA), Petroquímica Chilena, and Hotelera Nacional, S.A. (HONSA), which has a network of hotels in important tourist localities. CORFO's vast activities extend also to cellulose, fishing, fertilizers, seeds, sulphuric acid, electronics, computer service, motion pictures, and television. The Chilean Development Corporation also maintains important national-research and data-collecting institutes in natural resources, mechanized agricultural-equipment services, geological survey, fishing development, agriculture and livestock, forestry, technical cooperation and research, and professional and vocational training.

Land Reform

Until recently, Chile was an agricultural export nation. During the Californian and Australian gold rushes, miners ate food imported from Chile's Coast Range and Central Valley. So for a time did nitrate and copper miners of the Norte Grande and industrial workers in England. But now Chile imports food from abroad.

Many aspects of Chilean life styles and attitudes still reflect an essentially agrarian society. For centuries agriculture was organized around the large estate. The owner was responsible for the health and education of the resident farm population. With the arrival of social security, labor unions, and agrarian reform, however, the entire structure of farming both in the Central Valley and Chile as a whole has undergone a radical transformation.

In the past, the workers on the land (*inquilinos*) received a small house, a garden plot, and grazing rights for a few cattle. In exchange, they provided dawn-to-dusk manpower for plowing, seeding, fertilizing, weeding, irrigating, and harvesting the fields. Life for the *inquilino* was dreary and uneventful; poverty was common. The peasant did not expect and did not have the range of services available to factory workers. Generally speaking, agriculture was at a low level of production and static. The inability of the agricultural sector to keep pace with the rest of the national economy over the years changed Chile from an export to an import nation in foodstuffs. In 1969, almost one fifth of the total value of imports were agricultural compared to 2.6 per cent of total exports. Within the national economy, agriculture produced 12.1 per cent of income in 1960 compared with 7.5 per cent in 1969.

Recognizing that more and more of the national wealth was being diverted to food imports, the Chileans initiated drastic measures to try to improve the lot of the rural population as well as to increase productivity to keep pace with the rapidly increasing population. The government spent millions of dollars to make a careful inventory of food-producing resources. After aerial and field surveys were undertaken between 1961 and 1963, detailed land-capability maps were published by the Chilean Development Corporation for the entire national core area. Summary compilations of map information show 6.9 million acres of arable land in the region between the Aconcagua Valley and Puerto Montt, with only 1.2 million acres of good to excellent farmland. Comparing detailed population-distribution maps with land-capability maps, it becomes apparent that most of the highly productive soils (75 per cent) are already densely settled north of the thirty-sixth parallel, and that some lands, especially in the Coast Range, are overpopulated to the point of creating serious soil erosion. South of 36° S., soils of high capability are less intensively occupied. The significance of this situation is that Chile must seek ways of making the lands of highest capability produce higher yields and create better systems of land management on the marginal lands.

The grave problems facing the agricultural sector of the Chilean economy are easily recognized, but the proposed solutions differ widely. During the past decade, a series of agrarian reforms were directed specifically at the problem of production and the low socio-economic status of the landless peasantry. In 1963, the Catholic Church began a national program designed to convert its farms into worker-run organizations. Congress passed the first agrarian reform law the same year, establishing

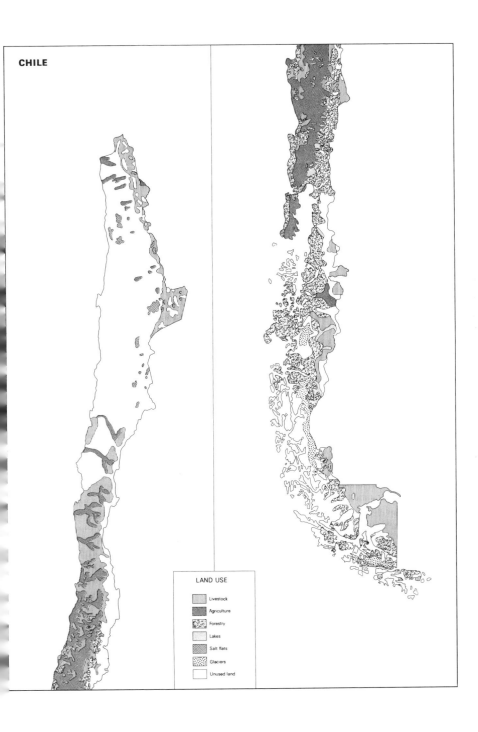

CHILE

LAND USE

- Livestock
- Agriculture
- Forestry
- Lakes
- Salt flats
- Glaciers
- Unused land

the Chilean Agrarian Reform Corporation (CORA) and redistributing family-sized parcels to peasant workers on government-owned land. President Eduardo Frei inaugurated a second agrarian-reform law in 1967 to correct what he characterized as "the concentration of land in a few hands, an inadequate and insufficient use of land resources, the monopolization of credit and other services by the few, and a paternalistic labor system which tended to abuse the peasant and prevented the development of a vigorous rural middle class." * At that time, there were 185,000 landless families out of a total 345,000 rural working families in Chile. Of the remaining families (160,000), 78 per cent owned only 5 per cent of the agricultural land. Conversely, 2 per cent of the total farms, each exceeding 2,470 acres, comprised 69 per cent of the land in farms.

The second law created *campesino* (rural) cooperatives, called *asentamientos,* under the administration of CORA from *fundos* expropriated because of large size, poor exploitation, or both. CORA was to provide a minimum of three (sometimes five) years of technical, financial, and administrative assistance while training the peasants to be fully productive and self-sufficient. The decision whether to remain in cooperatives or subdivide into family units was to be made by the *campesinos* after they proved their competence to farm. Until the advent of the Allende administration, it was common for them to elect to divide the land into individual units. By the end of 1970, there had been 1,412 expropriations involving over 10 million acres. Of these, 716,600 acres were irrigated and 1.5 million acres were nonirrigated farmland. Also included were 7.9 million acres in nonarable land.

The present Popular Unity government would initiate still a third agrarian reform if it could do so, but it lacks a majority in the Senate and the Chamber of Deputies. Its present policies mark it as substantially different from preceding administrations. President Allende has stated that "the fundamental aspect of Chile's agrarian problem is the extent of the peasant's dependence, which in turn puts him well behind the rest of Chile's underdeveloped society." † It is clear that he views the problem as basically social and only secondarily economic. Under President Frei, the announced policy was that "the efficient farmer need not fear expropria-

* Joseph R. Thome. "A Brief Survey of the Chilean Agrarian Reform Program." *Land Tenure Center Newsletter,* No. 28 (Sept., 1968–Feb., 1969), p. 1. Madison: The University of Wisconsin.

† Salvador Allende. "Perspectives on Agrarian Reform." *Ceres,* IV, no. 5 (Sept.–Oct., 1971), pp. 13–17.

This landscape in the Norte Chico (Little North) is semidesert. Shown here is an experiment to prevent erosion. Under the direction of government experts, local people dig ditches that follow the contour of the land. This project, sponsored by the United Nations, is designed to encourage volunteers to participate in rural community-development work.

tion." The philosophy and application of Frei's agrarian reform law have changed under President Allende. First, as defined by Frei's law, a *latifundio* is *any* holding in excess of 198 acres "under basic irrigation." Now *all* farms exceeding that size will be expropriated. President Allende declared a goal of 1,200 expropriations during his first year. By mid-1971, CORA had taken over 1,100 holdings. This does not mean that all farmers will be driven out of business, but that the privately owned and managed proprietorships must conform to basic size limits defined by law. The equivalent basic farm size could be about 1,000 acres in Cautín Province, for example, and ten times that far to the south in Magallanes. The different sizes are based on the varying productive qualities of the land. By 1976, the government plans to have expropriated over 17 million acres and to have resettled no fewer than 70,000 families.

What are the prospects for agriculture in this confused period? Except for family-run farms, which come under very specific size limits, much of the agricultural sector will be government-controlled and supervised. The many *asentamientos* will operate under the Agrarian Reform Corporation (CORA). Large, Soviet-style "state farms" will probably appear on marginal or submarginal lands unless *campesino* resistance proves too strong. The government will strictly control prices and wages at all levels. The medium-size, independent farms and the large *asentamientos* will continue to get government aid through reduced interest rates on farm credit at state-owned banks, and will get seed, breeding stock, farm machinery, and technical assistance through state agencies. Farm labor on privately owned farms will become more widely unionized. Government control will be felt in the area of foreign trade. The recent changes in agriculture indicate a highly structured system totally dominated by government and an abolition of the traditional play of the marketplace.

In July, 1972, President Allende announced a new economic plan. It will include government investments of over $760 million in the next two years to improve industrial and farm production. Most of the money will come from Communist countries. There will be three new milk-bottling plants, a new sugar refinery, and enough poultry farms to produce 100 million chickens a year (twice the present number).

Fisheries and Forestry

As of 1971, Chile ranked second in the tonnage of fish caught in South America (after Peru). The great bulk of its 1.5-million-ton catch is destined for industrial use as fishmeal or fish oil. These are export products, which somewhat obscure the fact that the Chileans are the greatest consumers of fish in South America: they eat forty pounds per person yearly, three times more than elsewhere in South America.

The cold coastal waters, influenced by the Humboldt Current, which sweeps northward from the Antarctic, teem with marine life. Because of the great latitudinal extent of the coastline, the varieties vary considerably. Between Antofagasta and Arica, pelagic fish such as anchovies, sardines, bonito, and tuna abound. In the northern fishing ports, large fleets of big, steel-hulled boats belong to firms dedicated to anchovies. From the fishing grounds between Curicó and Concepción and between Cautín and Valdivia come bottom fish, such as hake and cod. The main fishing centers along this section of coast are Talcahuano, San Antonio, and Valparaíso. The waters southward from Puerto Montt are noted for shellfish such as oysters and crabs. The Chilean production of oysters and scallops is just under 17 million pounds in an average year. CORFO regards oysters as having great prospects for export. In the past decade and a half the number of large fishing vessels quadrupled and small craft increased by half. The total catch increased fivefold. At present Chile is experimenting with cooperative programs with the Soviet Union, Cuba, and Eduador to expand production further.

Chile harvests wood both from natural forests and from plantations. The northern limits of natural forests begin with the Montaña adjacent to the Central Valley. Remnants of the original cover occur in open stands or woodlots throughout the tableland, and there are dense forests in the Lake District and nearby ranges. Four species make up three fourths of the sawn-timber volume in the natural forests. In order of importance, they are Coigüe, known commercially as Chilean cherry (*Nothofagus dombeyi*); Tepa (*Laurelia serrata*); Ulmo (*Eucryphia cordiofolia*); and Tineo (*Weinmannia trichosperma*). Until 1963, the major portion of sawn wood came from natural forests; since then, conifer plantations have been the chief source. Estimates in 1969 put the Monterey pine plantations at 686,980 acres, mainly in the Bío-Bío and Maule watersheds. The tree is fully grown in twenty-five years. CORFO plans to plant a minimum of 100,000 acres per year in pine, more than doubling the total planted area in pine by 1980, to meet the needs of the nation's fast-growing cellulose industry.

There are three large cellulose plants and two newsprint plants in the Bío-Bío region. Chilean economic planners see an excellent and growing market for kraft pulp. The value of Chilean exports of paper, cellulose, and newsprint in 1970 was $32 million; by 1973 Chile should be South America's largest producer of kraft cellulose.

Mineral Wealth and the Rise of Nationalism

As agrarian problems have dominated Chile's internal affairs in the twentieth century, problems related to minerals have played a key role in its foreign relations. Minerals bring in 87 per cent of the total value of exports, and more than three fourths of that export income comes from copper. Equally significant is the role played by two copper mines, Chuquicamata in the desert of Antofagasta Province and El Teniente in O'Higgins Province. "Chuqui" is one of the world's greatest open-pit copper mines; El Teniente is the world's largest underground copper mine. In 1968 and 1969 these two mines together produced two thirds of the nation's total copper—42 per cent by Chuquicamata and 25 per cent by El Teniente.

"Chuqui" was owned by the Anaconda Copper Company and the Teniente mine by the Kennecott Copper Corporation, and these were not
the only large mines owned and operated by foreign interests. Anaconda
also controlled the Potrerillos complex and the El Salvador mine at the
southern end of the Atacama Desert. The same mining interests discovered
a rich copper deposit, La Exótica, near Chuquicamata in 1960. Another
important discovery opened the Río Blanco mine near Los Andes in 1970
under the joint ownership of the U.S.-owned Cerro Corporation and
Chile's Copper Corporation (CODELCO).

In recent years the growing involvement of U.S. corporations in Chilean
national affairs has become a highly charged issue. Chileans are indignant
at seeing enormous national wealth going abroad that is sorely needed for
internal programs, and they feel a sense of frustration at having so high
a proportion of the nation's economy controlled by foreigners. These
feelings have been expressed by Chileans from all walks of life, not only
political extremists. Thus, the steady movement toward nationalization
of the copper mines in the past decade is an expression of changing
political attitudes, especially of increasing nationalism.

During the administration of Eduardo Frei, the Chilean government
agreed to take over a controlling interest (51 per cent) in the major copper
companies. CODELCO was set up to effect this change and did so by 1970.
With the election of President Allende, the pace accelerated; complete
nationalization went into effect with the approval of the Congress of Chile.
Immediately a controversy arose because President Allende declared that
no payments to the affected companies would follow the government's
assumption of complete ownership. Chile argued that they were "simply
exercising the inalienable right of a sovereign people to own [their] own
natural resources" and that it "was not an act of vengeance against any
group, nation, or country."* Moreover, the government stated that during
a sixteen-year period both Anaconda and Kennecott received "excess
profits," left "deficient and inoperable machinery and equipment," and
had inflated book values of worth. The copper companies, for their part,
point out that for four years of the period in question, they operated
in joint partnership with the Chilean government. Moreover, a United
Nations resolution requires that "appropriate compensation" be provided,
and not to do so is a violation of international precepts, according to
company documents. Kennecott, for example, declares that it paid taxes

* CORFO. "The First State of the Nation Address by President Salvador Allende
—May 21, 1971." *Chile Economic Notes*, No. 83 (July 26, 1971), pp. 1–2.

of 67 to 87 per cent, without depletion allowances, for over fifty years of operation, and that it faithfully complied with Chilean law. The copper controversy left diplomatic relations between Chile and the United States in a very delicate state. Bethlehem Steel Corporation fared somewhat better in negotiations relating to the nationalization of the Chilean iron and steel industry. The government of Chile will pay $8 million over ten years as compensation for assuming the corporation's share of the Pacific Steel Company operation near Concepción.

Iron mining became significant on a national scale in the 1920's and since that time production has climbed slowly but steadily. Before Pacific Steel's plant was opened at Huachipato in 1950 most production was exported. The largest mines are near the coast in the Norte Chico at El Tofo and El Romeral. These mines, once operated by a subsidiary of Bethlehem Steel, have been nationalized and are now part of the Pacific Steel Company complex. Other medium-sized mines account for half the total production, which amounts to about 11.4 million tons a year in the early 1970's. Over 90 per cent of the iron is exported.

Production of nitrate (*salitre*) from deposits in the Atacama Desert has been an important part of Chile's mineral economy for a half century, but in recent years the development of synthetic nitrates, foreign tariffs, and rising costs have helped curtail production. Output has declined steadily from about 1 million tons in 1966 to only 670,000 in 1970. The only important nitrate camps still functioning are at Pedro de Valdivia and María Elena in Antofagasta Province. With the sharp reduction in *salitre* exports, it may now be possible to produce specialty products such as lithium, potassium, borax, and iodine in significant commercial quantities. Chilean farms use a quarter of the present production for fertilizer.

Changing Sources of Energy

During the last thirty years, the sources of energy in Chile have changed dramatically. In 1940, two thirds of the total energy came from coal and wood. Today, petroleum supplies half of it, and hydroelectricity another quarter (see Table 18.1).

Chile is the largest producer of coal in South America, with an annual output of about 1.7 million tons. The nationalized mines, located on the

TABLE 18.1

SOURCES OF ENERGY IN CHILE, 1940–69

Year	Petroleum and Its Derivatives	Hydro-electricity	Coal	Wood	Other Sources	Total Energy Produced (millions kw-h)
1940	26.4%	11.6%	31.3%	30.1%	0.6%	6,531
1950	31.3	19.2	25.5	23.4	0.6	8,583
1960	43.0	25.3	16.4	14.8	0.5	11,765
1969	53.6	23.7	15.6	6.6	0.5	17,006

SOURCE: ENDESA, *Producción y consumo de energía en Chile*. Santiago, 1969.

shores of the Gulf of Arauco south of Concepción, account for 95 per cent of production. The Huachipato steel complex, a large market of small users, and a few large buyers, whose needs fluctuate with the climate, consume all production. Dry years make large demands on thermo-generating plants. There are an estimated 100 million tons of reserves in the Arauco-Concepción area and 350 million tons in Magallanes Province. On the basis of present rates and trends, it appears that Chile has approximately three centuries of known coal reserves for internal use.

Currently Chile produces about half its own needs in both natural gas and petroleum. It has begun modest export shipments of liquefied gas to other South American nations. The oil and gas fields lie on the eastern continental and northern Tierra del Fuego portions of Magallanes Province. The National Petroleum Enterprise (ENAP) has refineries at Concón, north of Valparaíso, Concepción, and Magallanes. The major commercial distributors are COPEC, a nationally owned enterprise, Exxon, and Shell.

Electrical-energy production is virtually all state-owned. Hydroelectric plants in the Andes near the Central Valley supply the heartland. Andean rivers have tremendous potential for future development of hydroelectric power, particularly the Bío-Bío watershed. At the nitrate center of Pedro de Valdivia in the desert north, the consumption of solar energy is estimated to be the equivalent of 55,000 tons of fuel annually. CORFO and the United Nations are jointly exploring the possibility of capturing geothermal energy in the geyser area of the Tatio Valley to supplement power needs in the copper mines of Antofagasta Province.

Future Prospects

Starting with the Christian Democratic administration and accelerating under the present Popular Unity government, Chile has been moving away from close political alignments with the West and opening up trade and diplomatic relations with the East. United States foreign assistance has declined steadily from a high point in the mid-1960's; U.S. aid continues, but meanwhile technical and financial assistance from the Soviet Union, Cuba, and, most recently, the People's Republic of China, is rising.

Within South America, the present government is working actively to improve relations with nations on its borders. With solid trade relations with the other member nations of LAFTA and the Andean Common Market (see pages 47–60), Chile should be able to further diversify its economy, especially its industry, apparently an objective of President Allende. Trade with Europe is likely to increase, and in the long run trade with the United States may once again rise.

Hemispheric relations are complicated by Chile's refusal to recognize the ban on relations with Cuba imposed by the Organization of American States (OAS). First the government of Eduardo Frei broke the ban on trade, then the government of Salvador Allende re-established diplomatic ties. Thus, long-standing relationships within the OAS have been severely tested.

One of the nation's most serious problems, affecting confidence at home and abroad, is inflation. The cost of living has gone up as much as 40 per cent per year. This situation has plagued Chile for three decades and has almost become a way of life. Price controls and currency-exchange restrictions, initiated by the present government in 1971, temporarily stayed the inflationary rise. In 1972, however, inflation reached 30 per cent in the first six months, provoking repeated strikes, demonstrations, and riots. Greater stability and confidence in the economy and a reduction of socio-economic inequalities could contribute greatly toward the solution of staggering internal problems. Real and extraordinary revolutionary processes are now in full swing—undertaken peacefully and under a constitutional government, whose representatives are chosen in regular and genuine elections. These processes are bringing changes unique in the history of South America.

Suggested Readings

ALLENDE, SALVADOR. "Perspectives on Agrarian Reform." *Ceres,* IV, no. 5 (May, 1971), pp. 13–17.

ANGELL, ALAN. "Chile: From Christian Democracy to Marxism?" *Current History,* XL, no. 354 (February, 1971), pp. 84–89. Briefly examines some political, social, and economic changes, and suggests that "Chile is not likely to see a straight march to a Marxist dictatorship."

CORFO. "The First State of the Nation Address by President Salvador Allende—May 21, 1971." *Chile Economic Notes,* No. 83 (July 26, 1971).

DEBRAY, RÉGIS. *The Chilean Revolution: Conversations with Allende.* New York: Pantheon, 1971 (translated from the French). Debray, a militant French leftist, discusses with Allende the latter's hopes for a peaceful socialist revolution. Debray questions the constitutional nature of Allende's revolution, and thus raises a primary question concerning "democratic communism": If Allende should lose the next election, will he voluntarily surrender power?

JEFFERIES, A. "Agrarian Reform in Chile." *Geography,* LVI, no. 252 (July, 1971), pp. 221–30. An evaluation of land-reform programs from the 1920's to the end of the Frei administration, concentrating on use of available resources, terms under which expropriated land may be held, and opposition from the landowning class.

McBRIDE, GEORGE McCUTCHEN. *Chile: Land and Society. Research Series No. 19.* New York: American Geographical Society, 1936 (reprinted 1971 by Octagon Books, New York). A classic historical study of Chile's societal groups.

PETRAS, JAMES. *Politics and Social Forces in Chilean Development.* Berkeley and Los Angeles: University of California Press, 1969. An examination of the interrelation of industrialization, modernization, social structure, and political organization.

PORTEOUS, J. DOUGLAS. "Urban Transplantation in Chile." *Geographical Review,* LXII, no. 4 (October, 1972), pp. 455–78.

PORTES, ALEJANDRO. "The Urban Slum in Chile: Types and Correlates." *Land Economics,* XLVII, no. 3 (August, 1971), pp. 235–48. Differentiates four types of settlements formed by migrants to urban areas of Chile, and analyzes their basic characteristics.

RACZYNSKI, DAGMAR. "Migration, Mobility, and Occupational Achievement: The Case of Santiago, Chile." *International Migration Review,*

VI, no. 2 (summer, 1972), pp. 182–99. Discusses the relationship between migration and occupational mobility in a large Chilean city.

RUDOLPH, W. E. *Vanishing Trails of Atacama.* New York: American Geographical Society, 1963. This account, by a mining engineer with many years of experience in the area, is still interesting. He comments on the changes in and development of Chile's Norte Grande desert.

SEERS, DUDLEY. "Chile: Is the Road to Socialism Blocked?" *The World Today,* XXVIII, no. 5 (May, 1972), pp. 202–9. A brief, interesting account of current political and economic conditions in Chile.

SWIFT, JEANNINE. *Agrarian Reform in Chile: An Economic Study.* Lexington, Mass: D. C. Health, 1971. A study of agrarian reform in Chile, emphasizing its effects on the redistribution of income and the strength of the industrial sector.

ZAÑARTU, S. J., and JOHN J. KENNEDY, eds. *The Overall Development of Chile.* Notre Dame, Indiana, and London: University of Notre Dame Press, 1969. A collection of provocative economic, sociological, and political essays, by Chilean and U.S. experts, on fundamental problems confronting Chile.

See also Suggested Readings for Part I, pp. 61–63.

INDEX

ABRAMEX nations, 48
Aconcagua Valley, 245, 252
Afobaka, 104–5
Africans. *See* Blacks
Aftosa, 222
Agency for International Development (AID), 40, 140–41, 211
Agrarian reform. *See* Green revolution; Land development, ownership, reform; Rural areas
Agricultural productivity, 32–34, 36, 40, 168, 176; in Argentina, 234, 239; in Chile, 252; in Ecuador, 131–33; in Guyana, 92; in Paraguay, 210, 213; in Peru, 154, 156, 158; in Uruguay, 221–22, 225
Agriculture: in ANCOM, 51; diversification of, 222–23, 250; expansion of, 33, 36–44, 151, 221, 254–56; oasis, 156, 235; plant diseases and, 36, 137, 222; reclamation in, 77, 91–92, 118; research in, 36, 39, 77, 178, 252; slash-and-burn (subsistence, shifting), 71, 109, 148, 164, 168, 213. *See also* under country; name of particular crop
Aguirre Cerda, Pedro, 242, 249
Albina, 100
Allende, Salvador, 249–50, 254–55, 256, 258, 261
Allesandri, Arturo, 249
Allesandri, Jorge, 249
Alliance for Progress, 8

Aluminum production, 86–87, 89, 103–5, 109
Alvarez Cabral, Pedro, 164
Amapá, 180
Amazon River and Basin, 130, 136, 159, 163, 168, 179–80, 190–92
Amerindians. *See* Indians (indigenous)
Andean Common Market (ANCOM), 47–63; industry in, 52–53, 119; nationalism of, 55–57, 59; trade within, 53, 133, 197, 239, 261; U.S. ties to, 51–52, 55–59
Andean Cordilleras, 53; in Argentina, 231; in Bolivia, 185, 190, 193; in Chile, 246; in Colombia, 112, 119; in Ecuador, 130; in Peru, 145
Andean Development Corporation, 58
Andean Petrochemical Agreement, 52
Andes Mountains. *See* Andean Cordilleras
Animal husbandry. *See* Ranching and animal husbandry
Antioquia, Antíoqueños, 112–18, 121–24
Antofagasta: Port, 196, 242, 243, 256; Province, 249, 257, 259, 261
Apure-Barinas, 73
Arauco, 260
Arequipa, 157
Argentina: agriculture in, 234–36, 239; climate and landforms of, 230–31; commerce of, 229, 234, 236–39; economy of, 229–30, 234–40; history of,

El Chocón (energy complex), 235, 236
El Teniente (mine), 257–58
Employment: foreign aid for, 30–31; marginal, 156; rural, 11, 29, 32–33, 36–40, 43–45, 159, 210–11, 233, 238, 247–48; strategies for, 22–27, 29–33, 36–46; technology and, 27–29, 31, 238; underemployment, 12, 23, 29, 86, 135, 210–11, 238, 247
Encarnación, 210–12
Energy sources: geothermal, 260–61; hydroelectric, 51, 77, 103, 118, 135, 138, 157, 158, 175, 195, 212, 235, 237; natural gas, 73, 194, 236, 260; Oil (*see* Petroleum Production); power corporations for, 51, 118, 260; solar, 260; thermoelectric, 73, 195
Erosion, 90, 193, 222, 231, 252
Esmeraldas, 133, 137
Essequibo River, 84, 88
Estancias, 208, 219–20
European Economic Community, 58, 102, 239
Expropriation, 71–72, 151–53, 200, 213, 254–55; of foreign-owned properties, 55, 73, 86, 198, 200, 258–59

Fabricato (corporation), 122–23
Federal Inspectorate of Works Against the Droughts (IFOCS), 171, 172
Fisheries, 101, 109, 153, 156, 224, 256–57
Flood control, 90–91, 95–100, 118
Food and Agriculture Organization (FAO), 33, 37
Foreign corporations, 31, 75, 85, 86–89, 109, 118, 123, 133, 151–53, 200, 258–59, 260
Foreign investment, 30, 31, 46, 55–57; in Argentina, 233, 236–37, 239; in Bolivia, 201; in Chile, 256, 258–59, 261; in Colombia, 120, 123–24; in Ecuador, 133; in Paraguay, 212; in Peru, 152–54; in Venezuela, 70, 73–74, 76
Forestry and its products, 52–53, 102, 109, 138, 164, 257
Foundation for the Development of

Mechanized Agriculture in Surinam, 101
France, 106–9, 111
Frei, Eduardo, 49, 249–50, 254–55, 258, 261
French Guiana: climate and landforms of, 107–8, 110; economy, 108–10; history, 106–7; Kourou Space Center, 109–10; peoples and population in, 108
Freyre, Gilberto, 170
Fruits and vegetables, 75, 86, 101, 109, 118, 133–34, 137, 180, 186, 192–93, 235, 245
Fundo, 245, 254

Galápagos Islands, 130
Galo Plaza, Lasso, 128
Ganso Azul, 159
Gauchos, 176, 232
Georgetown, 82, 89, 90
Germany (West), 197, 212
Goiás-Goiânia, 178
Gómez, Juan Vicente, 70
Goulart, João, 181
Grain. See Wheat and other grains
Great Britain. See United Kingdom
Green Revolution, 36–45, 101
Gross national product, 4, 22, 31; of ANCOM, 50; of Bolivia, 193; of Ecuador, 131; of Guyana, 86, 88; of Peru, 153; of Surinam, 105; of Venezuela, 73
Guaraní. See Indians (indigenous)
Guayaquil, 127, 138–39
Guayas River, 138
Guerrilla movements, 29, 225, 228
Guiana Highlands (Venezuela), 70
Guianas. See Guyana (formerly British Guiana); French Guiana; Surinam (formerly Dutch Guiana)
Guri hydroelectric plant, 77
Guyana: agriculture of, 85–86, 89–92; climate and landforms of, 84, 89; economy of, 85, 88–89; history of, 80–82; peoples and population in, 80–82, 89, 92

THE CONTRIBUTORS

RAYMOND E. CRIST is Professor of Geography, University of Florida.

KEVIN C. KEARNS is Chairman of the Department of Geography, University of Northern Colorado.

JOSEPH B. KELLEY was formerly Social Service Consultant at the Universidad Católica del Ecuador, and is now Professor and Associate Dean, School of Social Work, California State University, San Diego.

EDWARD P. LEAHY is Associate Professor of Geography, East Carolina University.

CORNELIUS LOESER is Assistant Professor of Geography, Northern Illinois University.

DONALD D. MACPHAIL is Professor of Geography, University of Colorado, Boulder.

DAVID A. MORSE was formerly Director General of the International Labour Organization, and is now a partner in the law firm of Surrey, Karasik, and Morse.

JAMES J. PARSONS is Professor of Geography, University of California, Berkeley.

ROBERT D'A. SHAW is on the staff of the Agriculture and Rural Development Division, International Bank for Reconstruction and Development.

RICHARD V. SMITH is Professor of Geography, Miami University, Oxford, Ohio.

ROBERT J. TATA is Associate Professor of Geography, Florida Atlantic University.

ROBERT N. THOMAS is Associate Professor of Geography, Michigan State University.

RANJIT TIRTHA is Associate Professor of Geography, Eastern Michigan University.

JAMES W. VINING is Assistant Professor of Geography, Western Illinois University.

KEMPTON E. WEBB is Professor of Geography, Institute of Latin American Studies, Columbia University.

MORTON D. WINSBERG is Associate Professor of Geography, Florida State University.